Environmental Justice i...

Urban and Industrial Environments
Series editor: Robert Gottlieb, Henry R. Luce Professor of Urban
and Environmental Policy, Occidental College

Environmental Justice in Latin America

Problems, Promise, and Practice

David V. Carruthers, editor

The MIT Press
Cambridge, Massachusetts
London, England

For information on quantity discounts, email special_sales@mitpress.mit.edu.

Set in Sabon by SNP Best-set Typesetter Ltd., Hong Kong. Printed (on recycled paper) and bound in the United States of America.

Library of Congress Cataloging-in-Publication Data

Environmental justice in Latin America : problems, promise, and practice / David V. Carruthers, editor.
p.   cm.—(Urban and industrial environments)
Includes bibliographical references and index.
ISBN 978-0-262-03372-5 (hardcover : alk. paper)—ISBN 978-0-262-53300-3 (pbk. : alk. paper)
1. Environmental justice—Latin America. 2. Environmental justice—Caribbean Area. I. Carruthers, David V.
GE235.L29E58   2008
363.70098—dc22

2007020848

10 9 8 7 6 5 4 3 2 1

Contents

Acknowledgments

This collection represents the tireless work of a diverse group of scholars, activists, professionals, scientists, and community leaders, as well as people from neighborhoods, farms, and factories around the world, inspired by a shared vision for a more just, sustainable, and democratic future. The people involved daily in Latin America's struggles for environmental justice have shared with us the hopes, challenges, frustrations, courage, and tenacity that make these stories real, and we are forever in their debt.

I am deeply grateful to the contributors who conducted the research and prepared the essays for this project. Thank you for your expertise, patience, dedication, and enthusiasm. I am also grateful to my colleagues at San Diego State University for your support and friendship.

Many people provided valuable guidance and suggestions in the preparation of this manuscript. I would particularly like to thank my wife, Janet, for her love and emotional support, and David Schlosberg and John Dryzek for wise advice and encouragement. Finally, I am grateful to Clay Morgan, Robert Gottlieb, and the patient and supportive people at The MIT Press.

Environmental Justice in Latin America

Introduction
Popular Environmentalism and Social Justice in Latin America

David V. Carruthers

Human history has always included the continuous alteration of our endeavors through the global movement of ideas in religion, politics, art, architecture, literature, cuisine, and so on. This is as true today for the passions and tactics of social-movement organizing as it is for the tools of academic analysis and methods of policy design. In the environmental arena, we tend to think of environmental activism, education, and policy as a story that began in the wealthy, industrialized North and has since traveled to nearly every part of the world. This received wisdom is mistaken, largely because of the way the story has been told and who the storytellers have been. In actuality, there have always been myriad forms of environmental consciousness, practice, and mobilization in most parts of the world, even if they have not always appeared in forms familiar to Western eyes. Such is the case with environmental justice.

Most readers recognize "environmental justice" as the rallying cry raised against environmental racism in US communities of color from the mid 1980s onward. Fusing civil rights activism with environmental health concerns, the environmental justice movement energized African American, Latino, and Native American resistance to industrial hazards and toxic threats concentrated in their communities. Environmental justice has been transformative, broadening the scope and altering the character and tactics of the US environmental movement (Bryant and Mohai 1992; Bullard 1993; Cole and Foster 2001; Westra and Lawson 2001). By launching a dialogue about race, class, and the unfair distribution of environmental hazards, environmental justice has also altered academic and political debates. Its language and ideas move between activist, scholarly, and policy circles, offering a critical framework for analyzing environmental inequities (Bullard 1994; Bryant 1995; Pellow 2000a; Mutz, Bryner, and Kenney 2002). Indeed, several authors believe it represents a paradigm shift, both in the larger environmental movement and in the study and practice of environmental politics (Novotny 2000; Taylor 2000; Rhodes 2003).

Narratives of social justice and environmental well-being also come together in many other forms and in many other places. Environmental justice, in fact, is an important part of the fabric of popular environmentalism in much of the world. Growing numbers of activists, scholars, and policymakers have been breaking open the environmental justice discourse, recognizing value in its language and methods, and drawing upon its symbols and assumptions to better understand and address environmental conflicts and concerns in a variety of global settings, from Europe to Asia and from Africa to South America (Adeola 2000; Byrne, Glover, and Martinez 2002; Agyeman, Bullard, and Evans 2003a). Analysts are also applying notions of environmental justice to the global distribution of environmental risks (such as climate change or toxic waste), highlighting the disproportionate negative environmental and social costs of global production borne by the communities of the global South (Kiefer and Benjamin 1993; Khor 1993; Agarwal, Narain, and Sharma 2002; Glover 2002; Sachs 2002).

This book contributes to an emerging effort to explore the promise and limits of environmental justice in Latin America and the Caribbean, both as a banner of popular mobilization and as a set of principles for analysis, interpretation, and policy. To what extent and in what forms have Latin America's popular movements fused environmental dimensions into community struggles for social justice? How do we recognize and analyze local or global forms of environmental justice consciousness and action? Do the analytical tools of environmental justice open the doors to useful understanding that we might otherwise not capture? The book explores these questions both conceptually and empirically, drawing lessons from a variety of studies of popular environmental movements and cases throughout urban and rural Latin America. Here, to set the context for this exploration, I first consider some of the challenges facing environmental justice research in Latin America. Next I turn to its unique potential for the region, rooted in diverse, localized meanings. In the third section of this introductory essay, I point toward the practice of environmental justice in Latin America, introducing the scope and content of the chapters to follow.

Research Challenges

In order to assess the ways in which environmental justice might be promoted, understood, or experienced in Latin America, or indeed in any global context, I begin by outlining some practical and conceptual difficulties.

Data and Resource Limitations

One basic challenge to environmental research in Latin America concerns the availability and quality of scientific data. The allegations of the US environmental justice movement gained credibility with a series of studies documenting disproportionate environmental burdens in poor communities of color, beginning with *Toxic Wastes and Race in the United States* (Commission for Racial Justice 1987). Analysts from geography, public law, social science, epidemiology, public health, and other fields have continued to use a wide variety of data and methodologies to document, analyze, and assess environmental inequities. The Emergency Planning and Community Right-To-Know Act of 1986, which led to the creation of the Toxics Release Inventory, means that US community activists can readily access information regarding hazardous substances in their neighborhoods.

In contrast, the paucity of systematic environmental and public health data in most Latin American and Caribbean countries presents an obstacle, at least to the research model familiar to US analysts. In spite of the rapid growth of industrial production and associated hazards in Latin America's cities, limited data are available for testing relationships between ethnicity or class and exposure to environmental risk. Demographic data can also be unreliable, particularly in industrializing cities with fast-growing, mobile immigrant populations. Recent decades have witnessed explosive production growth in export-processing zones throughout Mexico, Central America, and the Caribbean. These industrial export sectors are notoriously defensive and secretive, and government enforcement of hazardous-waste-disposal laws has been uneven at best. Studies that rely on industry or official statistics are likely to understate toxic threats significantly (Cohen and Méndez 2000). Right-to-know laws, if they exist at all, are typically limited in reach and efficacy (Naumann 2004). As several studies in this volume demonstrate, these constraints on the quantity and quality of data are systemic, resulting from enduring limitations on democratic space as well as pressures stemming from the imperatives of international economic integration.[1]

Limited funding for research or activism presents another challenge. While US environmental justice campaigns originate in poor neighborhoods with limited resources, the financial barriers to community activism are more daunting in the global South, where economic marginalization is more severe and fewer societal resources are available. Community groups in the United States or Europe can secure assistance from large environmental organizations, philanthropic foundations, and government entities, and can obtain material or logistical support from regional or national networks such as the Southwest Network for Environmental and Economic Justice (SNEEJ) and the Center for Health, Environment, and Justice (CHEJ). In contrast, formal environmental networks in most Latin American countries are nascent at best, and philanthropic and government support is much scarcer. Latin American environmental groups are less able to advance agendas on their own terms and tend to rely more on denunciation and defense (Kelly 2002).

Context, Concepts, and Strategies

Taking questions that have arisen in one geographic or social context and seeing what insights they might reveal elsewhere presents additional challenges. What does it mean to employ the language, tools, or assumptions of environmental justice in the context of Latin America? Concepts, discourses, movements, and policies emerge from specific political-cultural-historical experiences. Environmental justice in Latin America will not share the hypotheses, assumptions, images, or political ramifications that would be most familiar to US activists and analysts. Few of the major works in Northern environmental justice scholarship have been translated into Spanish or Portuguese; only a few Latin American authors approach their studies with the familiar language and concepts of Northern environmental justice traditions (Leff 2001; OLCA 2005). While many Latin American researchers and activists confront clear cases of environmental injustice, they operate with localized discourses and tactics. North American conceptions of popular environmental activism likewise overlook many forms of action and consciousness that are central to the Latin American environmental experience, such as struggles for land and defense of traditional seeds or agricultural practices.

Consider the question of race. Environmental justice emerged in the United States as an extension of the civil rights movement into the arena of environmental health. The environmental justice movement has drawn directly on the rhetoric, the organizational experience, and the institutions of the civil rights movement (Camacho 1998). If we think narrowly about environmental justice, only in parts of the Caribbean basin and Brazil would we find a comparable legacy of Afro-American slavery, segregation, and civil rights mobilization. Nevertheless, race-based struggles for rights and citizenship have been going on in Latin America for centuries. Indigenous identity replicates inherited social hierarchies and has long been a focal point of social justice mobilization. As several chapters in this volume illustrate, indigenous people face some of the most egregious environmental (and social) inequities in Latin America. Furthermore, as Juanita Sundberg argues, critical race theory reveals historically embedded processes of racialization that correlate to inequities in the distribution of environmental goods and bads, as well as unequal political representation.

Similarly, the socioeconomic and distributional assertions of US environmental justice will often not appear or hold the same way in other contexts. Analysts in the United States impose spatial maps of environmental hazards over race and income data to identify disproportionate siting of industrial hazards in poor and minority communities. However, clear correlations between race or poverty and environmental risk do not typically appear in Latin American cities. Instead, studies suggest that industrial hazards are distributed widely throughout metropolitan zones and outskirts. While factories and waste-storage facilities might be concentrated in industrial parks, in most cases they are dispersed across many neighborhoods of all social classes. The risks that lower-class and working-class urban Latin Americans face are not consistently greater than those faced by middle-class or upper-middle-class residents. While higher risks often face the poorest, most recent urban immigrants, this is largely due to growth patterns that produce inexpensive informal housing settlements near factories (Kopinak and Barajas 2002). This stands in contrast with deliberate policy decisions to impose environmental hazards on politically weak minority communities—the "perpetrator-victim scenario" that can mobilize community action in the United States (Pellow 2000b).

The relative lack of legal protection and the limited opportunities for democratic political participation are also important. Only since the late 1980s or the 1990s have Latin American governments begun to adopt environmental laws and institutions. Much of that policy architecture has been modeled along US or European lines. While democratic space has opened considerably since this process began, environmental groups in nearly every Latin American country still face considerably greater constraints on participation than their counterparts in the industrial democracies. Moreover, as we will see in the case studies throughout this volume, Latin America's environmental laws and institutions have not functioned as well in practice as on paper, in part because they cannot presuppose the regulatory capacity and political pluralism of the Northern contexts from which they were "imported" (Alfie Cohen and Méndez 2000; Carruthers 2001a).

The Unique Promise of Environmental Justice in Latin America

In spite of the aforementioned challenges, the authors represented in this volume see ample reason for optimism about the potential of environmental justice in Latin America. As a framework for analysis and as a discourse of political action, environmental justice reveals new insights and reframes important questions about Latin America's inherited problems of inequality and injustice. Such possibilities have been demonstrated in diverse global contexts. Studies and movements appear in many settings, including Canada, Scotland, New Zealand, Israel, Eastern Europe, India, Africa, and the Pacific Islands.[2] In Latin America, Brazil hosted the region's first international colloquium on environmental justice (in 2001) and is home to the Brazilian Environmental Justice Network (Roberts and Thanos 2003; Acselrad, this volume). Analysts have explored environmental injustices in mining, oil, agriculture, and development in Peru, Nicaragua, Ecuador, and elsewhere (Faber 2002; Roberts and Thanos 2003; Martinez-Alier 2003). One volume on Latin American environmental justice broadens the concept to consider cultural rights, indigenous knowledge, genetic resources, and citizenship (Leff 2001).

While environmental justice in Latin America is not anchored in the hazardous siting inequities that fueled its rise in the United States, environmental concerns are deeply woven into the fabric of Latin American popular mobilization for social justice and equity. Environmentalism in Latin America generally begins with a stronger social justice component than its counterpart in the United States (Faber 1993; Antal 2003; Roberts and Thanos 2003). Localized meanings of "environmental justice" inhere where environmental concerns intersect with strong traditions of social justice activism.

As with environmental justice movements elsewhere, popular environmentalism in Latin America takes shape in the arenas most directly salient to people's lives and livelihoods. Environmental resistance weaves into existing struggles for social justice because people face environmental threats in every corner of their daily lives. Environmental injustice is real to the millions who breathe the poisoned air of Mexico City, Santiago, and São Paulo. It is real to the farmworkers and day laborers who spend their days and nights in the pesticide-drenched fields of Mexican, Central American, and Chilean export agriculture. It is real on the eroded slopes of El Salvador's volcanoes and in the Andean foothills, where farmers struggle to eke out a living on depleted soil. It is real for indigenous peoples in Chiapas, Guatemala, the Amazon, and Patagonia, whose ancestral forests are disappearing before their eyes. And it is real in the shadows of the export factories of Mexico, Honduras, and Nicaragua, where shantytown families store drinking water in discarded chemical barrels and raise their children in a landscape leached through with heavy metals. In the language of the US movement, environmental justice claims arise where people "live, work, and play" (Novotny 2000).

Social Justice, Social Movements, and the Quest for Political Voice

In addition to *distributional* inequity, one of the pillars of environmental justice is a concern about *procedural* inequity, propelling a quest for greater political participation and more authentic citizenship (Hunold and Young 1998; Schlosberg 2003). Environmental grievances gain legitimacy when representatives of affected communities demonstrate not just disproportionate exposure but deliberate exclusion from the political decisions that determine the locations and the risk levels of environmental threats.

The aspiration for political voice is likewise essential to the Latin American social-movement experience. While complete analysis of the origins and impacts of the region's new social movements is beyond our purpose here, it does provide a backdrop. Grassroots resistance has endured from conquest and colonialism through independence and modernization, but we pay special heed to the popular movements forged in the context of Cold War repression. Social movements emerged throughout Latin America as pillars of resistance to late-twentieth-century authoritarianism and went on to play vital roles in the democratic transitions of the 1980s and the 1990s. The region has since experienced explosive growth in popular movements demanding greater voice in all matters of social justice, including labor, gender, community health, human rights, and the environment (Alvarez, Dagnino, and Escobar 1998; Lievesley 1999; Eckstein and Wickham-Crowley 2003). Strong, diverse traditions of education, organization, and networking are built into the experience of popular resistance in virtually every country in Latin America, presenting an existing populist organizational infrastructure within which justice and environment narratives readily interweave.

David Schlosberg explores the pluralistic character of the environmental justice movement with reference to Deleuze and Guattari's rhizome metaphor. Rhizomes are a type of root system that spread underground in all directions; rather than producing a single stalk, they sprout in multiple locations, connecting in ways that are not always visible from above (Schlosberg 1999, pp. 96, 120). This is an apt metaphor for social-movement networking in Latin America, where generations of activists learned to work beneath the surface during the dark years of authoritarianism and military dictatorships. As environmental consciousness and activism have exploded across a democratizing Latin America, they have spread in this "rhizomatic" fashion among multiple social-movement networks, demonstrating connection, heterogeneity, and multiplicity. Thus, a diverse mosaic of existing popular struggles with an unmistakably environmental cast has evolved throughout Latin America. I can only begin to scratch the surface here.

The urban popular movements and shantytown dwellers' organizations that have emerged in virtually all Latin American cities testify to the failure of development strategies that dispossess rural citizens at a pace that outruns the ability of urban expansion to absorb them. Neighborhood associations in urban and peri-urban communities increasingly organize and educate people to confront pressing environmental health hazards, alongside traditional issues of education, land titles, crime, and public services (Gilbert 1994; Collinson 1996; Alfie Cohen 2003; Roberts and Thanos 2003).

Women's movements are remapping social relations throughout Latin America in human rights, community health, labor, and other campaigns for justice. As in the United States, women often take the lead in Latin America's environmental justice campaigns precisely because injustices obtain in ways that threaten their households, their workplaces, and their children's health (Hofrichter 1993; Di Chiro 1998). This link between gender and environmental health is represented in hundreds of women's grassroots and community organizations throughout Latin America.

Independent labor movements in Latin America's labor-surplus economies still struggle to secure basic rights and protections for workers. Central to many of these struggles is a growing awareness of the inhumanity of workplaces in which unprotected toxic exposures are an unacceptable price to pay for employment (Williams 2002; Anner 2003). At the intersection of labor, human rights, gender, environment, and public health, the global anti-sweatshop movement demonstrates broad recognition of workplace injustices in the world economy.

Latin America has a strong tradition of academic activism, spawning generations of "organic intellectuals" who keep one foot in the academy and another in the activist community. They lead, support, or lend technical expertise to the tens of thousands of non-governmental organizations

(NGOs) that have exploded on the scene to address virtually every dimension of social and environmental injustice. Agronomists and forest ecologists lend support to rural grassroots groups, as do attorneys, epidemiologists, and toxicologists in contaminated cities (Reilly 1995; Brooks and Fox 2002; Hogenboom, Cohen, and Antal 2003).

Indigenous rights have been a powerful catalyst to mobilization throughout the region as native communities battle the forces that threaten to fragment them, displace them, and drive them toward cultural disintegration. Not only are Indian leaders and their environmental allies revaluing the inherited ecological wisdom of their ancestors; struggles for indigenous recognition and autonomy are often inseparable from environmental and resource claims (Carruthers 1997; Apffel-Marglin 1998). Environmental injustices can be glaring, as in the ongoing conflicts with the international oil companies that have contaminated indigenous lands in Ecuador and Colombia (Martinez-Alier 2003; Roberts and Thanos 2003).

Campesino identity and farmworker identity have long been pillars of political participation in rural Latin America, particularly where peasants' demands for justice figure in national histories of revolutionary violence. Now despoiled landscapes, poisoned watersheds, agricultural chemicals, and other rural environmental problems share the platform with such traditional peasant issues as land, credit, and commodity prices (Paré et al. 1997; Roberts and Thanos 2003; Wright 2005). Global sustainable-agriculture and fair-trade movements represent national and cross-national solidarity with *campesinos* who suffer from environmental and economic injustices.

Human rights struggles have tremendous salience for Latin Americans, with decades of authoritarianism looming large in their recent pasts. Human rights activism and legislation increasingly incorporate "environmental rights," and human rights campaigns have an established international reach (Adeola 2000; Leff 2001; Agyeman, Bullard, and Evans 2003b).

Finally, the popular church of liberation theology has been a powerful force in the struggle for social justice, with significant political ramifications in Nicaragua, Mexico, Brazil, and elsewhere. In theology, policy, and daily practice, Christian Base Communities have linked environmental stewardship to human rights and equity (Faber 1993, 2002; Esteva and Prakash 1998).

These movements provide a mere glimpse into the many ways that environmental concerns mesh with the quest for social justice in numerous, interlocking arenas of contemporary popular participation in Latin America. This takes the form of a web of networked organizations, all demanding greater voice in the political decisions that affect people's lives. Many of these activists might not identify themselves first as environmentalists, nor might outside observers first see them as such. Yet all are increasingly mobilized to action by inter-related social, economic, and environmental injustices.

Environmental Justice and Global Justice

In addition to histories of state repression and the quest for more vital democracies, we must also consider Latin American social mobilization in the context of today's backlash against the "Washington Consensus" agenda of economic liberalization. Since the debt crisis of the early 1980s, virtually all Latin American governments have actively embraced (or acquiesced to) the mandates of international creditors and financial institutions, implementing strict packages of "free-market" restructuring policies to stabilize currencies, reduce inflation, shrink the role of the state in the economy, introduce greater competitiveness, create a favorable climate for corporate investment, and eliminate barriers to trade. Though the controversies surrounding this economic program lie beyond my scope, it has provoked widespread resistance across Latin America as people have reacted against crippling austerity programs, worsening economic polarization, the erosion of basic economic security, the collapse of small farms and businesses, and insurmountable household debt. Sophisticated, multi-faceted campaigns to constrain or renegotiate the process, character, and terms of international economic integration are now central to the region's politics (Chalmers 1997; Broad 2002; Finnegan 2003; Fisher and Ponniah 2003).

Social, economic, and political relationships between Latin America and the industrial North increasingly reflect the forms, tensions, and consequences of global neoliberalism. With deepening economic and corporate integration, solidarity links to the South present dense countervailing concentrations of the myriad "transnational advocacy networks" that have arisen with various aspirations to humanize the workings of the global economy (Keck and Sikkink 1998; Brooks and Fox 2002; Hogenboom, Cohen, and Antal 2003). An important thread of this story began in the early 1990s, when a network of labor and citizen's campaigns from Mexico, the United States, and Canada rose to oppose and ultimately renegotiate the content of the North American Free Trade Agreement (NAFTA).[3]

In 1999, transnational citizen activism captured the world's attention with street protests of the World Trade Organization's ministerial conference in Seattle. Since then, a broader global justice movement calling for debt relief and for reform of the institutions and rules of global trade and finance has made its presence felt at meetings of regional and international institutions in Washington, Prague, Genoa, Cancún, Miami, and elsewhere. Though the movement is complex, controversial, and multifaceted, it has articulated and projected coherent arguments, images, and assumptions about the injustices of the world economy, including environmental inequities.

Activism and scholarly debate over the costs and consequences of economic globalization incorporate important elements of the environmental justice discourse writ large (Anand 2004). Environmental injustices are not "relegated to local failures in wealthy nations" but are instead "symptomatic of systemic tendencies of globalization" (Byrne, Martinez, and Glover 2002, p. 8). Global systems of production and distribution parcel out costs and benefits with profound inequity. Special benefits accrue to highly mobile international capital (mostly based in the North), as well as to domestic subsidiaries and locally allied industrial and agricultural elites. Consuming classes in both the North and the South enjoy an expanding cornucopia of inexpensive manufactures and foods. But the "poor neighborhoods of color" on a planetary scale—the peasant villages and working class communities of the global South—pay disproportionate human and environmental costs in the form of low-wage labor and unchecked environmental devastation. Without corrections, free-trade regimes reward the producers who most effectively push the negative externalities of production onto nature, the poor, and future generations (Khor 1993; Weissman 1993; Shiva 1997; Glover 2002).

Globalized notions of environmental justice take a variety of additional forms. "Ecological footprinting" assesses the load of different human lifestyles on ecosystems, highlighting the disproportionate ecological damage caused by the world's overconsumers (Durning 1992; Rees and Westra 2003). Wolfgang Sachs (2002) argues that the world's poor endured inequality when they could aspire to a larger "slice of the cake," but ecological constraints have undermined that premise; the world economy has become a zero-sum game in which benefits to the wealthy come directly at the cost of social and ecological injustices to the poor. William Rees and Laura Westra (2003) refer to an "ecological apartheid" that segregates the world's peoples along class and ethnic lines. Within the larger global movement for debt relief, Friends of the Earth and Acción Ecológica launched a campaign for repayment of the "ecological debt" that rich countries owe to the poor for the colonial and post-colonial legacies of accruing their own wealth at the cost of Southern poverty and ecological devastation. The "International Right to Know Coalition," comprising more than 200 environmental, human rights, and social justice organizations, promotes laws requiring global corporations to disclose environmental and labor information about their operations abroad.

The Practice of Environmental Justice in Latin America

Environmental justice is clearly global. Rather than framing it principally as a US movement experience that has migrated abroad, we should focus on forms of environmental justice as they have unfolded in Latin America, on their own timelines, with their own language and their own historically grounded circumstances. While policy transplants from a Northern template have often been disappointing, dysfunctional, or ineffective in implementation in the South, elements of other countries' environmental experiences have in fact appeared in creative new forms in Latin America. These are not simple transplants; they have evolved as hybrid fusions of imported notions with local, indigenous ideas or experiences. We can identify hundreds of illustrative examples: biosphere and nature reserves (particularly those which consciously reject the "wilderness" profile and seek instead to integrate residents as stakeholders), ecological tourism, traditional medicine, sustainable agriculture, social forestry, fair-trade organizations, creative tax policies, and even locally appropriate innovations in urban planning (such as the innovations in greenbelts, public transportation, and waste management made by the Brazilian city of Curitiba—see Collinson 1996 amd Roberts and Thanos 2003).

According to Joan Martinez-Alier (2003), environmental justice is but one element of a larger "environmentalism of the poor" that can be found everywhere in the world. Daniel Faber (2002) presents the "revolutionary ecology" of Nicaragua's Sandinista government in the 1980s as a model infused with principles of equity and social justice alongside more traditional environmental notions of resource conservation. There is likewise a substantial literature on the defense of inherited ecological knowledge among indigenous peoples; traditional knowledge informs myriad experiments with sustainable agriculture, social forestry, and even ecological management of resources for small artisans (Bray 1995; Carruthers 1997, 2001b; Apffel-Marglin 1998). This book argues that we should view environmental justice in this mold—as a malleable discourse that presents elements of both Northern and Southern forms of environmental consciousness. In scores of cases across Latin America and the Caribbean, we find claims for justice already embedded in myriad indigenous, independent forms of popular environmentalism. The language, principles, tactics, and questions posed by environmental justice present an opportunity to reveal new insights, new ideas, and new ways of understanding the tremendous social and environmental challenges facing the region. "In this sense, the discourse of environmental justice may be seen as a unifying process, bringing together diverse situations and sharing understandings and experiences." (Agyeman, Bullard, and Evans 2003b, p. 9)

Organization of the Book

The chapters in part I address the larger conceptual issues evoked by environmental justice as a discourse, a social movement, or an analytical construct in the Latin American context. Juanita Sundberg explores the relationship between race and the environment in Latin American social movements. She dispels the idea that race is marginal or irrelevant, arguing instead that it is a key variable for environmental justice research in the region. Peter Newell turns our attention to the global economy, exploring the controversial relationships between trade, social justice, and the environment. Global economic, cultural, and conceptual integration place issues of North-South justice at the center of the discussion about the global future. Newell finds the demands of environmental justice—equity, recognition, and participation—increasingly framing Latin American social debates over the virtues and perils of globalization. Henri Acelsrad, in his account of an environmental justice movement in the South, discusses domestic and international contributions to the evolution of Brazilian environmental consciousness. As one of the co-founders and organizers of the Brazilian Environmental Justice Network, Acselrad has been a scholarly observer, an activist, and a participant in this process.

Parts II and III take us in a more empirical direction with a series of case studies from Latin America and the Caribbean. Recall that the perception of unjust exposure to industrial hazards fueled much of the North American environmental justice experience. In Latin America, there is a sense of injustice with regard to the unfair distribution of environmental burdens associated with rapid industrial development. Part II offers four studies that demonstrate issue mobilization around the perils of industrial development. Latin American leaders have eagerly embraced industrialization as the quickest path to modernity and economic security. Powerful public and private interests have imposed a fast-paced, largely unregulated process of industrial development on inherited class hierarchies and ethnic fault lines, seldom pausing to consider, let alone constrain, the consequences for human, social, and environmental health. Though the local language and expressions vary, social justice and environmental health concerns are increasingly fused in the popular sector's response to industrial hazards.

Carlos Reboratti begins part II by taking us through a series of environmental conflicts in Argentina, demonstrating similar social and political tensions over an array of industrial and infrastructural "mega-development" projects. Chapters 5–7 explore environmental justice in Mexico, a country whose rapid industrial development and deep integration with its northern neighbors might imply a strong environmental justice consciousness. Sarah Moore's study of environmental risks and solid-waste management in Oaxaca offers a sobering assessment of the limited quality of citizenship in the Mexican policy process. In chapter 6, I look at the US-Mexico border, which offers an intensified local illustration of global injustices in the distribution of costs, benefits, and risks. My study looks at the industrial-waste hazards of the border region's export assembly plants and at northern Mexico's role as an export platform to meet the energy needs of the United States. Jordi Díez and Reyes Rodríguez derive important lessons from the absence of environmental justice mobilization in a community facing serious health hazards and pollution from a northern Mexican mineral and chemical enterprise. Their study demonstrates how cultural, institutional, and contextual barriers can seriously constrain popular environmental mobilization in Latin America.

Part III offers a departure from the familiar North American traditions of environmental justice scholarship, helping to flesh out the book's assertion that there is indeed a distinctively Latin American environmental justice framework emerging—one that adopts varied languages and takes myriad localized forms, merging local environmental and health concerns with the language and the tactics of justice mobilization. Throughout Latin America's history, social injustice has been inextricably linked with grossly inequitable access to land and natural resources. Perpetual conflicts between landed elites and land-poor peasants explain much of the region's contentious and violent political history, from conquest through colonialism and independence, and at every turn in the modern era. Part III focuses on the power and politics of land and resources, which infuse social justice struggles with environmental values. It opens with Michele Zebich-Knos's analysis of the politics of competing land uses in Latin America, where environmental values vie with traditional extractive industries for access to land. The expansion of national and private parklands may present opportunities for more equitable revenue sharing, particularly through ecological tourism. Wendy Wolford takes us to Brazil, which suffers under one of the world's most inequitable structures of land distribution. She traces collective mobilization for land and resource justice, demonstrating the localized pursuit of distributional and procedural equity. In Bolivia too, national and local conceptions of injustice in the use of natural resources have fueled massive social discontent in recent years, as Tom Perreault chronicles. With a variety of resistance strategies to challenge the privatization of natural gas and of water, Bolivians are testing the boundaries of citizenship and are asserting livelihood rights. Many advocates view the closure of the US Navy's bombing range in Vieques, Puerto Rico as a significant victory for a Latin American environmental justice movement. Yet Katherine McCaffrey documents Vieques as an incomplete, ongoing struggle for environmental justice and political accountability. McCaffrey shows how the conversion of the former bombing range to a wildlife preserve not only continues to estrange islanders from the land but also allows the US military to elude responsibility for a toxic legacy of unexploded ordnance and chemical and industrial waste. The volume concludes with a comparative examination of the control of water resources in Chile, Bolivia, and Mexico. Stephanie Wickstrom traces decades of water policy in the three countries, exploring the politics of control, access, and exclusion. Wickstrom's study demonstrates the value of cross-national analysis, applying the lessons from the three countries comparatively to assess the problems and prospects of environmental justice in the region.

Combined, these studies suggest that, although environmental justice research and activism present risks and challenges, they also hold tremendous potential. Environmental justice has firm roots in Latin America, locally, nationally, and transnationally. The discourse of environmental justice highlights macro issues of global injustice North to South, yet takes on localized meanings appropriate to the many parts of the world in which it now appears. Like the activists, advocates, and analysts who operate under its banner, we have every reason to expect that environmental justice will continue to present openings for a more just and sustainable future for Latin America and the Caribbean.

Notes

1. In debt-burdened Latin American and Caribbean countries, state austerity often translates into chronic underfunding of environmental institutions, undercutting enforcement and efficacy. Indeed, limited state regulatory capacity is an enduring feature of the business climate in much of the region, valued by transnational or domestic industrial interests not accustomed to constraints.

2. On environmental justice studies and movements around the world, see Westra and Lawson 2001, Adamson, Evans, and Stein 2002, and Agyeman, Bullard, and Evans 2003a. See also Fritz 1999, Adeola 2000, and Anand 2004.

3. Although this "fair trade campaign" did not see its proposed "just and sustainable alternative" to the NAFTA enacted, its members' efforts were indispensable in pressuring the US Congress and the Clinton administration to require the NAFTA signatories adopt parallel side agreements, ensuring basic protections against labor abuses and environmental destruction (Brooks and Fox 2002).

References

Adamson, Joni, Mei Mei Evans, and Rachel Stein, eds. 2002. *The Environmental Justice Reader*. University of Arizona Press.

Adeola, Francis O. 2000. Cross-national environmental injustice and human rights issues: A review of evidence in the developing world. *American Behavioral Scientist* 43, no. 4: 696–706.

Agarwal, Anil, Sunita Narain, and Anju Sharma. 2002. The global commons and environmental justice: Climate change. In *Environmental Justice*, ed. J. Byrne et al. Transaction.

Agyeman, Julian, Robert D. Bullard, and Bob Evans, eds. 2003a. *Just Sustainabilities: Development in an Unequal World*. MIT Press.

Agyeman, Julian, Robert D. Bullard, and Bob Evans. 2003b. Joined-up thinking: Bringing together sustainability, environmental justice and equity. In *Just Sustainabilities*, ed. J. Agyeman et al. MIT Press.

Alfie Cohen, Miriam. 2003. The rise and fall of environmental NGOs along the US-Mexico border. In *Cross-Border Activism and Its Limits*, ed. B. Hogenboom et al. Center for Latin American Research and Documentation.

Alfie Cohen, Miriam, and Luis H. Méndez. 2000. *Maquila y movimientos ambientalistas: Examen de un riesgo compartido*. Grupo Editorial Eon.

Alvarez, Sonia, Evelina Dagnino, and Arturo Escobar, eds. 1998. *Cultures of Politics/Politics of Cultures: Re-Visioning Latin American Social Movements*. Westview.

Anand, Ruchi. 2004. *International Environmental Justice: A North-South Dimension*. Ashgate.

Anner, Mark. 2003. Defending labor rights across borders: Central American export processing plants. In *Struggles for Social Rights in Latin America*, ed. S. Eckstein and T. Wickham-Crowley. Routledge.

Antal, Edit. 2003. Cross-border relations of Mexican environmental NGOs in Tijuana-San Diego. In *Cross-Border Activism and Its Limits*, ed. B. Hogenboom et al. Center for Latin American Research and Documentation.

Apffel-Marglin, Frederique. 1998. *The Spirit of Regeneration: Andean Culture Confronting Western Notions of Development*. Zed.

Bejarano, Fernando. 2002. Mexico-US environmental partnerships. In *Cross-Border Dialogues*, ed. D. Brooks and J. Fox. Center for US-Mexico Studies, University of California, San Diego.

Bray, David Barton. 1995. Peasant organizations and "the permanent reconstruction of nature": Grassroots sustainable development in Mexico. *Journal of Environment and Development* 4: 185–204.

Broad, Robin, ed. 2002. *Global Backlash: Citizen Initiatives for a Just World Economy*. Rowman and Littlefield.

Brooks, David, and Jonathan Fox, eds. 2002. *Cross-Border Dialogues: US-Mexico Social Movement Networking*. Center for US-Mexico Studies, University of California, San Diego.

Bryant, Bunyan. 1995. *Environmental Justice: Issues, Policies, Solutions*. Island.

Bryant, Bunyan, and Paul Mohai, eds. 1992. *Race and the Incidence of Environmental Hazards: A Time for Discourse*. Westview.

Bullard, Robert D. 1993. *Confronting Environmental Racism: Voices from the Grassroots*. South End.

Bullard, Robert D., ed. 1994. *Unequal Protection: Environmental Justice and Communities of Color*. Sierra Club Books.

Byrne, John, Leigh Glover, and Cecilia Martinez. 2002. *Environmental Justice: Discourses in International Political Economy*. Transaction.

Byrne, John, Cecilia Martinez, and Leigh Glover. 2002. A brief on environmental justice. In *Environmental Justice*, ed. J. Byrne et al. Transaction.

Camacho, David E. 1998. *Environmental Injustices, Political Struggles: Race, Class, and the Environment*. Duke University Press.

Carruthers, David. 1997. Agroecology in Mexico: Linking environmental and indigenous struggles. *Society and Natural Resources* 10: 259–272.

Carruthers, David. 2001a. Environmental politics in Chile: Legacies of dictatorship and democracy. *Third World Quarterly* 22, no. 3: 343–357.

Carruthers, David. 2001b. The politics and ecology of indigenous folk art in Mexico. *Human Organization* 60, no. 4: 356–366.

Chalmers, Douglas A., et al., eds. 1997. *The New Politics of Inequality in Latin America: Rethinking Participation and Representation*. Oxford University Press.

Cole, Luke W., and Sheila R. Foster. 2001. *From the Ground Up: Environmental Racism and the Rise of the Environmental Justice Movement*. New York University Press.

Collinson, Helen. 1996. *Green Guerrillas: Environmental Conflicts and Initiatives in Latin America and the Caribbean*. Monthly Review Press.

Commission for Racial Justice, United Church of Christ. 1987. *Toxic Wastes and Race in the United States*.

Di Chiro, Giovanna. 1998. Environmental justice from the grassroots: Reflections on history, gender, and expertise. In *The Struggle for Ecological Democracy*, ed. D. Faber. Guilford.

Durning, Alan. 1992. *How Much Is Enough? The Consumer Society and the Future of the Earth*. Norton.

Eckstein, Susan, and Timothy Wickham-Crowley. 2003. *What Justice? Whose Justice? Fighting for Fairness in Latin America*. University of California Press.

Esteva, Gustavo, and Madhu Suri Prakesh. 1998. From global to local: Beyond neoliberalism to the international of hope. In *Grassroots Postmodernism*, ed. G. Esteva and M. Suri Prakesh. Zed.

Faber, Daniel. 1993. *Environment under Fire: Imperialism and the Ecological Crisis of Latin America*. Monthly Review Press.

Faber, Daniel. 2002. A revolution in environmental justice and sustainable development: The political ecology of Nicaragua. In *Environmental Justice*, ed. J. Byrne et al. Transaction.

Finnegan, William. 2003. The economics of empire: Notes on the Washington Consensus. *Harper's Magazine*, May: 41–54.

Fisher, William, and Thomas Ponniah, eds. 2003. *Another World Is Possible: Popular Alternatives to Globalization at the World Social Forum*. Zed.

Fritz, Jan Marie. 1999. Searching for environmental justice: National stories, global possibilities. *Social Justice* 26, no. 3: 174–190.

Gilbert, Alan. 1994. *The Latin American City*. Russell.

Glover, Leigh. 2002. Globalization.com v. ecological justice.org: Contesting the end of history. In *Environmental Justice*, ed. J. Byrne et al. Transaction.

Hofrichter, Richard, ed. 1993. *Toxic Struggles: The Theory and Practice of Environmental Justice*. New Society.

Hogenboom, Barbara, Miriam Alfie Cohen, and Edit Antal. 2003. *Cross-Border Activism and Its Limits*. Center for Latin American Research and Documentation.

Hunold, Christian, and Iris Marion Young. 1998. Justice, democracy, and hazardous siting. *Political Studies* 46, no. 1: 82–95.

Keck, Margaret, and Kathryn Sikkink. 1998. *Activists beyond Borders: Advocacy Networks in International Politics*. Cornell University Press.

Kelly, Mary E. 2002. Cross border work on the environment. In *Cross-Border Dialogues*, ed. D. Brooks and J. Fox. Center for US-Mexico Studies, University of California, San Diego.

Khor, Martin. 1993. Economics and environmental justice: Rethinking North-South relations. In *Toxic Struggles*, ed. R. Hofrichter. New Society.

Kiefer, Chris, and Medea Benjamin. 1993. Solidarity with the Third World: Building an international environmental justice movement. In *Toxic Struggles*, ed. R. Hofrichter. New Society.

Kopinak, Kathryn, and Maria Del Rocio Barajas. 2002. Too close for comfort? The proximity of industrial hazardous waste to local populations in Tijuana Mexico. *Journal of Environment and Development* 11, no. 3: 215–247.

Leff, Enrique, ed. 2001. *Justicia ambiental: Construcción y defensa de los nuevos derechos ambientales, culturales, y colectivos en América Latina*. PNUMA.

Lievesley, Geraldine. 1999. *Democracy in Latin America: Mobilization, Power and the Search for a New Politics*. Manchester University Press.

Martinez-Alier, Joan. 2003. Mining conflicts, environmental justice, and valuation. In *Just Sustainabilities*, ed. J. Agyeman et al. MIT Press.

Mutz, Kathryn M., Gary C. Bryner, and Douglas S. Kenney, eds. 2002. *Justice and Natural Resources: Concepts, Strategies, and Applications*. Island.

Naumann, Talli. 2004. *The Environmental Right-to-Know Movement*. Inter-hemispheric Resource Center.

Novotny, Patrick. 2000. *Where We Live, Work, and Play: The Environmental Justice Movement and the Struggle for a New Environmentalism*. Praeger.

OLCA (Observatorio Latinoamericano de Conflictos Ambientales). 2005. *Justicia ambiental: un derecho irrenunciable*.

Paré, Luisa, David Bray, John Burstein, and Sergio Martínez, eds. 1997. *Semillas para el cambio en el campo: Medio ambiente, mercados, y organización campesina*. Imagen Textual.

Pellow, David N. 2000a. Environmental inequality formation: Toward a theory of environmental justice. *American Behavioral Scientist* 43, no. 4: 581–601.

Pellow, David N. 2000b. African American labor at the margins: Exploring the emergence of environmental health hazards in the workplace. *Research in the Sociology of Work* 9: 95–114.

Rees, William E., and Laura Westra. 2003. When consumption does violence. In *Just Sustainabilities*, ed. J. Agyeman et al. MIT Press.

Reilly, Charles A., ed. 1995. *New Paths to Democratic Development in Latin America: The Rise of NGO-Municipal Collaboration*. Lynne Rienner.

Rhodes, Edwardo Lao. 2003. *Environmental Justice in America: A New Paradigm*. Indiana University Press.

Roberts, J. Timmons, and Nikki Demetria Thanos. 2003. *Trouble in Paradise: Globalization and Environmental Crisis in Latin America*. Routledge.

Sachs, Wolfgang. 2002. Ecology, justice, and the end of development. In *Environmental Justice*, ed. J. Byrne et al. Transaction.

Schlosberg, David. 1999. *Environmental Justice and the New Pluralism: The Challenge of Difference for Environmentalism*. Oxford University Press.

Schlosberg, David. 2003. The justice of environmental justice: Reconciling equity, recognition, and participation in a political movement. In *Moral and Political Reasoning in Environmental Practice*, ed. A. Light and A. deShalit. MIT Press.

Shiva, Vandana. 1997. *Biopiracy: The Plunder of Nature and Knowledge*. South End.

Taylor, Dorceta. 2000. The rise of the environmental justice paradigm. *American Behavioral Scientist* 43, no. 4: 508–580.

Weissman, Robert. 1993. Corporate plundering of Third World resources. In *Toxic Struggles*, ed. R. Hofrichter. New Society.

Westra, Laura, and Bill E. Lawson. 2001. *Faces of Environmental Racism: Confronting Issues of Global Justice*. Rowman and Littlefield.

Williams, Heather. 2002. Lessons from the labor front: The Coalition for Justice in the Maquiladoras. In *Cross-Border Dialogues*, ed. D. Brooks and J. Fox. Center for US-Mexico Studies, University of California, San Diego.

Wright, Angus. 2005. *The Death of Ramón González: The Modern Agricultural Dilemma*. University of Texas Press.

I

Environmental Justice in Latin America?
Global and Conceptual Challenges

1

Tracing Race: Mapping Environmental Formations in Environmental Justice Research in Latin America

Juanita Sundberg

Trabajo como negro para vivir como blanco. [I work like a black to live like a white.]
—saying common in Mexico

In a recent volume, Ariel Dulitzky of the Inter-American Commission on Human Rights of the Organization of American States argues that Latin America is a region in denial about racial discrimination and racism. Dulitzky (2005, p. 40) cites a statement issued by South American officials in 2000: "The Presidents [of South America] view with concern the resurgence of racism and of discriminatory manifestations and expressions *in other parts of the world* and state their commitment to preserve South America from the propagation of said phenomenon." In Dulitzky's view, national mythologies of racial harmony such as *mestizaje* [racial mixing] in Mexico and racial democracy in Brazil conceal the place of race in organizing social relations, while also masking official policies of whitening in colonial and post-colonial contexts.

Despite such national mythologies, Dulitzky (ibid., p. 48) argues, many people experience race as "a decisive factor in determining chances and opportunities to succeed in [Latin American] society." Arguably, many people also experience race as a significant factor in shaping access to natural resources; exposure to environmental hazards (pesticides, toxic waste) and natural hazards; access to environmental benefits (clean air, water, fertile soils); and determinations of who counts in environmental policy formulation, implementation, and enforcement. However, researchers have tended to treat studies of race as discreet from such environmental issues. Consequently, there is little understanding of how race intersects with environment to create socio-environmental inequalities in Latin America.

In this chapter, I demonstrate why race should be included as a key variable in considerations of human-environment relations in Latin American countries. Systems of racial classification, I argue, have drawn upon and come into being through *environmental formations*, by which I mean the historically specific articulations between environmental imaginaries,[1] legal frameworks for allocating natural resources, and patterns of environmental transformation driven by the broader political economic context. Tracing the ways in which racial hierarchies and environmental formations articulate promises to inspire fresh interpretations of the ways in which race works to organize and rationalize environmental inequality.

Given debates about the place of race in organizing social relations in Latin America, I begin with a review of differing conceptualizations of race and racism and outline the implications of each for the study of environmental justice in Latin America. I then draw on several empirical examples from the colonial era to the present in order to illustrate how attitudes toward, relations with, and claims to natural resources enter into the production of social and political distinctions and define membership in the national body. I conclude by synthesizing my approach and presenting some points of departure for environmental justice research in Latin America. Ultimately, my goal is to provoke new questions about the ways in which exclusionary discourses and practices work in and through the environment, but also how they are naturalized, and come to appear justifiable and indeed necessary.

Before I begin, it is important to define my terms. First, I use the term *environmental justice* to delineate an investigative approach, not a normative state that scholars might bring to Latin America. As this chapter is directed at scholars interested in developing environmental justices as an approach in Latin America, I occasionally use the terms "us" or "we" to refer to this group. Second, I draw from David Theo Goldberg (1993, p. 81) to define race as a concept that "serves to naturalize the groupings it identifies. In articulating as natural ways of being in the world and institutional structures in and through which such ways of being are expressed, race both establishes and rationalizes the order of difference as a law of nature." This definition recognizes that racial categories are not dependent upon notions of biological difference, but may incorporate a wide range of cultural expressions. Third, in keeping with the schema outlined by Nancy Appelbaum, Anne Macpherson, and Karin Rosemblatt (2003b, p. 2), I use 'race' when referring to "a contingent historical phenomena that has varied over time and space," and 'racialization' to refer to the "the process of marking human differences according to hierarchical discourses." From these definitions, I hope it is clear that my intent is not to reify racial categories as natural, but to understand how they come into being.

What Is the Place of Race in Organizing Social and Environmental Relations?

My desire to develop a framework appropriate for studying the articulations between race and environment in Latin American contexts is driven by the frustrations I experienced in my dissertation research. While doing fieldwork in Guatemala, I struggled to make sense of the ways in which conservation projects directed by US-based non-governmental organizations (NGOs) keyed into and reproduced pre-existing social hierarchies (Sundberg 1998a). In particular, I suspected I was seeing racial hierarchies at work, but was not sure how to study them. I now believe there is no mystery as to why I was unprepared theoretically to analyze how processes of racialization organized social and environmental relations in Guatemala. Simply put, as a privileged white United Statesian, I was not taught to *see* or *feel* race. Rather, I was taught—if it was mentioned at all—that "races" do not exist, in the sense that scientific evidence does not support the notion that human beings are divided up into distinct races, each with its own geography and bio-cultural characteristics.

My inability to see and feel race was compounded by my training in the discipline of geography, which stands accused of being nearly silent on how hegemonic racial formations operate at systemic levels to shape space, place, and environment (Bonnett 1997; Kobayashi and Peake 2000). Geography's quiet may be a consequence of the discipline's origins in colonial and imperial projects mapping and classifying difference. Another important factor, argues Laura Pulido (2002), is the ethnic composition of geography departments in North America. (See also Mahtani 2004.) As the dominant socio-spatial experience in geography, whiteness shapes what is regarded as a problem or issue worth analyzing and "skews our intellectual production" (Pulido 2002, pp. 45, 46).

Puzzled by what I saw with untrained eyes, I began to search for tools with which to analyze the place of race in organizing socio-spatial and environmental relations. In what follows, I outline two principal perspectives on race and racism as found in current debates in studies of race and environmental justice. I place the first group within a liberal social science paradigm, while the second is grouped under the umbrella of critical race theory.[2] In this brief review, my goal is to focus on how assumptions about the place of race will shape the study of environmental injustices in Latin America.

Liberal paradigms, which predominate throughout the Americas, tend to frame racial thinking as a phenomenon of the past, when science fostered a belief in the biological or genetic differences between different groups of people (Winant 2001). In North American democracies, legislation is seen as having rectified the inequities of the past and citizens are called upon to help build a tolerant, "color-blind" or multicultural society (D'Souza 1991). Racism is defined as conscious discrimination against people of color, and racists are framed as stuck in the past or as extremists. Indeed, court rulings in the United States increasingly restrict legal definitions of racism by requiring proof of intentionality (Delgado and Stefanic 2000). From such perspectives, *procedural change* is assumed to produce *social change*, thereby eliminating barriers to citizenship (Pulido 1994). In this "post-racial" context, race is discredited as a valid analytical category.

In contemporary Latin American countries, Dulitsky (2005) argues, racial discrimination is officially denied in four ways. First, Latin American governments argue that racial discrimination and segregation was never legislated in the region (ibid., p. 45). This claim is based upon the notion that liberal philosophical ideals directed the region's break with Spanish colonialism and led to the establishment of universal citizenship within the new nations. The implication of such claims is that racism only exists if codified in the legal system. Second, Latin American regimes attribute existing discrimination to poverty; thus, for instance, the government of Peru claims: "Today, practically every Peruvian is of mixed blood and a racial problem no longer exists. Instead, there exists a problem of economic underdevelopment in certain sectors of the population." (cited in Dulitzky 2005, p. 44) Third, Latin American leaders and intellectuals point to nation-building narratives of inclusion based upon homogenizing identities: "we are all Mexicans," "we are all *mestizos*," or "we are all white" (Graham 1990; Radcliffe 1996; Wade 1997). Carol Smith (1999) argues, for instance, that North American anthropologists followed official narratives about the absence of racial discrimination against indigenous peoples in Guatemala because they had the option of becoming *ladinos*,[3] an identity category predicated on being non-indigenous. (See also Warren 2000.) Finally, Dulitzky (2005) suggests, governments tend to respond to charges of racism by labeling such acts as isolated incidents motivated by individuals or small groups.

In contrast to liberal thinkers, critical race theorists point out that, although races do not exist as facts of nature and are not regarded as valid scientific categories, processes of racialization continue to organize social relations and define who counts in the body politic (Delgado and Stefanic 2000; Appelbaum et al. 2003a). Rather than an "antiquated" or "irrational" way of organizing human kind, racial thinking is framed as formative of and intimately woven into the very fabric of modern social formations, such as colonialism, nationalism, capitalism, and liberal democracies (Goldberg 1993; Winant 2001; Silverblatt 2004). Since their very inception, critical theorists contend, liberal democracies at once proclaimed liberty and justice for all *and* restricted citizenship on the basis of class, gender, and racial hierarchies (Winant 2001). Even in contemporary established democracies, not all are equal under the law (Delgado and Stefanic 2000). Although race is only one variable, it is crucial to the production of inequality. In Goldberg's (1993) view, race "prompts the exclusion of others by making it thinkable to deny or ignore their respective claims." Racial thinking, Goldberg argues, provides a powerful rationale for *why* inequalities or injustices between groups of people are socially and legally acceptable.

As scholars illustrate, racial thinking was formative of and integral to the Spanish colonial bureaucratic and legal structure (Silverblatt 2004); post-colonial framings of citizenship in Latin America are built on this structure (Appelbaum et al. 2003a; Graham 1990; Radcliffe and Westwood 1996; Wade 1997). Liberals may have called for universal rights; however, visions of the proper citizen were rooted in Creole ideals of "whiteness and masculinity," characterized by "literacy, property ownership, and individual autonomy" (Appelbaum et al. 2003b, p. 4). Those who did not conform to these ideals (women, Indians, *mestizos* [mixed-race people], former slaves) were framed as biologically and racially inferior and therefore incapable of taking on the rights and responsibilities of citizenship (Dore and Molyneux 2000; Wade 1997). Moreover, national mythologies of inclusion are shown to be fundamentally exclusionary, in that they intend to promote whitening through European immigration, miscegenation (*mestizaje*), assimilation, and in extreme cases genocide (Bonnett 2000). Despite official and popular claims that mestizaje and assimilation represent democratizing or equalizing forces, whiteness is privileged in Latin American societies and is the "essential ingredient to obtain better social, employment, and education opportunities in a white-dominated world" (Dulitzky 2005, p. 49; see also Bonnett 2000).

New social movements in Latin America challenge liberal notions that racial thinking is an antiquated practice ameliorated by progressive politics. Indigenous, black, feminist, gay and lesbian, and environmental movements—to name only a few of those on the scene—contest hegemonic conceptions of who counts as a political actor, what counts as a political issue, and where politics happens (Alvarez, Dagnino, and Escobar 1998). In particular, indigenous and Afro-descendents movements have sparked intense debates on nation-building projects predicated on homogenous and homogenizing conceptions of the citizen as *mestizo* or *ladino* (Bianchi et al. 1999; Brysk 2000; Hooker 2005; Warren and Jackson 2002). In the context of these movements, numerous Latin American countries have ratified new constitutions containing language recognizing the multiethnic, pluricultural, or multilingual nature of their societies, while others have awarded specific rights to indigenous and

Afro-descendent populations including collective land rights (Van Cott 2000, 2005; Hooker 2005).

Relevance of Debates on the Place of Race for Environmental Justice in Latin America

What do these differing conceptions imply for research on environmental inequality? If racism is viewed through a liberal lens as an isolated event, an aberration within a color-blind or *mestizo* society, then scholars must demonstrate proof that policies or decisions *intend* to discriminate against racialized communities. Current definitions of environmental racism in the United States, for instance, are informed by this liberal social and legal context. For example, Bunyan Bryant's (1995, p. 6) definition "refers to those institutional rules, regulations, and policies of government or corporate decisions that *deliberately* target certain communities for least desirable land uses . . . based upon prescribed biological characteristics" (emphasis added). Francis Adeola (2000, p. 688) also uses the word 'deliberate' in her definition. In short, proof of racist intent must be provided to argue that inequality is tied to racial thinking.

In contrast, if race and processes of racialization are regarded as constitutive of socio-spatial relations at systemic, structural levels, studies of environmental inequality will not be concerned to prove that racism exists (Pulido 1996). Rather, they will attempt to analyze how race *works* with and through other axes of power at multiple scales to organize and rationalize environmental decision making and its unequal effects.

Pulido's study of environmental racism in Los Angeles offers an example of this approach. Pulido (2000, p. 15) begins with an analysis of racial formations in the United States; she names the hegemonic formation "white privilege" to encompass the "structures, practices, and ideologies that reproduce whites' privileged status." Within this racial formation, Pulido argues, racism is not confined to intentional acts of discrimination, for white privilege is an unconscious form of racism: "whites do not necessarily *intend* to hurt people of color, but because they are unaware of their white-skin privilege, and because they accrue social and economic benefits by maintaining the status quo, they inevitably do." Environmental racism in Los Angeles, Pulido concludes, is an effect of myriad individual and institutional decisions intended to protect white privilege.

It is incumbent upon those of us wishing to study environmental injustices in Latin America to seriously examine the relevance and utility of differing theoretical frameworks. How has our institutional training taught us to see, feel, and interpret race? What might liberal versus critical frameworks make visible? What is rendered invisible? In my own attempts to examine inequality in Guatemala, I have found restricted conceptions of race and racism very limiting, for they seem to close off the entire realm of social relations from analysis; it is as if the social order is a closed book and no questions need to be asked about how subjects are constituted through everyday discourses and practices. In my view, the political and theoretical questions inspired by new social movements are crucial to the study of how environmental inequality comes into being: how are social subjects constituted as members of, or marginal to the national body? How have these categories come into being at particular historical junctures? And, I would add, how do these categories articulate with and through environmental formations? In the next section, I illustrate how these questions might inspire fresh interpretations of environmental inequality in Latin America.

Race and Environmental Formations: Exploring the Articulations in Latin American Contexts

Critical race theorists point to the role of legal frameworks in constituting social subjects; new social movements draw our attention to the ways in which every day discourses and practices constitute systems of racial classification at multiple and intersecting geographical scales, including the body, home, neighborhood, nature, and nation. To trace the articulations between race and environmental formations, I propose a methodological approach that works backward from a particular issue or event to ask how social groups are categorized, who is included or excluded in the body politic and on what grounds, and how this shapes spatial and environmental practices. Thus, instead of starting with pre-given or taken-for-granted categories like "indigenous people" or "such and such ethnic group" within "such and such" geographical area, we might begin by exploring how differently situated historical actors bring these categories into being in the context of three critical fields of social and political action: legal frameworks delimiting access to rights and resources, systems of classification constituting subjects and their social and geographical place in society, and environmental formations. How these three elements articulate will be different in time and place, considering the unique histories, national imaginaries, populations, and geographies of individual countries.

To demonstrate the potential insights to be gained from this approach, I engage with a series of empirical examples selected from the work of scholars working in historic and contemporary contexts. In doing so, I do not pretend to outline a comprehensive or exhaustive theory that applies to all of Latin America at all points in time. My goal is much more modest: to identify the social fields important to this line of inquiry in the hopes of provoking new questions about the ways in which exclusionary discourses and practices work in and through the environment. Likewise, my approach is informed primarily by scholarship on Spanish-speaking Latin America, wherein Spanish colonial policies and administrative bureaucracies left an indelible imprint on governance, cultural practices, and environmental formations throughout the region. Brazil and especially the Caribbean—shaped as it is by layers of European colonialism—are largely outside my purview (which is not to say that my approach offers nothing to students of these regions). I offer this approach, not as theory about or a model of environmental justice in Latin America, but an invitation.

In the following discussion, I rely upon Appelbaum, Macpherson, and Rosemblatt's (2003b) timeline delineating distinct colonial and post-colonial national projects in Latin America; each of these periods drew upon particular understandings of race. However, this periodization is not meant to indicate radical shifts, for racial discourses and practices are marked by continuity and change and are always being contested. Approaching racial constructs historically in a particular socio-political space allows for an understanding of such continuities, shifts, and contestations. I begin with the colonial era precisely because post-colonial racial thinking builds upon, contests, and reconfigures colonial constructions.

Colonial Articulations

Spanish colonialism is viewed as formative of modern racial thinking (Goldberg 1993; Winant 2001). The encounter with societies and landscapes previously unknown to the conquerors was productive of new ways of thinking about the nature of human beings, governance systems, human-land relations, and the environment. Although the colonists encountered diverse groups of people with differing languages, economies and governance structures, the conquest led to a process of social homogenization, thereby producing unified categories of "Spaniards" and "Indians" where none had existed previously (Quijano 2000; Dussel 1995).

After the initial conquest, the Spanish crown outlined clear legal and fiscal rights and responsibilities for the different categories of people residing in the two separate republics: Spanish and Indian (Bakewell 2004; Silverblatt 2004). In brief, Spaniards had rights to indigenous labor within a specified geographical space and the fruits of that labor. Indians were obliged to pay tribute to the Spanish crown; were governed by a native authority at the local level; had rights to communal land; and were regarded as minors under the law, which made the crown responsible for their protection (Chambers 2003). Those individuals born of mixed heritage were organized into different categories. They held a nebulous legal status, which often depended upon local interpretations of the law; they were, however, exempt from the rights and responsibilities held by Indians. Slaves were governed by a different set of laws.

Throughout the Spanish colonial era, then, the legal system created racial categories to organize socio-spatial relations, including access to rights, resources, living spaces, education, jobs, and protection from harm. In time, categories of people and their corresponding rights and responsibilities came to appear as fixed characteristics inherent to that group (Silverblatt 2004). Spaniards and Creoles came to see themselves as rightful governors and cultural, social, and economic leaders, while Indians came to appear as simple, without education, and suitable only for labor. And yet the boundaries between social groups were often difficult to define, given processes of *mestizaje* [racial mixing] as well as flexibility in interpretations (Appelbaum et al. 2003).

Of relevance to this chapter is how elite conceptions of appropriate resource management informed processes of racialization and vice versa. Although very little research specifically examines this issue, the articulations between race and environmental formations in the colonial era appear contradictory. The colonial system clearly privileged Spaniards, who assumed rightful ownership of the bodies and labor of "Indians" as well as natural resources. This group also presumed to define "appropriate" land use; inappropriate land use was tied to the notion of irrationality or the incapacity to be rational (Sluyter 1999). At the same time that the category "Indian" implied legalized abuse and race-based social and political exclusion, however, it also promised rights to natural resources and protection by the Crown. In some cases, the right to communal land was crucial to the autonomy of indigenous societies and formed the basis for collective identities tied to language, cosmology, land-use practices, etc.

Two examples highlight the differing implications of racialized environmental formations. In early colonial Mexico, Spanish attempts to appropriate native land—despite legislation intended to protect it—were accomplished by naming native agricultural fields and orchards as *baldíos*, a term used in Spanish law to mean wastelands, as in idle, unimproved lands (Sluyter 1999). Through this process, colonists were able to claim lands for grazing, which they considered a rational use of the landscape. Although it is commonly argued that Spaniards may not have recognized native land use, Andrew Sluyter (1999) found archival evidence in Veracruz demonstrating that native communities contested the utilization of Spanish categories in legal cases, thereby showing them to be the culturally specific categories they were. In other cases, some native communities deployed Spanish categories to claim lands for ranching; yet, their success demonstrates how Spanish "categories became the taken-for-granted, be-all and end-all measures of productive land use" (Sluyter 1999, p. 391).

In a study from late colonial Arequipa, Peru, Sarah Chambers (2003) demonstrates the ways in which individuals legally classified as indigenous, regardless of their parentage, negotiated this category in relation to changing environmental formations. In the late colonial period, Arequipa's white elite had appropriated significant landholdings around the city, leading to less communal land and conflicts over access to that land. Those individuals categorized as "Indian" received less and less land or none at all, yet were still required to pay a head tax. In this context, some individuals petitioned to have their identity legally changed to Spanish (Chambers 2003, p. 35). In 1803, the *cacique* of one village complained that many of the "Indians" were trying to exempt themselves from paying tribute by claiming to be Spanish. He reported: "All the Indians . . . want to become Spaniards, some because they dress in the Spanish style, others because they learn Spanish trades such as Barbers, tailors etc., or because their color is somewhat pale, or because they style their hair, or because their godparents are Spanish and have them baptized in the Cathedral, and finally because they change their Indian surnames and take on Spanish ones." (cited in Chambers 2003, p. 38) The *cacique* warned that soon there would be no Indians left to pay tribute. Ultimately, in Arequipa, appropriation of communal lands served to further elite-driven ideologies and processes of *blanqueamiento* or whitening of the population by eliminating or minimizing indigenous identities and practices, as well as the special rights ascribed to them under the law.

Though these cases are revealing, there are many questions that remain to be fully explored about the articulation between legal frameworks, systems of social classification, and environmental formations in the colonial era. How did elites define cultural ecological traits in ways that furthered exclusionary practices, as in continued attacks on communal lands? Did indigenous communities develop counter-discourses in attempts to protect or claim rights?

Early Independence

In the early nineteenth century, the newly independent republics faced the challenge of "creating citizens out of colonial subjects and forging national communities from colonial societies marked by stark social divisions" (Appelbaum et al. 2003b, p. 4). Generally speaking, nation building in Latin America was predicated upon creating a homogenous ethnic community (Radcliffe and Westwood 1996). As in all nations, that ethnicity had to be produced, its boundaries defined (Anderson 1991). Therefore, the early nation-building era is characterized by debates over who should be included within the newly emerging polities and under what conditions. Those drawing upon and contributing to classical liberal philosophy—the Liberals—asserted democratic ideals and suggested that citizenship should replace all other identities (caste, religious), making all equal before the law (Sanders 2003, p. 60). Conservatives, on the other hand, sought to preserve colonial hierarchies and tended to create "racialized forms of subordinate inclusion, even as they emphasized caste divisions over common citizenship" (Appelbaum et al. 2003b, p. 4).

As noted above, liberal visions of universal citizenship were underwritten by race, gender, and class hierarchies, which restricted who was eligible for citizenship (Dore and Molyneux 2000). Within paradoxical liberalism, then, whiteness became the socio-cultural standard against which other social categories were measured and racial diversity was framed as an obstacle to democratization (Bonnett 2000). Debates centered on whether or not these racial and cultural "impediments" could be overcome with *blanqueamiento* or whitening through civilizing projects and racial improvement (Stepan 1991). Some leaders shared Simón Bolívar's belief in social improvement, meaning that racially inferior individuals could be educated and extended citizenship over time. Others suggested that national progress depended upon the extermination of those deemed inferior—for instance, Domingo Sarmiento specific targeted the indigenous peoples of the Pampas.

Of particular relevance to this chapter is how elite visions of "appropriate" human-land relations were used to define membership in the nation. Through what narrative strategies did Creoles install whites (however defined) as entitled to develop the land and its resources? How did elites codify these beliefs into law, thereby structuring the spatialities of Latin American nations and institutionalizing racialized conceptions of property regimes and resource-management practices deemed "appropriate" to national progress? How did elites envision the destiny of those social groups engaged in "inappropriate" human-land relations? In turn, how did social groups deemed "inappropriate" contest these visions and/or demand rights to the fruits of citizenship and national progress? These questions were at the center of nation-building projects in the late nineteenth century.

Late-Nineteenth-Century and Early-Twentieth-Century Nation Building
After the instabilities of the early independence era, political and economic leaders sought to consolidate power and create order to stimulate
economic development and international trade. In particular, leaders
promoted the expansion of plantations and cultivation of commodities
of value on the global market, often in concert with foreign individual
entrepreneurs or interests like the United Fruit Company. Always under
threat, indigenous communal lands now came under unyielding attack.
As I show, however, this conflict cannot be analyzed in terms of political
economy alone, as debates about rights to land became primary sites for
reconfiguring systems of racial classification and membership in the body
politic.

In a fascinating study of Colombia's Cauca region from 1849 to 1890,
James Sanders (2003) illustrates how indigenous groups negotiated shifting notions of citizenship and land. In the Cauca, those groups classified
as Indians lived in *resguardos* or communal lands to which they had
rights since the colonial era. Sanders (ibid.) found that elites attacked the
resguardos as institutions unsuitable for a republican nation; some suggested that they "doomed Indians to backwardness and barbarism and
prevented them from entering modern society as productive individuals,
thus condemning them to poverty." Liberals advocated the dismantling
of communal lands and the creation of a land market to which all had
"equal" access. In this way, shifting notions of race were attached to
environmental formations: communal lands and special rights constituted backwardness; private property meant modernity and productivity.
Archival evidence suggests that the Cauca's Indians defended their rights
to lands and local governance in a unique way: they "amalgamated an
older discourse of community and appeals to authority with a new
republican discourse of rights and citizenship" (ibid.). Sanders found that
other indigenous groups in Colombia were less successful in unlinking
ideas of backwardness from the institution of communal land and the
land-use practices carried out therein.

In mid-nineteenth-century Guatemala, indigenous communities also
found themselves framed as obstacles to progress when white and *ladino*
elites identified coffee production as Guatemala's ticket to economic
development and progress. In this context, indigenous rights to commu-

nal land came under attack (Cambranes 1985, p. 88). On a discursive level, Liberal elites attacked indigenous management of communal lands by suggesting they were uncultivated and unproductive; Indians were represented as lazy and unwilling to work. "It is a pity to see such great areas of uncultivated lands in the hands of the natives, who neither cultivate them nor let them be cultivated," one Political Chief wrote in 1875 (cited Cambranes 1985, p. 257).

After gaining power in 1871, the Liberals used legislative means to do away with communal lands. In 1873 and 1877, new legislation effectively allowed those renting communal lands from indigenous communities to claim ownership of the property. In addition, communal lands were made available for appropriation and privatization by redefining the very meaning of the term "cultivation" to refer to coffee, sugar cane, fodder, and cacao plantations (Cambranes 1985, p. 252). Land cultivated with other crops was rendered "uncultivated." Further legislation institutionalized forced labor for indigenous people.

The following quotation from a departmental Political Chief (1873) is indicative of how land use and property were tied to racial categorizations (cited in Cambranes 1985, p. 253):

In Santa Lucia, a great part of the common public land has been granted to the *ladino* class, and what before was uncultivated land has been transformed into beautiful and productive *fincas*, where people can go to work in order to get what they need . . . and what is more, there is hope for progress in this beneficial transformation of the Indians.

As this quotation suggests, the appropriation of indigenous lands was justified in terms of racialized discourses that named indigenous communities as "backward," indigenous land-use practices as "unproductive," and indigenous lands as "uncultivated." Moreover, private property and coerced labor were framed as beneficial to indigenous people in that they were intended to cultivate values and land-use practices appropriate to a nation defined as productive and white. In sum, the primary documents cited by Jorge Cambranes suggest that debates about land use in late-nineteenth-century Guatemala became important sites for defining the national body as *ladino* and white. The exclusion of indigenous people from the body politic and the sacrifice of their political rights were inscribed within the very concepts of productive land use. As such, national economic development goals coincided with goals of *blanquea-miento* or whitening (Taracena 2002). Liberal, *ladino* nation-building projects were in place in Guatemala until the 1940s.

While there is much to explore in this period and every country is distinct, these brief examples from Colombia and Guatemala hint at the importance, indeed the necessity of historical research on the articulations between race and environmental formations in Latin America. Historical approaches allow for the analysis of patterns of inequality over time, thereby exposing if and how particular social groups were consistently denied access to rights and resources or if and how certain groups were disproportionately burdened with the costs of national progress and development.

Mid- to Late-Twentieth-Century Contests over Power, Citizenship, and Environment

In the mid to late twentieth century, Latin American countries witnessed significant contests over power and the contours of citizenship; these struggles challenged established social relations and long-standing systems of racial classification (Yashar 1998; Sieder 2002). After World War II and the Holocaust, Latin American leaders, scientists, and intellectuals abandoned explicit discourses of race (Stepan 1991). However, as Appelbaum et al. (2003b, p. 8) assert, they did not "abandon the assumptions that underlay racial thinking." Rather, the authors argue, the concept of ethnicity came to dominate discourses about those social groups who did not conform to national visions of the ideal citizen, coded as either *mestizo*, *ladino*, or white. Discourses of ethnicity fit nicely with emerging ideologies of modernization and development, which are underwritten by the notion that backward cultural traits bind certain groups to tradition and therefore under-development. According to modernization theory, these traits must be overcome in order for such groups to be integrated into modern national economies (Saldaña-Portillo 2001; for evidence of the continuing relevance of this approach, see Harrison 2000).

Of relevance to this chapter is how historical actors have drawn upon racializing discourses to push for, negotiate, or contest changing environmental formations, characterized by the expansion of agri-businesses, agrarian reform, colonization of so-called "empty" or "idle" lands, to sustainable development projects and the creation of protected areas (Goett 2006; Gordon, Gurdian, and Hale 2003; Sawyer 2004; Sundberg 2003; Stephen 2002). What does the changing place of race in organizing citizenship in Latin American societies mean for struggles over resources? Who is deemed as expendable for the sake of economic development and why? How are perceived differences in environmental practices used to promote or further social and environmental exclusions? Conversely, how are they used to make claims for inclusion?

Here I draw from my research on the cultural politics of conservation in Guatemala to illustrate the ways in which racial thinking informs the daily practices of a movement that many associate with progressive goals. My ethnographic research reveals how Guatemala's system of protected areas was the outcome of high-level, exclusive negotiations between elite Guatemalans and United Statesians representing environmental non-governmental organizations and the US Agency for International Development (Sundberg 1998b; 2003). These groups assumed authority and ownership of the process on the assumption that other Guatemalans did not have the appropriate training and education to understand conservation. In this context, Guatemalan park administrators deployed authoritarian and coercive means to implement the Maya Biosphere Reserve.

In approaching the discourses and practices of authoritarian conservation, I began by examining how political subjects in Guatemala are constituted in relation to environmental formations. As I noted in the previous section, nation-building projects in Guatemala sought to create a *ladino* body politic that excluded indigenous people. Although suffrage was extended to all in the mid twentieth century, exclusionary social practices presented barriers to the exercise of citizenship for the majority of people (Taracena 2002; Sieder 1999). Thus, who came to count as a legitimate environmental decision maker in conservation projects was determined by an exclusionary social order that positioned indigenous people and poor *ladino campesinos* as mentally incapable of taking on rights and responsibilities due to lack of formal education and essentialized cultural traits like communal resource management (Sundberg 2003).

I also asked how hegemonic visions of nature determine who may and may not participate in conservation decision making, or who may or may not have access to resources within the boundaries of the reserve. In Guatemala, US-based non-governmental organizations formed alliances with elite Guatemalan professionals with training in the biophysical sciences (ecology, biology, zoology, botany) and law. Such partnerships legitimize the presence of international NGOs in Latin America (Christen et al. 1998). However, it is important to ask how the rhetoric of partnership in conjunction with the biological sciences (as scientific and therefore universal languages) obscures the power relations, such as parallel systems of racial classification and class alliances, that make these arrangements possible and indeed viable across multiple socio-spatial scales. Through such partnerships, these groups produced a vision of nature in the Maya Biosphere Reserve as pristine (Sundberg 1998b). This vision determined how conservation projects were formulated, where conservation happened, under what conditions, and at whose expense. While none of the social groups residing within the newly created reserve shared this vision, it had the effect of privileging some while furthering the exclusion of others.

Given that past nation-building projects in Guatemala have attempted to whiten the national body through civilizing projects and racial improvement, it is also important to ask if and how conservation reconfigures these goals. At a national scale, the creation of the Maya Biosphere Reserve was intended to promote the "rational" use of natural resources (USAID 1989, p. 1). As rationality has long been used to define what counts as legitimate land management, this goal may be viewed as an effort to modernize and whiten cultural landscapes by eliminating those human-land relations defined as backward or inappropriate. At the local level, NGO environmental education projects may be seen as a means of social improvement by erasing ethnically coded cultural traits and human land relations to produce modern visions of nature and land use.

I also found that the discourses of conservation were appropriated to make claims for inclusion (Sundberg 2006). For example, the Itzaj, an indigenous community residing within the boundaries of the Maya Biosphere Reserve, was left out of decision-making circles because of local and national level systems of racial exclusion. And yet, a group of Itzaj and their supporters found that the discourses and practices of conservation offered new modes of representing their relationship to the forest. In short, these men appropriated North American visions of native peoples as living in harmony with nature to make claims about access to and control over resources. When articulated with new discourses of indigenous rights, conservationist discourses provided members of this social group with powerful tools to claim rights and resources in post-civil-war Guatemala.

Concluding Remarks and Points of Departure

This chapter outlines an environmental justice approach for Latin America. To this end, I explore a set of historical articulations between racial and environmental formations from the colonial era to the present. These brief examples serve to illustrate the importance of race as a critical variable in organizing inequality in Latin American societies and, likewise, how systems of racial classification come into being through environmental formations.

This theoretical and empirical exploration of the place of race leads me to summarize what I see as a point of departure for research on environmental injustice in Latin America: un-mapping how systems of racial classification come into being in relation to environmental formations and vice versa. As a methodology, un-mapping allows us to de-naturalize taken-for-granted socio-spatial and environmental categories by analyzing how historical actors bring them into being in the context of three critical fields of social and political action: legal frameworks delimiting access to rights and resources, systems of classification constituting subjects and their social and geographical place in society, and environmental formations. In this way, we treat race and natural resource management as the products of dynamic social relations, rather than reify them as individual characteristics, pre-given categories, or practices determined by nature. This approach promises to open up new areas of investigation and significantly enrich the study of environmental inequality in the region.

I offer this approach as a point of departure and as an invitation. Asking how racial processes work with and through environmental formations will help to understand not only how exclusionary discourses and practices work, but also how they come to appear justifiable and indeed necessary. What is more, tracing how social and environmental formations come into being is to rob them of their naturalness—one of their primary sources of power—thereby revealing their potential for re-configuration.

Notes

1. By "environmental imaginaries" I mean ideas about nature and its appropriate management, as in resource-management practices and property regimes.

2. The term "critical race theory" is usually used to delineate a field of critical legal studies; here, I use the term more broadly to include those social scientists that subscribe to radical perspectives on the place of race in North American societies.

3. *Ladino* is the term used for a person of mixed European and indigenous descent; it can also refer to an indigenous person who no longer identifies him or her self as such. The term, however, is not synonymous with *mestizo*, used in other contexts like Mexico where nation-building projects in the early twentieth century celebrated the notion of mixed heritage.

References

Adeola, Francis. 2000. Cross-national environmental injustice and human rights issues: A review of evidence in the developing world. *American Behavioral Scientist* 43: 686–706.

Alvarez, Sonia, Evelina Dagnino, and Arturo Escobar. 1998. Introduction: the cultural and the political in Latin American social movements. In *Cultures of Politics/Politics Of Culture*, ed. S. Alvarez et al. Westview.

Anderson, Benedict. 1991. *Imagined Communities*. Verso.

Applebaum, Nancy, Anne Macpherson, and Karin Alejandra Rosemblatt, eds. 2003a. *Race and Nation in Modern Latin America*. University of North Carolina Press.

Applebaum, Nancy, Anne Macpherson, and Karin Alejandra Rosemblatt. 2003b. Introduction. In *Race and Nation in Modern Latin America,* ed. N. Applebaum et al. University of North Carolina Press.

Bakewell, Peter. 2004. *A History of Latin America: 1450 to the Present.* Blackwell.

Bianchi Clara Arenas, Charles Hale, and Gustavo Palma Murga, eds. 1999. *¿Racismo en Guatemala? Abriendo el debate sobre un tema tabú.* AVANSCO.

Bonnett, Alastair. 1997. Geography, "race" and whiteness: invisible traditions and current challenges. *Area* 29: 193–199.

Bonnett, Alastair. 2000. *White Identities: Historical and International Perspectives*. Prentice-Hall.

Bryant, Bunyan. 1995. *Environmental Justice: Issues, Policies, and Solutions*. Island.

Cambranes, Jorge. 1985. *Coffee and Peasants: The Origins of the Modern Plantation Economy in Guatemala, 1853–1897*. Institute of Latin American Studies.

Chambers, Sarah. 2003. Little middle ground: the instability of a Mestizo identity in the Andes, eighteenth and nineteenth centuries. In *Race and Nation in Modern Latin America*, ed. N. Applebaum et al. University of North Carolina Press.

Christen, Catherine, Selene Herculano, and Kathryn Hochstetler. 1998. Latin American environmentalism: comparative views. *Studies in Comparative International Development* 33, no. 2: 58–87.

Casaús Arzú, Marta Elena. 1999. La metamorfosis del racismo em la elite de poder en Guatemala. In ¿*Racismo en Guatemala? Abriendo el Debate sobre un tema tabú*, ed. C. Arenas Bianchi et al. AVANSCO.

Delgado, Richard, and Jean Stefancic, eds. 2000. *Critical Race Theory: The Cutting Edge*. Temple University Press.

D'Souza, Dinesh. 1991. *Illiberal Education: The Politics of Race and Sex on Campus*. Free Press.

Dulitzky, Ariel. 2005. A region in denial: racial discrimination and racism in Latin America. In *Neither Enemies nor Friends*, ed. A. Dzidzienyo and S. Oboler. Palgrave Macmillan.

Dussel, Enrique. 1995. Eurocentrism and modernity. In *The Postmodernism Debate in Latin America*, ed. J. Beverley et al. Duke University Press.

Dzidzienyo, Anani, and Suzanne Oboler. 2005. *Neither Enemies nor Friends: Latinos, Blacks, Afro-Latinos*. Palgrave Macmillan.

Goett, Jennifer. 2006. Diasporic Identities, Autochthonous Rights: Race, Gender, and the Cultural Politics of Creole Land Rights in Nicaragua. Ph.D. dissertation, University of Texas.

Goldberg, David T. 1993. *Racist Culture: Philosophy and the Politics of Meaning*. Blackwell.

Gordon, Edmundo, Galio Gurdian, and Charles Hale. 2003. Rights, resources, and the social memory of struggle: Reflections on a study of indigenous and black community land rights on Nicaragua's Atlantic coast. *Human Organization* 62, no. 4: 360–381.

Graham, Richard. 1990. *The Idea of Race in Latin America, 1870–1940*. University of Texas Press.

Hooker, Juliet. 2005. Indigenous inclusion/black exclusion: Race, ethnicity and multicultural citizenship in Latin America. *Journal of Latin American Studies* 37: 285–310.

Harrison, Lawrence 2000. *Underdevelopment Is a State of Mind. The Latin American Case. Updated Edition.* Madison Books.

Kobayashi, Audrey, and Linda Peake. 2000. Racism out of place: thoughts on whiteness and an antiracist geography in the new millennium. *Annals of the Association of the American Geographers* 90: 392–403.

Mahtani, Minelle. 2004. Mapping race and gender in the academy: The experiences of women of colour faculty and graduate students in Britain, the US and Canada. *Journal of Geography in Higher Education* 28: 91–99.

Mignolo, Walter. 2000. *Local Histories/Global Designs: Coloniality, Subaltern Knowledges, and Border Thinking.* Princeton University Press.

Nelson, Diane. 1999. *A Finger in the Wound: Body Politics in Quincentennial Guatemala.* University of California Press.

Pulido, Laura. 1994. Restructuring and the contraction and expansion of environmental rights in the United States. *Environment and Planning A* 26: 915–936.

Pulido, Laura. 1996. A critical review of the methodology of environmental racism research. *Antipode* 28, no. 2: 142–159.

Pulido, Laura. 2000. Rethinking "environmental racism": White privilege and urban development in Southern California. *Annals of the Association of American Geographers* 90, no. 1: 12–40.

Pulido, Laura. 2002. Reflections on a white discipline. *The Professional Geographer* 54: 42–49.

Quijano, Anibal. 2000. Coloniality of power and Eurocentrism in Latin America. *International Sociology* 15: 215–232.

Radcliffe, Sarah. 1996. Imaginative geographies, postcolonialism, and national identities: Contemporary discourses of the nation in Ecuador. *Ecumene* 3, no. 1: 23–42.

Radcliffe, Sarah, and Sallie Westwood. 1996. *Remaking the Nation: Place, Identity and Politics in Latin America.* Routledge.

Razack, Shrene. 2002. When place becomes race. In *Race, Space, and the Law*, ed. S. Razack. Between the Lines.

Sanders, James. 2003. Belonging to the great Granadan family: Partisan struggle and the construction of indigenous identity and politics in Southwestern Colombia, 1840–1890. In *Race and Nation in Modern Latin America*, ed. N. Applebaum et al. University of North Carolina Press.

Sawyer, Suzana. 2004. *Crude Chronicles: Indigenous Politics, Multinational Oil, and Neoliberalism in Ecuador.* Duke University Press.

Sieder, Rachel. 1999. Rethinking democratization and citizenship: Legal pluralism and institutional reform in Guatemala. *Citizenship Studies* 3: 103–118.

Sieder, Rachel, ed. 2002. *Multiculturalism in Latin America: Indigenous Rights, Diversity, and Democracy.* Palgrave Macmillan.

Sluyter, Andrew. 1999. The making of the myth in postcolonial development: material-conceptual landscape transformation in sixteenth-century Veracruz. *Annals of the Association of American Geographer* 89: 377–401.

Smith, Carol. 1999. Interpretaciones Norteamericanas sobre la raza y el racismo en Guatemala. In *¿Racismo en Guatemala?* AVANSCO.

Stepan, Nancy. 1991. *"The Hour of Eugenics": Race, Gender, and Nation in Latin America.* Cornell University Press.

Stephen, Lynn. 2002. *Zapata Lives! Histories and Cultural Politics in Southern Mexico.* University of California Press.

Stonich, Susan. 1993. *"I Am Destroying the Land!" The Political Ecology of Poverty and Environmental Destruction in Honduras.* Westview.

Sundberg, Juanita. 1998a. Strategies for authenticity, space, and place in the Maya Biosphere Reserve, Petén, Guatemala. *Conference of Latin Americanist Geographers Yearbook* 24: 85–96.

Sundberg, Juanita. 1998b. NGO landscapes: Conservation and communities in the Maya Biosphere Reserve, Petén, Guatemala. *Geographical Review* 88, no. 3: 388–412.

Sundberg, Juanita. 2003. Conservation and democratization: Constituting citizenship in the Maya Biosphere Reserve, Guatemala. *Political Geography* 22: 715–740.

Sundberg, Juanita. 2006. Conservation encounters and trans-culturation in the "contact zones" of empire. *Cultural Geographies* 13, no. 2: 239–265.

Taracena, Arturo. 2002. *Etnicidad, estado, y nacion en Guatemala, 1808–1944.* CIRMA.

Van Cott, Donna Lee. 2000. *The Friendly Liquidation of the Past: The Politics Of Diversity in Latin America.* University of Pittsburgh Press.

Wade, Peter. 1993. *Blackness and Race Mixture: The Dynamics of Racial Identity in Colombia.* Johns Hopkins University Press.

Wade, Peter. 1997. *Race and Ethnicity in Latin America.* Pluto.

Warren, Jonathan. 2000. Masters in the field: White talk, white privilege, white biases. In *Racing Research, Researching Race,* ed. F. Twine and J. Warren. New York University Press.

Warren, Kay, and Jean Jackson. 2002. *Indigenous Movements, Self-Representation, and the State in Latin America.* University of Texas Press.

Winant, Howard. 2001. *The World Is a Ghetto: Race and Democracy since World War II.* Basic Books.

Yashar, Deborah. 1998. Contesting citizenship: Indigenous movements and democracy in Latin America. *Comparative Politics* 31: 23–42.

2

Contesting Trade Politics in the Americas: The Politics of Environmental Justice

Peter Newell

Anti-globalization movements in many parts of the world have made trade justice a central plank of their demands for a world trading system that is fairer to the world's poor while promoting sustainable development (Curtis 2001; TJM 2007). The concept of trade justice places questions of equity and access centrally in discussions about the winners and losers from trade. At the same time, the discourse and practice of environmental justice is gaining popular currency (Agyeman 2005; Pellow and Brulle 2005; Bullard 2005). The term is helpful in understanding the disproportionate impact of environmental degradation on the lives of poorer communities in the global North and South. This chapter shows that there exists an increasingly intimate relationship between the pursuit of trade and environmental justice, one which is recognized and acted upon by a growing number of social and environmental activists in Latin America. Insofar as struggles around access to resources and the location of hazard are increasingly affected by global and regional relations of production, trade affects the pursuit of environmental justice, altering the rules of the game and the strategic challenges faced by those seeking to defend the interests of poorer groups. Likewise, issues, discourses and strategies from the experience of the environmental justice movement increasingly feature in contestations around trade policy, who benefits from trade, and who has a right to make policy. How these notions relate to one another in the context of Latin America, where trade policy and the movements that have sought to contest its social and environmental impacts have assumed an increasingly high profile in the region's politics, is the subject of this chapter.

While acknowledging the role of those groups that have sought to pursue their notion of environmental justice through channels of institutional reform available to them within the main trade agreements in the region, namely the North American Free Trade Agreement (NAFTA), Mercosur, and the draft Free Trade Area of the Americas (FTAA) (Audley 1997; Tussie and Newell 2006), this chapter focuses on the relationship between trade and environmental justice as it is articulated by those contesting the current framing of trade debates in Latin America. This is done through appeals to notions of environmental justice which embody a different understanding of the social ecology of trade, posing questions about who benefits from trade and who bears the social and environmental costs of liberalization in more fundamental ways. By contesting the distribution of gain and risk that results from liberalization, these groups raise important environmental justice concerns, though in ways which reflect the unique nature of trade politics in Latin America.

Environmental Justice in Context

Activist and academic interest in the notion of environmental justice has been strongly shaped by the US context in which many of its defining struggles took place (Bullard 1990). The bulk of the literature continues to focus on the United States, despite emerging interest in poorer communities' struggles for environmental justice in South Africa (McDonald 2002) and India (Newell and Lekhi 2006). For example, environmental justice struggles in Latin America have attracted less attention despite significant attention to environmental politics in general within the region (Collinson 1996; Garcia 1991; Gumarâes 1995; Hall 2006).

Environmental justice is taken to mean the "distribution of environmental goods and environmental bads among human populations" (Dobson 1998, p. 20), a definition that consciously excludes issues of justice *to* the environment.

Environmental justice can be understood both as a discourse of popular mobilization and as a set of principles for analysis and interpretation. It provides a rallying cry for socially marginalized communities disproportionately exposed to polluting industry and destructive investment practices. The frames employed in the analysis and practice of these movements also serve to highlight key questions of equity, justice, and participation in the study of environmental politics. This chapter demonstrates the way in which viewing trade policy in Latin America through the lens of environmental justice reveals much about who benefits from the prevailing organization of trade policy and how, and about which social groups and environments are expected to absorb the costs of economic expansion. Therefore, it helps us to understand the sources and manifestations of resistance to trade liberalization we are witnessing across the region. The purpose is not to assess whether environmental resistance movements in Latin America fit with models of environmental justice developed in other, particularly North American, contexts. Nor is it to compare the success of environmental justice mobilizing in the two regions. The purpose is to develop the analytical value of EJ concepts and praxis in relation to trade politics, and to do so in the context of Latin America where these have received little attention to date.

There is in fact a long history of environmental justice struggles in Latin America, even if they are not named in those terms. Insofar as the term describes an environmentalism of the poor, contesting risk allocation and the distribution of gains from resource exploitation, making linkages to other social justice movements and profiling race and class concerns in the politics of struggle, there are many examples that would fit this broad category (Martinez-Alier 1991; 2002). This is particularly the case for movements protesting the abuse of indigenous peoples' rights (Crabtree 2005; Kimerling 1996). Indigenous peoples and *campesino* groups are often at the forefront of contesting land claims of economic producers, often inhabiting resource-rich areas opened up for investment, whether it be gold mines in Peru, copper mines in Chile, or areas of Amazonia in Brazil. Insofar as trade agreements enable the expansion of regional and global market actors into new areas of the continent, bringing them into contact and conflict with existing regimes of resource control and property rights, it is unsurprising that trade liberalization intersects with existing patterns of inequality and marginalization to produce vocal opposition to its expansionist ambitions. Insofar as trade liberalization forms derives from a broader process of commodification, extraction, and exploitation that characterizes many poorer groups' relations with the state in Latin America, these groups are contesting the process and the means of securing liberalization, including the allocation of property rights and the displacement of people, the opening up of new areas to exploration and investment, and a new politics of service delivery in which access for the poor is far from secure. In this sense, the current debate about trade liberalization has to be understood as part of a broader historical pattern of resource exploitation and the denial of land claims and rights claims that this presupposes.

Despite the long history of social movement mobilization in Latin America (Alvarez et al. 1998; Eckstein 1989), it remains the case that processes of globalization and regionalization have brought new threats to the livelihoods of the poor in the region that have prompted new forms of mobilizing and organizing. Indeed, emerging themes of environmental justice within struggles for trade justice are indicative of this changing landscape, which, while informed and shaped by broader historical and material struggles, brings to the fore a novel combination of analytical and practical dimensions.

Contesting the Process

The new regional trade politics of Latin America have brought about a series of challenges for diverse movements that have begun to organize under banners that include environmental justice. Trade accords dealing with control of natural resources (gas, water, etc.), agriculture, and knowledge (through intellectual property rights [IPR] provisions) align the interests of regional and global capital in conflict with those of indigenous peoples and social-justice-oriented environmental groups. Mainstream environmental groups such as those that supported the NAFTA agreement, meanwhile, have sought to improve environmental provisions within the existing agreements, their aim being greater balance between trade and environmental objectives without perceiving, in many cases, inherent incompatibility between the two.

Among those opposed to the NAFTA agreement, and in response to the enhanced mobility provided to capital through the accord, transnational connections were formed from 1991 on, with groups such as Coalition for Justice in the Maquiladoras aiming to internationalize awareness of citizen trade campaigns. The MODTLE (Mobilization on Development, Trade, Labor and the Environment) was established as a tri-national dialogue among activists from all three NAFTA countries. Such campaigns were able to connect to groups with greater resources and different approaches to lobbying (groups such as Development Gap) that helped community groups to testify at the US trade commission on NAFTA, for example. There has, therefore, been an enormous amount of transnational activism around trade issues from border-organizing around NAFTA (Icaza 2004; Wise et al. 2003) to more recent trans-American protests that focused on "summits of the Americas." These have involved environmental groups, labor activists, and an increasing tide of indigenous activism across the region, broadening framings of environmental politics to incorporate social justice concerns.

In relation to the Mercosur agreement, one issue that has engaged activists has been the broader "ecological footprint" of Mercosur. If the infrastructural developments proposed for the region in order to enhance integration are not managed responsibly, the environmental consequences could be devastating. For example, the Inter-American Development Bank (IDB) has identified a mixture of transport, hydroelectric power projects, and gas pipelines as essential foundations of an infrastructure for integration. Coalitions of NGOs successfully encouraged the IDB to withdraw funding for the controversial *hidrovia* proposal to construct a water superhighway on the River Plate system. The provision of alternative environmental and economic assessments and a legal case brought by coalitions of opponents in Brazil and Argentina (and backed by the Brazilian government) were crucial to the stalling of this Mercosur initiative (Hochstetler 2003). There is significant and renewed commitment by governments across the region, however, to improve energy, transport, and telecommunications in order attract foreign investors. Activists from Latin America and Europe are now joining forces to challenge a swathe of new infrastructural projects planned across the region funded by the European Investment Bank and Andean Investment Corporation, the IDB, and private investors under the banner of Integración de la Infraestructura Regional Sudamericana (IIRSA 2006). Activists such as Amigos de la Tierra in Paraguay have joined forces with counterparts in Europe, part of the BankWatch coalition, to contest the expected displacement of peoples, social upheaval and environmental destruction that will ensue (BankWatch 2006). Environmental justice concerns regarding the rights of indigenous peoples, issues of property rights (over traditional medicines), land acquisition, and the pollution such projects would bring to poorer communities have been prominent in the campaign.[1] For example, Brazil has already started work on two hydroelectric projects on the Madera River which have been condemned by movements in Brazil. Hugo Chávez's backing for a vast pipeline that will link Venezuela with Brazil at huge financial and environmental costs has been criticized by indigenous groups who, Buxton claims, "more fundamentally question a developmental model based on western-style industrialization" (2007, p. 6). Pablo Solón, an activist from Bolivia, speaking at the Cumbre Por la Integración de los Pueblos (a counter-summit to the South American Community of Nations summit held in Cochabamba in December 2006), claimed that social movements were working at "closing the veins of Latin America," a direct reference to Eduardo Galeano's (1973) book *The Open Veins of Latin America* about how colonial and then imperial powers established structures for the looting of the region's natural resources. Processual concerns have also been raised in relation to the lack of information made available about the projects and, in particular, the ways in which concerns for commercial confidentiality have been allowed to take precedence over rights to information.

If NAFTA and Mercosur were sources of alarm, the scope of the proposed Free Trade Area of the Americas causes even greater concern for environmental justice activists. It seeks to address every major industry, commodity and trade issue. So far, a series of commissions have been established in areas relevant to the environment, such as agriculture and intellectual property rights. Agriculture was considered so important a sector for negotiation that it not only has a special commission, but is also covered by the work of other commissions on subsidies, dumping, and compensation. Liberalization of services also includes "environmental services" such as water, controversial in light of the experience to date of water privatization in Argentina and Bolivia. The national treatment provisions are what concern many activists, where companies from all countries in the region will be afforded the same entitlement to provide services on a commercial basis. Also, it is alleged quotas or prohibitions on the export of resources such as water for environmental reasons will be considered protectionist (Acción Ecológica 2004).

At FTAA meetings in Buenos Aires and Quebec there have been explicit inter-governmental statements in support of the trade in genetically modified organisms (GMOs), prompting concerns among activists that the FTAA will provide new momentum to the spread of GMOs in the region (Global Exchange 2004). Increased use of GMOs would be against the expressed reservations of Bolivia and other countries about the technology's social and environmental impacts, and would be driven by the need for the United States, Canada, and Argentina (the world's three largest producers and exporters of GMOs) to find new markets for products rejected in Europe and parts of Asia. This issue has been raised by *campesino* groups in countries (including Mexico, which has already experienced contamination of non-GM crops by transgenic varieties) that are centers of origin for maize and other crops. The same groups have registered concern that IPR provisions within the FTAA might continentalize North American patenting provisions, overriding communal and indigenous peoples' rights (Acción Ecológica 2004).

Opposition to the FTAA within civil society has been widespread, reflecting both what is at stake in political and economic terms and the number of countries and associated civil societies involved. A large number of anti-FTAA movements have developed positions that place themselves outside the process. The forms of protest in many ways mirror, and build on, experiences of global campaigning around trade issues in the World Trade Organization. Alliances between a plurality of interests, held together through exchange of information and formulation of positions over the Internet, combined with joint demonstrations around key summits such as those held at Quito and Quebec, are indicative of this form of mobilizing. Within these coalitions, environmental groups critical of the process and skeptical about the compatibility of trade liberalization with sustainable development have articulated concerns that resonate with a broader critique of neo-liberal development models. There are the familiar concerns about the potential for mobile capital to exploit lower environmental standards and about the environmental impact of increased volumes of trade. As Acción Ecológica of Ecuador argues (2004), "ALCA implies a direct increase in the consumption and therefore production of fossil fuels, this implies an increase in CO_2 emissions which the United States does not want to control." Relatedly, there is concern that the FTAA, by reforming the legal base of energy policy in the region, will increase exploration for and extraction of fossil fuels, with further social impacts on the poorer indigenous communities that inhabit these areas.

Links to Rural Social Movements

By challenging elite control of trade policy (centered in national capitals) and by engaging only well-networked civil-society groups supportive of trade liberalization, the involvement of rural social movements in trade activism has helped to strengthen environmental justice components of critiques of regional trade policy. For a set of reasons already alluded to, *campesino* and indigenous peoples' groups have become increasingly involved in regional debates about trade policy. Their strong ties to agriculture, their proximity to resource rich areas and dependence on resource economies, and their sensitivity to issues of property rights and access to affordable services mean that trade agendas that have broadened to cover these issues necessarily affect their livelihoods. As organizations of the poor, such groups do not have the political clout or the resources of some of their counterparts in the labor and environmental movements, but they have sought to make their voices heard through traditional patterns of protest, resistance and confrontation with the state.

The literature on environmental justice often emphasizes the different cultures of protest that poorer groups bring to environmental politics; a distrust of institutions and the law that is reflected in self-help strategies of protest and resistance (Cole and Foster 2001). In the Latin American context, Philip Oxhorn (2001, p. 174) is right to claim that "in many ways, indigenous movements present the most fundamental challenges for understanding the quality of democratic regimes and for theories of social movements" and that "their distinctly non-western experience, history of violent abuse, and understanding of rights in collective rather than liberal-individualist terms all seem to set them apart from other movements, and perhaps even from the context of civil society in which they are frequently placed."

In some settings, indigenous movements have identified themselves by their ethnic or community identities. In other instances, they have formed alliances with women's and environmental movements, in the latter case against large projects such as hydroelectric dams in Brazil (Navarro 1994). Often broader critiques are explicitly articulated, such as in the case of the Zapatistas of Mexico, who are expressly critical of NAFTA. Indeed, the Zapatista movement is in many ways a product of the effect of neo-liberal reforms on the rural poor in Mexico, which turned those people against the governing PRI (Institutional Revolutionary Party)—a party they traditionally had supported. While the struggles of such groups center on land claims and demands for better living conditions, they articulate, according to Teubal and Rodriguez, "more important social currents against the contemporary global model of neo-liberalism" (2002, p. 195).

This background provides an entry point to understanding the roles that *campesino* and indigenous peoples' movements play in regional trade debates. Clearly opposed to many of the central tenets of the liberalization process, such movements are outsiders in the process, though they can lay claim to a much broader constituency of support than most environmental groups. They have raised objections about provisions of the proposed FTAA that have specific implications for *campesinos* and indigenous peoples (Guerrero 2005; Estigarribah 2005). Issues of particular concern include agricultural reforms and the removal of subsidies, fears about further consolidation of power in the hands of large food producers and measures to strengthen IPR protection, in particular the ability to register private property claims over communally held resources in the manner permitted by the WTO TRIPs accord (Acción Ecológica 2004). Where regional efforts to secure these provisions have stalled (as in the case of the FTAA), the United States has sought to promote new export opportunities and protect investor rights through bilateral trade agreements, such as the one recently concluded with Peru (which demands IPR protection along US lines, allowing for the patenting of genetic resources and traditional knowledge, and which calls for the harmonization of Sanitary and Phytosanitary provisions). This will make it easier to get GMO varieties accepted in the market by reducing the scope of government leeway to raise social-economic concerns not based on "sound science." Activists have raised concerns about the threat this poses to the more than 6 million subsistence farmers in Peru who grow potatoes (for which Peru is a center of origin), exacerbating the potential costs of contamination by GM varieties (de Wit 2006).

Amid existing controversies over rights of access and compensation for the appropriation of genetic material (especially in Mexico and other biologically rich countries, where many controversies about access and benefit sharing have already unfolded), IPRs have been viewed variously as new a form of colonialism or at the very least as a commodification of knowledge rights (Sanchez et al. 2004). Similarly, conflicts around the privatization of water in Bolivia, where Cochabamba was flashpoint in a violent conflict that ended in a water multinationals' leaving the country (Ceceña 2005), form the background to current concerns about service sector liberalization within the FTAA and the CAFTA and access to resources of national (geo-) strategic importance, such as gas (Crabtree 2005). Again, these are natural-resource struggles that embody many other elements and in which "the environment" as conventionally understood features as just one part, often a minor part.

Global connections in campaigning become apparent when opposition to the FTAA is re-framed as a broader struggle against the global industrialization and intensification of agriculture, or against privatization of public services the world over. Connections have been forged, for example, to international campaigns against GMOs, which also have a regional resonance given the centrality of Argentina and Brazil to the global GM debate. According to Teubal and Rodriguez, "various *campesino* movements have successfully articulated in recent years an authentic global movement" (2004, p. 197). Such movements are grounded in opposition to TNC control of agriculture (including patenting and bio-piracy), to free trade in agricultural produce (especially dumping), and to the use of hormones and transgenics and in favor of food security and food sovereignty. The umbrella group Via Campesina provides a clear articulation of this position and demonstrates its global connectivity through involvement in the World Social Forums, for example. Coalition building of this sort and a range of protest activities have been the main strategies adopted by *campesino* movements, often aided by the financial support of sympathetic groups in Europe and

North America that have funded trips by *campesino* groups to major anti-FTAA demonstrations (Newell et al. 2006).

Regional dynamics are important to understanding the politics of mobilization, the agendas around which groups cohere, and the possibilities of transnational cooperation. On the environment, competing views over the nature of the relationship between sustainable development and free trade have persisted, reflecting the broader ideological divisions discussed above. At times, such differences were amplified by conflicts between protest cultures which bring together groups of such divergent social profiles as middle class students and *campesino* groups (Ruben 2004). There has been a general asymmetry in participation during the FTAA summits, where there has been a much stronger presence of environmentalists from North America than from organizations from Latin America. These dynamics reflect the experience during the NAFTA negotiations and the broader politics of transnational collaboration that characterized that process, but they inevitably serve to enhance the profile of narrowly defined environmental concerns at the expense of giving space to broader environmental justice critiques of trade policy in the region.

Democratizing Trade Politics

Amid accusations that rich clubs of economic elites have crafted the terms of agreements that serve narrow economic interests, it is unsurprising that there have been calls to democratize trade policy in Latin America, to open it up to a plurality of participants, interests and agendas, and to revisit fundamentally the question of who and what trade is for. But the technical, expertise-led, legal nature of trade negotiations, combined with the reciprocal bargaining that lies at the heart of the brokering of trade deals, present high barriers to the meaningful engagement of citizens and of organizations claiming to act on their behalf. There have been a number of attempts to involve elements of civil society in trade policy in Latin America (Newell et al. 2006), often as a reaction to crises of legitimacy amid objections to the secrecy in which decisions are taken. Responses have taken a range of forms.

The result has been a series of formal institutional channels of participation designed to include supporters of trade liberalization, separated from the formal trade negotiations and undertaken in an ad hoc manner. Groups that question the purpose, pace or appropriateness of trade liberalization find themselves excluded from the forums in which trade policy is debated. Some efforts have been more serious than others in their outward attempts to create spaces for civil society, but all reproduce a liberal democratic version of participation as consultation about decisions already made, information about processes from which groups are excluded, and about agendas that have already been determined.

When it comes to serious debate about "the social ecology of trade" (that is, trade as an inevitable part of broader social and ecological systems that determine its viability and sustainability and whose maintenance should be the starting point for debates about which trade and for what purpose), the policy process as currently organized does not work. It is unsurprising, therefore, that activists across the region have rejected participation and engagement on such narrow and predetermined terms in favor of diverse strategies of protest and resistance. Social movements and other political actors have transcended the politics of formal state bargaining over tariff reductions, in cases where trade negotiations determine access to water and life-saving medicines, where they determine the viability of rural livelihoods and pass judgment on whose knowledge counts and can be privately owned. Politics, morality, and social and ecological sustainability are at stake, and much activism is geared toward ensuring they are addressed as such with the Hemispheric Social Alliance, promoting, for example, a "social agenda" for regional integration that goes beyond merely defining the region as an economic unit and a commercial opportunity.

The narrow form of democratizing trade policy, understood as bringing more voices and actors into a set of institutions and policy processes whose purpose and process are already established, is a far cry from "ecologizing democracy," which requires us to recognize the broader and multiple social and ecological systems that support and will be affected by the expansionist ambitions of trade policy and set up policy spaces and processes that can cope with the complexity that flows from this relationship. This understanding stands in contrast to current attempts either to negate the relevance of the social and environmental impacts of trade policy or to press these issues into the service of trade liberalization. Side agreements without meaningful enforcement, procedures for citizens to bring legal claims once harmed by polluting industry (such as those included in the NAFTA agreement), or the suggestion "drop box" in which activists can deposit ideas about improvements to the FTAA negotiations, without any obligation on the part of negotiators to respond to these, hardly count as a serious effort to engage with civil society, let alone democratize trade policy in any meaningful sense. Many such mechanisms reproduce the WTO logic that only groups with a "legitimate" interest in the organization's work, defined as having a "direct interest in issues of production, distribution and consumption" by the Mercosur agreement, are entitled to a say. Groups are regarded as a "valuable resource" in making the case for trade liberalization in the public domain. The political function of the FTAA's Committee of Government Representatives on Civil Society (since they are clearly unable to represent themselves) is made clear in the draft text of the agreement: "to build broad public understanding of and support for hemispheric trade liberalization."

Inevitably such mechanisms serve to reproduce inequalities within civil society. Those who have a clear grasp of the legal and economic framing of the agreements, who have the resources to participate and the e-capacity to engage in "virtual consultations" (often capital-based), and who, most critically, are willing to support the institution's goals and objectives may make use of such mechanisms. The vast majority of civil-society organizations, and certainly those better placed to claim that they represent the citizens who are most affected by trade agreements, often with fewer resources, little or no e-capacity, frequently not capital-based and critical of the processual and distributional elements of trade policy, will not.

In the short term, the project of democratizing trade policy remains a valid one, using existing spaces to open up broader debates about what types of trade are desirable, not as an end in themselves, but justified by their ability (or not) to serve broader social and environmental goals. The contribution of groups critical of the current framing of debates about the relationship between trade liberalization and the environment as a mutually supportive one, is to contest the boundaries and objectives of the discussion and the means by which it is conducted. In this regard there has been common ground between groups across the region on the need for enhanced transparency in the deliberations in the run-up to and during the summits of the Americas and for improvements in mechanisms for the participation of civil society. Demands around civil-society participation have continued to be made through the Peoples' Summits that led to the Hemispheric Social Alliance, a network, officially founded in 1999, of those groups most critical of the summits of the Americas, and of the FTAA in particular. Over the course of the summits of the Americas, the HSA has been strengthened by groups' frustration with the lack of openings within formal processes and the failure to meaningfully act on the promising rhetoric regarding civil-society participation that peppered early ministerial drafts. Agreement has been possible within the HSA on the core themes of official recognition of the social forums and inclusion on the official agenda of issues of labor rights, human rights and the environment (Botto and Tussie 2003:41). At the summit of Santiago in 1999, the HSA was able to generate a document that laid out alternatives to the programs being promoted within the FTAA (Alternativas para las Américas: Hacia la construcción de un acuerdo hemisférico de los pueblos). The HSA maintains links to other networks that cover *campesino* concerns such as the Coordinadora Latinoamericana de Organizaciones del Campo (CLOC), a regional network, based in Ecuador, that coordinates the work of organizations working with *campesinos*, indigenous communities, rural workers, and small producers (Korzeniewicz and Smith 2003). The meeting point with broader HSA agendas is issues such as economic justice, food sovereignty and sustainable agricultural development.

From Trade Justice to Corporate Accountability: Contesting Impacts

For those groups either excluded from or choosing to remain outside the formal arenas of trade policymaking, engagement with trade policy is often more indirect. Living with the repercussions of trade liberalization and the exposure of rural economies to regional and global markets, much campaigning energy is directed toward holding newly mobile external economic actors to account. Often without the support of the state, in reality often in conflict with the state, poorer groups adopt a range of community-based informal strategies of corporate accountability in order to secure social and environmental justice (Garvey and Newell 2005). Rather like their counterparts in North America, Latin American environmental justice activists seek to contest industrial, trade, and planning processes that affect them profoundly, but from which they are wholly excluded, in which new investors are lured to new areas with promises of cheap labor, abundant land, and natural resources and with promises of minimal controls on environmental pollution.

Newly acquired capital mobility has altered the power dynamics between corporations and communities to the advantage of the former. Activists have employed new tactics to contest forms of "economic blackmail" where communities are played off against one another as companies seek the best deal in terms of low levels of taxation and regulation, and a cheap labor force. There are, of course, traditions of this sort of campaigning which pre-date NAFTA's entry into force, but the opportunities created by NAFTA for such practices have been expanded and consolidated. Struggles around NAFTA's chapter 11 have been particularly significant in this respect. In August 2000 the California-based Metalclad corporation used chapter 11 provisions to sue the Mexican government for $16.7 million for rejecting its proposal to build a hazardous-waste facility in an already "highly contaminated" community (Roberts and Thanos 2003). There is a clear environmental justice element to this organizing when it seeks to contest the location of hazardous forms of production in poorer communities. In instances such as this, it was the local government that was sued for attempting to regulate pollution, whereas in many environmental justice struggles in the United States and elsewhere local groups are often in conflict with a government eager to attract new investment of whatever form. There are, indeed, many such cases in Latin America where local opposition to resource investors has been overridden by a government determined to attract investors. The Canadian mining company Manhattan Minerals Corporation ran into controversy over its continuing development of a mine in the Tambo Grande district of Peru requiring the relocation of 2000 families (Haslam 2003) even though 98.7 percent of local voters had voted against the project in an Oxfam-organized plebiscite held in the local municipality in June 2002. The involvement of an international NGO, particularly of Oxfam's standing, helped to focus international attention on the project and build linkages to international mining campaigns in Canada.

Often opposition has formed to mega-projects that provide the infrastructure necessary to realise the projected gains from trade accords. Mobilizations in relation to Mercosur's *hidrovia* project were mentioned above, and across the region there has been opposition to the proposed Plan Puebla Panama (PPP) as well as associated biological corridors bringing together a range of indigenous peoples and environmental groups (Paz 2005; Cortez and Pare 2006). In many demonstrations, explicit links have been articulated by activists between the FTAA, the CAFTA, and the PPP, which are understood as parts of a common project of imperial resource control.

A more recent environmental conflict in the Mercosur region has been the dispute over the paper mills in the Uruguayan coastal city of Fray Bentos proposed by the Finnish company Botnia and initially involving ENCE (Empresa Nacional Celulosa España). It would be the largest single investment in Uruguay's history (La Razon 2006). Under the banner of La Asemblea Ciudadana Ambiental de Gualeguaychú, environmental activists in Argentina have mobilized around the probable release of waste contaminants from the new factories into the rivers which they share with Uruguay, demanding at minimum a full environmental assessment before production commences. Other concerns include acid rain created by the factories and the stench generated by the plants. Their concerns have been lent credibility by the track record of ENCE in Valdivia, Chile and in Spain where the company has faced fines; sites campaigners in Argentina have visited through activist networks (*Página 12* 2006). These forms of pressure from within Argentina and in Europe succeeded in persuading the Spanish company to withdraw from this particular investment, while the Finnish company Botnia continues to pursue the project.

Groups critical of the factories have been able to form alliances and assemblies with environmental activists in Uruguay and garnered significant public support for their campaign to see the plants closed down altogether. Activists claim the 40,000 people that marched on this issue is unprecedented in the region for an environmental campaign (*Página 12* 2006). Protest tactics have involved forming pickets and blockading roads and bridges that connect Uruguay and Argentina at the height of the holiday season, mimicking tactics adopted by the *piqueteros* movement of the unemployed in Argentina and other social justice movements across the region. The drastic actions are a response to the fact that initial work has begun on the construction of the factories. The conflict is even said to have caused tensions between the two countries leaders, Néstor Kirchner and Tabaré Vázquez, with Uruguayan officials claiming that the actions of the protesters threaten Mercosur and the achievements of regional integration (*Página 12* 2006). To reject the expansion of the industry in the area would also be to go against World Bank recommendations, made over twenty years, that the South of the country be developed in this way. This is in spite of concerns that the paper factories, keen to relocate in Uruguay to avoid European regulations requiring changes in production, are engaging in "pollution flight."

In this context new opportunities have arisen through the development of mechanisms of participation at the regional level and information and communication technologies enabling forms of transnational activism and a new politics of investor accountability. As with other forms of trade justice activism, poorer communities in Latin America have been able to form alliances, however virtual, with groups sympathetic to their plight and keen to expose the consequences of rapid liberalization in the absence of adequate social and environmental safeguards as well as acts of corporate irresponsibility by Northern-based firms adopting double-standards when they operate in developing countries (Friends of the Earth 2003; WDM 1998). Often such campaigning serves to globalize localized resource struggles that pre-date regional trade accords but which acquire renewed significance in light of them.

Campaigns against the oil producers Chevron and Texaco, among others, for their role in extracting resources from contested land in Ecuador provide one example (Kimerling 1996). A report from the 1980s about Texaco's operations in Ecuador documented that 3.2 million gallons of toxic waste were being spilled from the company's operations every day. Legal battles have taken on international dimensions, with US legal activists working with indigenous peoples' groups against an Ecuadorian government anxious not to scare off would-be oil investment. The company is facing a class action suit in the United States and consumer boycotts organized by Acción Ecologica and Rainforest Action Network. In June 1994, Ecuador's twelve indigenous peoples' groups united to shut down the whole country for two weeks, protesting "decades of environmental destruction and social irresponsibility" (Roberts and Thanos 2003, p. 170).

Another oil-related case is that of Los Angeles-based Occidental Petroleum and the U'wa people of Colombia, who threatened mass suicide if "Oxy" was allowed to go ahead with plans, developed in 1995, to drill for oil on U'wa land. Highlighting the importance of identity-politics to environmental justice claim-making in Latin America, the U'wa people issued a declaration: "We would rather die, protecting everything we hold sacred rather than lose everything that makes us U'wa." (Garcia and Vrendenburg 2003) Rights enshrined in legal conventions combined with communication technologies that enable communities at the frontline of these forms of resistance to be in touch with groups sympathetic to their aims has created a public relations nightmare for firms hoping to contain localized conflicts with groups whose resources they are seeking to access. For example, Amazon Watch and the Action Resource Center organized a non-violent direct action against Occidental's headquarters in Los Angeles when protesters "installed" a 23-foot mock pipeline in Occidental's lobby. As Roberts and Thanos suggest, "with the globalization of investment capital has also come the globalization of communications and human rights law" (2003, p. 190). This has enabled the forging of links between struggles that are "inextricably linked" such as those for indigenous rights and environmental sustainability.

While patterns of trade liberalization bring to the fore new corporate accountability struggles, for many of these movements, old battles continue with state-owned and small and medium-sized firms that are less mobile, less equipped to take advantage of investor access and provisions in trade agreements, but no less polluting as a result. Campaigns against the state-owned firm PEMEX in Mexico, where an explosion in 1984 in Ixhuatapec was reported to have killed more than 500 people, and similar incidents in Brazil testify to this (Roberts and Thanos 2003). Foreign-owned transnationals such as Occidental and Shell are often more vulnerable to indigenous activism than Latin-American state-owned companies, such as CVG-EDELCA in Venezuela, since they are more accountable to global publics and more likely to be influenced by transnational organizing. If anything, trade liberalization has brought extra challenges for poorer communities, not just new ones.

Conclusion

Insofar as the notion of environmental justice foregrounds questions of social justice; distribution, participation, equity, conflict, race and class, it provides a loose but helpful analytical frame for understanding mobilizations currently taking place and the form mobilizations might take in the future. Advancing an environmentalism of the poor (Martinez-Alier 2002), the livelihood struggles of many of these groups share in common the strategies, values and experiences of many other social and environmental justice movements across the world, but perhaps especially in the majority world. Though debates on environmental justice are often framed by the unique experiences from which they derive in the United States, the patterns of social exclusion they identify in resource conflicts and decision making on environmental questions find parallel in struggles in Latin America. Though configurations of race, ethnicity, and class assume different forms, the sources of struggle and the contests over strategy that these produce demonstrate similarities which make it worth viewing environmental movement engagement with trade policy in Latin America through the lens of environmental justice. The point then has not been to adopt a template cast primarily by the environmental justice movement in the United States and to assess the fit of activism around trade and environment in Latin America. Rather, the chapter has shown that the experiences and theoretical resources accumulated by activists and scholars resonate with and help to make sense of emerging environmental justice conflicts over trade in Latin America.

An environmental justice frame broadens, deepens, and contests the environmental politics of trade in Latin America. Conventional understandings of the environment are embedded in explicitly political and historical contexts by "indigenous ecology's" emphasis on knowledge politics (Carruthers 1996). Questions of access and entitlement are highlighted and patterns of discrimination in resource use and exploitation are rendered visible and contestable. The "social ecology of trade," which many movements advance by approaching trade-environment relationships from the perspective of rights, embedding environmental issues within a broader framework of social justice thinking, also raises questions about the relationship between democracy and the market. Insofar as governments across the region are seen to be more sensitive to the needs of foreign capital than to broader social needs or notions of the public interest, they will face crises of legitimacy. "Delegative democracy" (O'Donnell 1994) may work for those given the power to defer to state leaders the authority to act in their name. For many others, and conflicts around trade policy seem to reflect this profoundly, there is a missing social contract (Bresser Pereira and Nokano 1998), where trade agreements are concluded without regard for those whose resources are being negotiated or whose livelihoods will be adjusted by the process. As long as such a scenario prevails, we can expect greater and more intense forms of conflict over trade policy, not just aimed at democratizing the market but about economic democracy; a more fundamental debate about who the economy should serve and how.

The narrow framing of the trade agenda in Latin America means that those formalized spaces that do exist for participation are unlikely to be accessible or useful for groups advancing environmental justice claims. Being cast as outsiders will make it more likely that they will seek alliances with other movements affected by trade policy. In this sense, environmental justice concerns regarding trade can be considered part of, but run the danger of being subsumed within, broader critiques of trade liberalization under the umbrella of coalitions such as the HSA. A number of strategic dilemmas flow from this situation regarding possible alliances with other movements and the role of environmental justice within those; the extent to which engagement in trade policy, even from a position of opposition and contestation, plays to the strengths and agendas of environmental justice movements and whether transnational protest politics around environmental justice are possible and desirable given the traditionally localised nature of struggles, even if in practice they manifest and reflect transnational dimensions.

There are shared resources and support that can be derived from belonging to coalitions such as the HSA which allow for the articulation of a range of inter-related, though not always internally consistent, demands from platforms with greater profile and further reach than individual movements could achieve on their own. Perhaps most significantly, as has been argued here, it is more often the case that there is an identifiable environmental justice element to existing campaigns around land, health and indigenous rights rather than an easily discernible self-identified EJ movement in its own right, despite the increasing uptake of that discourse. The challenge may be to connect in politically meaningful and strategically relevant ways, localized campaigns of an explicitly environmental justice nature with regional movements whose agendas feature environmental justice as just one element of a broader spectrum of concern regarding regional trade policy.

From the negotiation of trade rules through largely closed inter-governmental processes to the investments which ultimately result in firms taking advantage of new opportunities to access markets, consumers, and resources, we see a growing but shifting civil-society response to the perceived injustices of trade policy as it is currently conceived and implemented in Latin America. Those opposed to its content or processual elements include a diverse set of movements with a range of agendas that often compete and conflict, but which share concerns around equity, participation, and justice. Those groups approaching this critique from the perspective of environmental justice have successfully highlighted the disproportionate social and environmental costs that marginalized groups are expected to bear in the name of "development" from which they rarely benefit. They have raised crucial questions about the sustainability, in both a social and an environmental sense, of prevailing trade models within the region and they have forced policy elites to appreciate the level of concern and discontent about the model of economic development they are promoting for Latin America. The new political landscape across the region, the stalled status of the FTAA negotiations, and the heightened unpopularity of "free" trade's strongest advocate in the region, President George Bush, may have the combined effect of creating a window of opportunity for the agenda pursued by environmental justice groups and their allies across a range of similarly concerned social movements to get a more serious hearing than has been the case to date.

The continued marginalization of environmental justice concerns within state and regional politics concerning trade policy will continue to be a barrier toward the achievement of a trade agenda that is more responsive to the needs of poorer groups and the imperatives of sustainable development, but the validity of the arguments that environmental justice advocates articulate and the mounting evidence of increased inequalities combined with environmental destruction resulting from existing trade policies, will surely serve to keep the question of trade and environmental justice on the region's agenda for some time to come.

Acknowledgment

Portions of this chapter draw on Newell 2007.

Note

1. Source: discussion with Beatriz Sivero of Amigos de la Tierra, Paraguay, at "Enlazando Alternativas 2" conference, Vienna, May 11, 2006.

References

Acción Ecológica. 2004. Area de Libre Comercio de las Américas. http://www.accionecologica.org.

Agyeman, Julian. 2005. *Sustainable Communities and the Challenge of Environmental Justice*. New York University Press.

Alexander, Lucy. 1996. Colombia's Pacific Plan: Indigenous and Afro-Colombian communities challenge the developers. In *Green Guerillas*, ed. H. Collinson. Latin America Bureau.

Alvarez, Sonia, Evelina Dagnino, and Arturo Escobar, eds. 1998. *Cultures of Politics, Politics of Cultures: Re-Envisioning Latin American Social Movements*. Westview.

BankWatch. CEE Bankwatch Network 2006. http://www.bankwatch.org.

Botto, Mercedes, and Diana Tussie, eds. 2003. *El ALCA y las cumbres de las Americas: Una nueva relacion publico-privada?* Biblos.

Bresser Pereira, Luiz, and Yoshiaki Nakano. 1998. The missing social contract: Governability and reform in Latin America. In *What Kind of Democracy? What*

Kind of Market? ed. P. Oxhorn and G. Ducatenzeiler. Pennsylvania State University Press.

Bullard, Robert D. 1990. *Dumping in Dixie: Race, Class and Environmental Quality.* Westview.

Bullard, Robert D., ed. 2005. *The Quest for Environmental Justice: Human Rights and the Politics of Pollution.* Sierra Club Books.

Buxton, Nick. 2007. Latin America's future debated at parallel summits. Frontline Latin America Colombia Solidarity Campaign.

Carruthers, David V. 1996. Indigenous ecology and the politics of linkage in Mexican social movements. *Third World Quarterly* 17, no. 5: 1007–1028.

Ceceña, Ana. E. 2005. *La guerra por el agua y por la vida.* Asoc. Madres de la Plaza de Mayo.

Cole, Luke, and Sheila Foster. 2001. *From the Ground Up: Environmental Racism and the Rise of the Environmental Justice Movement.* New York University Press.

Collinson, Helen, ed. 1996. *Green Guerillas: Environmental Conflicts and Initiatives in Latin America and the Caribbean.* Latin America Bureau.

Cortez, Carlos, and Luisa Paré. 2006. Conflicting rights, environmental agendas and the challenge of accountability: Social mobilization and protected natural areas in Mexico. In *Rights, Resources and the Politics of Accountability*, ed. P. Newell and J. Wheeler. Zed.

Crabtree, John. 2005. *Patterns of Protest: Politics and Social Movements in Bolivia.* LAB books.

Curtis, Mark. 2001. *Trade for Life: Making Trade Work for Poor People.* Christian Aid.

De Wit, Inti Montenegro. 2006. FTA means deeper poverty in Peru. Biosafety Information Centre Third World Network. http://www.biosafety-info.net.

Dobson, Andrew. 1998. *Justice and the Environment.* Oxford University Press.

Eckstein, Susan, ed. 1989. *Power and Popular Protest: Latin American Social Movements.* University of California Press.

Estigarriba, Lucía Elizabeth 2005. El ALCA y sus consecuencias en la economía campesina paraguaya. In *El ALCA y sus peligros para América Latina*, ed. J. Estay and G. Sánchez. CLACSO.

Friedman, Elizabeth J., Kathyrn Hochstetler, and Anne Marie Clark. 2001. Sovereign limits and regional opportunities for global civil society in Latin America. *Latin American Research Review* 36, no. 3: 7–37.

Friends of the Earth. 2003. *UKplc in Latin America* Briefing.

Galeano, Eduardo. 1973. *Open Veins of Latin America.* Monthly Review Press.

Garcia, M, ed. 1991. *Ambiente, estado y sociedad. Crisis y conflictos socioambientales en América Latina y Venezuela.* Universidad Simón Bolívar-Centro de Estudios del Desarrollo.

Garcia, Percy, and Harrie Vredenburg. 2003. Building corporate citizenship through strategic building in the oil and gas industry in Latin America. *Journal of Corporate Citizenship* 10: 37–49.

Garvey, Niamh, and Peter Newell. 2005. Corporate accountability to the poor? Assessing the effectiveness of community-based strategies. *Development in Practice*, June 15 (no. 3–4): 389–404.

Gedicks, Al. 1996. Native peoples and sustainable development. In *Green Guerillas*, ed. H. Collinson. Latin America Bureau.

Girvan, Norman. 1976. Corporate Imperialism and Copper in Chile. In Girvan, *Corporate Imperialism*. Monthly Review Press.

Global Exchange. n.d. Top ten reasons to oppose the Free Trade of the Americas.

Guerrero, César, and Enrique Ortiz. 2005. El ALCA y la agricultura: Un análisis crítico del caso Colombiano. In *El ALCA y sus peligros para América Latina*, ed. J. Estay and G. Sánchez Estay. CLACSO.

Guimarães, Roberto P. 1995. *The Eco-Politics of Development in the Third World: Politics and Environment in Brazil*. Lynne Rienner.

Hall, Anthony, ed. 2006. *Global Impact Local Action: New Environmental Policy in Latin America*. Institute for the Study of the Americas.

Haslam, Paul. A. 2003. Surplus values: The Americas at a crossroads in the corporate social responsibility debate. FOCAL policy paper, Canadian Foundation for the Americas.

Hochstetler, Kathryn. 2003. Fading green? Environmental politics in the Mercosur Free Trade Agreement. *Latin American Politics and Society* 45, no. 4: 1–33.

Icaza, Rosalba. 2004. Civil society in Mexico and regionalization: A framework for analysis on transborder civic activism. CSGR Working Paper 150/04, Warwick University.

IIRSA. 2006. Iniciativa para la Integración de la Infraestructura Regional Suramericana. http://www.iirsa.org.

Kimerling, Judith. 1996. Oil, lawlessness and indigenous struggles in Ecuador's Oriente. In *Green Guerillas*, ed. H. Collinson. Latin America Bureau.

Korovkin, T. 2001. Reinventing the communal tradition: Indigenous peoples, civil society and democratization in Andean Ecuador. *Latin American Research Review* 36, no. 3: 37–69.

Korzeniewicz, Roberto Patricio, and William Smith. 2003. Redes transnacionales de la sociedad civil: Entre la protesta y la colaboración. In *El ALCA y las cumbres de las Americas*, ed. M. Botto and D. Tussie. Biblos.

Martinez-Alier, Joan. 2002. *The Environmentalism of the Poor: A Study of Ecological Conflicts and Valuation*. Edward Elgar.

Martinez-Alier, Joan. 1991. Ecology and the poor: A neglected dimension of Latin American history. *Journal of Latin American Studies* 23: 621–639.

McDonald, David A., ed. 2002. *Environmental Justice in South Africa*. Ohio University Press and University of Cape Town Press.

Navarro, Zander. 1994. Democracy, citizenship and representation: Rural social movements in Southern Brazil, 1978–1990. *Bulletin of Latin America* 13, no. 2: 129–154.

Newell, Peter. 2007. Trade and environmental justice in Latin America. *New Political Economy* 12, no. 2: 237–259.

Newell, Peter, and Rohit Lekhi. 2006. Environmental (in)justice, law and accountability. In *Rights, Resources and the Politics of Accountability*, ed. P. Newell and J. Wheeler. Zed.

Newell, Peter, et al. 2006. Civil society participation in trade policymaking in Latin America: Reflections and lessons. Working Paper 267, IDS.

O'Donnell, Guillermo. 1994. Delegative democracy. *Journal of Democracy* 5, January: 55–69.

Oxhorn, Phillip. 2001. From human rights to citizenship rights? Recent trends in the study of Latin American social movements. *Latin American Research Review* 36, no. 3: 163–183.

Página 12. 2006. Puentes cortados, 8/1/06: 1–5. Buenos Aires.

Paz, F. M. 2005. Participación, cultura y política. Reflexiones sobre la acción colectiva en el corridor biológico Chichinautzin, Morelos. *Mirada Antropológica* 3–4: 9–25.

Pellow, David N., and Robert Brulle, eds. 2005. *Power, Justice, and the Environment: A Critical Appraisal of the Environmental Justice Movement*. MIT Press.

Polanco, Héctor Díaz. 1997. *Indigenous Peoples in Latin America: The Quest for Self-Determination*. Westview.

Roberts, J. Timmons, and Demetria Thanos. 2003. *Trouble in Paradise: Globalization and Environmental Crisis in Latin America*. Routledge.

Ruben, Justin. 2004. Demonstrators in Quito say 'No' to the Free Trade Area of the Americas (FTAA). GoEcuador.com.

Sanchez Rubio, David, Alfaro Solorzano, and Isabel V. Lucena Cid, eds. 2004. *Nuevos colonialismos del capital: Propiedad intelectual, biodiversidad y derechos de los pueblos*. Icaria and Fundación Iberoamericano de Derechos Humanos.

Teubal, Miguel, and Javier Rodríguez. 2002. *Agro y alimentos en la globalización: Una perspectiva crítica*. La Colmena.

Trade Justice Movement. 2007. http://www.tjm.org.uk/.

Wise, Timothy, Hilda Salazar, and Laura Clausen, eds. 2003. *Confronting Globalization: Economic Integration and Popular Resistance in Mexico*. Kumarian.

World Development Movement. 1998. Law unto themselves: Holding multinationals to account. Discussion paper.

3

Grassroots Reframing of Environmental Struggles in Brazil

Henri Acselrad

The current notion of an environmentalist movement in Brazil covers a wide variety of organizations with different degrees of formal structure, ranging from bodies with relatively stable sources of funding to smaller, less stable groups whose actions are confined to particular circumstances. Most environmentalist associations, here taken to mean those whose explicit aim is environmental protection, passed through an initial stage without a legal structure; they were created with specific aims and activities, but also gave voice to a variety of protests from individual citizens, from informal neighborhood groups, and from victims of what were seen as environmental impacts. In their initial stages, these associations' most common targets were localized problems affecting the lives of local communities, either in cities, where the urbanization process leads to tenancy conflicts associated with the effects of overcrowding and the construction of infrastructure and industrial plant, or in rural areas, where the expansion of capitalist activities and the installation of major investment projects destabilize traditional lifestyles.

The environmentalist movement in Brazil is generally considered to have evolved through two major stages: an initial phase of protest and public awareness building and a subsequent phase of greater institutionalization and involvement in the debate on public policy. The movement began with actions to protect endangered fauna and flora, then moved on to exert pressure against the perceived overuse of mechanical and chemical methods in agriculture, water pollution, the destruction of essential ecosystems and for protection of the landscape heritage. In the second half of the 1970s, the major cities saw the emergence of small militant groups devoted to denouncing urban degradation and to protecting remnants of the native vegetation, such as the Atlantic Forest (which runs through most of the coastal states). The Amazon region also began to engage the interest of environmental groups in southern and southeastern Brazil, who made it a symbol of the fight against the kind of development blamed for the growing environmental degradation in the country. The movement against the construction of nuclear power plants gained strength in the late 1970s, helped to a considerable extent by the scientific community, especially in its questioning of the nuclear agreement between Brazil and Germany (CIMA 1991, p. 93).

Many environmental associations arose during the military dictatorship of the 1970s. One of the most extensive national protest campaigns carried out by environmentalists—the Goodbye Sete Quedas campaign against the drowning of the Sete Quedas waterfalls—took place under the military regime. With the return of the country to democracy after 20 years of military dictatorship, environmental action groups grew in number, while they lost their earlier power of influence over the people, who had seen these groups as a means of voicing their free will during the period of authoritarianism (Urban 2001).

The 1980s was a prolific decade for environmental groups. In the south and southeast they played an important role in fighting for state laws to regulate pesticide use and opposing the construction of nuclear plants. The National Environment Council (Conama), which controls the National Environment System (SISNAMA), was set up in 1981 with representatives of ministries, of state governments, and of four nongovernmental organizations appointed by the federal government. Its mission included the establishment of standards regulating motor vehicle pollution, general legislation on conservation units, and criteria for declaring areas critical. A 1985 decree changed Conama's statutes, increasing the part played in it by the Brazilian states and by civil society. Its 67 members henceforth included "representatives of five legally constituted civil-society bodies working directly or indirectly with the preservation of environmental quality, one of which to represent each geographical region of the country."[1] They were elected by a group of recognized associations drawn from a register of environmental bodies.

The greatest test of the environmentalist movement's ability to place its demands at the level of political decision making came during the preparation of the Constitution in 1988. A significant number of measures demanded by the movement were incorporated, and an environmentalist was actually elected to the Constituent Assembly, showing that the movement had gained some influence, particularly through the experience of developing alliances with broader sectors of society. Its action had already been shown at state and municipal levels with the election of a number of militants when free legislative elections were restored in 1982. Nonetheless, environmental issues were only superficially included in party programs and platforms and were little integrated into longer-term economic or social policies.

A question that has always vexed the organizations involved in the Brazilian environmental debate is how they can commit to campaigning for environmental protection without ignoring the obvious priorities of combating poverty and underdevelopment. In other words, how can the environment be put forward as a legitimate issue when all too often environmental concerns are seen as obstacles to tackling unemployment and overcoming poverty? How can environmental organizations deal logically and in a socially acceptable manner with the environmental implications of fighting social inequalities and promoting economic development?

Right from the start, an internal split developed within environmentalism that was directly related to whether or not the fight against inequality was integrated with the goals of the environmental struggle. The connection between environmentalism and economics clearly had been underestimated during the movement's early years. Its relationship with social justice, however, gained particular importance from the mid 1980s on, culminating during the run-up to the 1992 Rio de Janeiro UNCED (United Nations Conference on Environment and Development, the "Earth Summit") in the creation of a new networking body—the Brazilian NGO and Social Movements Forum for the Environment and Development. It was an attempt to incorporate environmental issues within the broader debate that criticized and sought alternatives to the dominant development model. It marked the beginning of an ongoing dialog, as yet unfinished, aiming at drawing up common policies with trade union activists, the landless rural workers' movement, communities displaced by dam construction, deprived urban community movements, rubber tappers, exploiters of forest products, and the indigenous movement.

The literature suggests that the main change that occurred in Brazilian environmentalism in the 1990s was the internal division caused by a move toward institutionalization. New organizations that arose during that period were run by professional technical and administrative staff and were systematically able to raise funding. They defined their areas of activity more precisely, had specific targets, and carried out internal performance assessments. A major debate was launched at this time regarding the new identity of those who claimed to be part of the environmentalist movement. Whether they were amateur or professional, informal or institutionalized, however, these proved to be merely external aspects of more substantive splits in the environmentalist movement in the period following the 1992 Earth Summit. It was increasingly divided between para-state pragmatism and criticism of the dominant development model, between being an instrument of ecological modernization and a social actor involved in the expansion of human rights. Those bodies and movements in Brazil which, from 2000 onward, began in some way to associate their activities with the notion of environmental justice certainly belong to the second group, since they are more combative than professional and more involved in critically discussing public policy than in providing governments with technical advice.

UNCED-1992 and the Splits in Environmentalism

The period between 1986 and 1992 was marked by the debate on the relationship between the environmentalist movement and politics, both at a national level, at which the debate revolved around the new Constitution, and internationally, with the new agenda brought in with the preparations for the United Nations Conference on Environment and Development to be held in Rio de Janeiro in June 1992. Several interstate meetings were organized to debate the relevance of founding a Green Party and how they could take part in developing the new Constitution. At the first National Meeting of Autonomous Ecological Organizations, held in Belo Horizonte in May 1986, a range of different schools of thought could be distinguished within the environmentalist movement;

in broad terms, there were fundamentalists, realists, eco-modernizers, and eco-socialists. Close cooperation was established between environmental organizations in Brazil and the United States, and several Brazilian activists attended multilateral meetings between 1986 and 1988, where they criticized the social and environmental impacts of World Bank-funded development projects in Brazil, particularly in the Amazon region.

In May 1990, the Brazilian Preparatory NGO Forum for the Civil Society Conference on Environment and Development was set up in São Paulo. By April 1992 it had held eight national meetings, by which time 1200 organizations had joined. The establishment of the Forum marked the intention to include environmental issues in the more general protests at the country's development model, and also to leverage the international dimensions of such criticism through the networks that were organizing and promoting the International NGO Forum held in parallel to the official UN government-level conference in Rio de Janeiro in 1992. The first signs of grassroots environmentalism were also developing at that time, comprising community associations, urban and rural trade unions involved with environmental problems that affected the poorest members of the population most of all, as well as organizations of traditional communities defending their means of social reproduction from the predatory advance of the expanding capitalist frontier.

The environment and justice were discussed within what was later renamed as the Brazilian NGO and Social Movements Forum in the run-up to the Earth Summit. The main challenge for the hundreds of organizations that had joined it was how to overcome the prevailing dissociation between development issues and environmental ones. That there was mistrust between environmentalist and "development" NGOs was clear throughout the efforts to gather ideas and actions together within a single organizational body. Despite its success in supporting the participation of non-governmental organizations from around the world in the parallel debate to the official UN conference, the Brazilian NGO Forum found it difficult to maintain its public visibility afterward. As well as the differences in mindsets and guiding policies of the various member bodies, the Forum also contained major inequalities in its members' levels of organization (Herculano 1996), and faced funding difficulties that were critical for an organization attempting to work on a national scale. Thematic or regional networks worked best within its structure, since their activities were more focused and they were more able to contribute to the public debate in their specific areas. Some of these networks' contributions revealed their considerable lobbying potential.[2]

At the same time, the establishment of bodies like the National and State Environment Councils created opportunities for NGOs to influence government environmental policymaking. These Councils, which had started appearing in the 1980s, were seen at first as a means for disseminating social demands, intra-state networks, proposed social pacts, or the government's reworking of demands from social movements or pressures from interest groups. Although the organizations represented in this kind of forum varied widely in the resources that they could devote to action, suggesting that their expectations of participation were doomed to failure, the discourse of public-private partnership and of civil society involvement in government policymaking continued, particularly from the early 1990s onward. It seemed that participative bodies might provide new ways to produce land-use policies, in which the various ecological systems or urban configurations could be associated with particular cultural systems and social actors whose knowledge and goals would provide democratic, pluralistic content to decision-making processes. However, the potentially democratic institutions provided for in Brazil's legislation and environmental policy framework did not live up to such promises.[3] Conama's resolutions, for instance, do not determine the use of public funds or define investment priorities. They merely rule on how certain activities should be performed, or not. Devoid of any political weight, the Environment Councils' decision-making powers were thus trivialized; despite their intentions of encouraging participation, they became dominated by proposals for technical standardization relating to the environment, thus contributing to the growing technicality of environmental policymaking and the increasing frustration among civil-society organizations at being unable to influence policy through formal institutional channels (Acselrad 1996, p. 15).

In the immediate wake of the UN Conference, a certain change could be seen both in the sensitivity of some environmentalist groups to social issues and in the attitudes of traditional "development" NGOs to environmental concerns. In the mid 1990s, however, environmental issues began to decline somewhat in the public eye, at the same time as there was a crisis in international funding for Brazilian NGOs. A widening split not unconnected with this crisis then developed between organizations devoted to environmental protest and those carrying out projects and advisory work in the environmental field. Multilateral banks and the government itself invested in moving from "confrontation to collaboration,"[4] in an attempt to turn ecological campaigning into an internalized aspect of the partnership between civil society and governments. The profile of the Green Party became more clearly defined through its "erratic" behavior (Viola and Boeira 1990, p. 70), confined to electoral activities that had little connection with the demands of social organization and struggle. In contrast, there was growing support for an "informal" environmentalist movement, developed by groups that had appropriated the environment theme without any formal reference to basic ecological thinking or action.

This other kind of environmentalism, more concerned with social issues, began to appear in the mid 1980s. In the midst of the return to democracy after two decades of military power, there was growing criticism of the dominant development model, which was seen as both favoring the concentration of wealth and being environmentally predatory. Despite the consensual nature of the transition by which the elite organized the country's emergence from authoritarianism, the end of the military regime raised hopes that the cracks appearing in the power block would lead to progress in rendering the State more democratic and socializing politics. It was assumed that the reinvigoration of social movements would allow a "new politics" to emerge, with the citizens partaking of control of the political elites through new channels of communication with the State. It was assumed that topics formerly regarded as private, moral, or economic would become political. Thus it was hoped that citizens would acquire greater influence over the exercise of government authority. In this context, the ecology discourse as expounded in the public sphere tried to question the cultural values and models within which the divergent interests has traditionally been defined, by acting in a public arena that was larger than that of the State.[5] Thus it was that a series of issues began to take shape at the grassroots level that gradually, by a dual process of renaming and rearrangement of forces, were recognized as being "environmental" in nature.

Running counter to the dominant socioecological project, another territory was being marked out by social struggles on at least three different fronts. In regions on the front line of expanding capitalism that were being taken over for raw material and commodity production, the model met with resistance from social actors linked to the exploitation of forest products and subsistence activities, who organized themselves to defend their traditional lifestyles against the expansion of land speculation, monocultures, or major hydroelectric and mining projects.[6] In depressed areas abandoned by development policies favoring "competitive inclusion" in the world market, farm workers linked to food production put pressure on the authorities to invest in infrastructure and to provide rural credit facilities that would enable them to remain in areas increasingly affected by desertification and the concentration of land ownership. In the core areas of modernization, movements arose to change the urban, industrial and agricultural development models, to combat industrial pollution, to expand water supply and sewerage services, and to promote farming methods that were less dependent on chemicals and mechanization.

The growing strength of this grassroots environmentalism was to a great extent responsible for the uniqueness of the Brazilian experience compared with other parts of the world. It is known that the environmentalist movement in most countries tended to expand at times of strong economic growth. Comparative studies suggest that when there is an economic downturn, the pressure for policies, legislation and standards to protect the environment falls off. The opposite happened in Brazil (Viola 1997, p. 28). The economic downturn of the 1980s coincided with a rise in the activity and visibility of its environmentalist groups. This inverse correlation between economic growth and collective environmental action is certainly associated with the transition from a dictatorial regime to a formal democracy, a process that coincided with the recession. However, it also points to the predominantly non-Malthusian nature of the Brazilian environmentalist movement.[7] That is not to say that neo-Malthusian ideas did not underlie a number of branches of Brazilian environmentalism, particularly conservationist ones, but the sheer size of the country, the signs of a highly concentrated system of land ownership and exceptionally high levels of social inequality, and the persistent fall in the birth rate from the 1970s onward argued strongly against any proposal based on a condemnation of economic and demographic growth.

The environmentalist discourse of the "lost decade" of the 1980s centered on a criticism of the adverse effects of the development model adopted in the country, with regard both to the social asymmetries that it entailed and to the predatory nature of the environmental practices that it promoted, especially the destabilization of local sociocultural lifestyles at the front line of capitalist expansion. It is even possible that the grassroots environmentalist movement was not more ferocious in its criticism because the economic stagnation that typified the 1980s and lasted into the 1990s hampered the consolidation of any significant alliances between the environmentalist and trade union movements. The unemployment rate in Brazil's greatest metropolis, São Paulo, grew steadily over these two decades: in its broadest definition it reached 20.3 percent in April 1999. With the implementation of neoliberal policies throughout the 1990s, job numbers in industry fell by 48 percent while receipts in this sector rose by 45 percent, significantly shifting the balance of power in social conflicts in the employer's favor. Although crucial trade unions like the CUT formally acknowledged the environmental question and even set up their own National Environment Commission in the early 1990s, there were few situations in which the unions felt strong enough to engage in environmental battles. Unions in the oil industry were an exception. Deregulation, the relative weakening of state control over the sector, and the outsourcing of work meant that, even after the major setback of the 1995 strike, they were willing to speak out: in some states they blew the whistle on the joint dangers of increased accident rates at work and of oil spills. In this particular case, the environmental issue was associated with defense of the state-owned company as a "national asset": the fact that the principal Brazilian oil company was state-owned should mean that any irregularities should not be hushed up but rather put right. This consistent stand taken by the trade unions was crucial, in that they fought for the company as a public asset while seeking to protect Guanabara Bay, the nation's heritage, from being degraded by the company itself. Since the company "belonged to the people," the unionists claimed, it should be more socially responsible, not less, and it was unacceptable for the company to make enormous profits by exposing workers to risks both within the company and outside (Acselrad and Mello 2002).

The difficulty that certain observers have had in recognizing such latent alliances between the environmentalist and unionist movements is due to a restrictive view that tends to associate environmentalism with the version that is totally opposed to economic growth. Such a reductionist attitude has led some analysts to consider the obvious inequality in the country to be a "factor that isolates environmentalism," since addressing it would mean "adopting programs to stimulate economic growth, based on the unlimited expansion of the economically active sector of the population, and extension of the equally unlimited benefits of the Welfare State to the universe of the workers." The analysts conclude: "This, perhaps, has been the most difficult problem for environmentalism to solve in recent years."[8] This statement might possibly apply to the restricted circle of neo-Malthusian ecologists. Throughout the environmental debate that has raged over the last three decades, however, no movement can be identified that has openly condemned economic growth or supported the "spurious sustainability" that might be considered to be associated with economic stagnation and unemployment, as a kind of beneficial environmental by-product from a neo-Malthusian viewpoint. Instead, the environmental debate has focused in various ways on a criticism of the development model adopted by the country's ruling classes, especially because it is based on the intensive and extensive exploitation of natural resources, i.e. the expropriation of non-capitalist social forms, and also because it does not adequately meet the basic demands of the already mostly urban population.[9] Even at a time of low economic growth, environmental struggles were justified by the spread of speculative land use, by the environmental impacts of the collapse in public investment, by the environmental agencies' loss of their policing powers, by the proliferation of illegal logging in reserves, and by the transformation of food-producing areas into monocultures for export.

Ferreira (1999, p. 46) points out that "in Brazil in the 1990s, the political environmentalism of previous decades turned itself to directly solving problems considered urgent, adopting an approach designed to produce what might be called a 'parainstitutional' form of action, in a consensual effort to use interdisciplinary technical-scientific knowledge for social ends, with a view to the sustainability of natural systems." Although much of the environmental discourse in the 1990s appeared to be associated with action in specific projects in order to obtain immediate practical results, it is not at all clear that such pragmatism effectively "replaced" the politicized environmentalism of protest and social criticism. What one can say is that part of the "non-grassroots environmentalist movement" responded favorably to the consensus-seeking discourse put out by multilateral agencies, which defended the public-private partnership, rejected the national sphere in favor of the local sphere,[10] and favored fragmentary actions over the structured consistency of political action. The pragmatism of professionalized environmentalism, according to Ferreira, "could count on a perverse factor in post-industrial societies, which is their structural inability to absorb young people ready to enter the job market: NGOs represent a real alternative for absorbing highly qualified labor" (1999, p. 50). On the other hand, however, apart from being a solution to the funding difficulties of organizations in crisis and the availability of professional teams, the "replacement" of protest by technical-scientific action associated with the discourse of localism and the use of consensus-forming techniques is a goal that multilateral bodies, governments and polluting enterprises all have in common. In a recent report on Brazil, the World Bank states that it "recognizes its role as a catalyst in the promotion of civil society participation" (Garrison 2000, p. 71). It thus wants to take pre-emptive action to capture the movements protesting the dominant development model within what has been called "ecological modernization."[11] The incorporation of "non-grassroots" environmentalist organizations into the ecological modernization process has occurred particularly through their involvement in consultancy activities or certain forms of what is termed "environmental education." As Fabiani points out, "where Ecology advances, the environmentalist movement retreats," suggesting that the advance of the scientific and educational discourse of Ecology leads to a certain dilution of the environmentalism as a social movement (Fabiani 1885, p. 90). This rule seems to be strongly guiding the strategies of governments, multilateral bodies and polluting enterprises in relation to the more conventional branches of environmentalism. Just as environmental policies often tend to be replaced by a gigantic research project, because of the scientific uncertainty that characterizes socioecological changes (Boehmer-Christensen 1994), there is clearly a predominant tendency today to transform the Brazilian environmentalist movement into part of a major environmental education program. This has not been successfully applied to grassroots environmentalism, however, which has reframed its objectives so as to innovatively incorporate "environmental justice" issues.

The Environmental Justice Issue as It Developed in Brazil

The term "environmental justice" refers to a movement that seeks to attribute new meaning to the environmental question. It has resulted from the specific appropriation of environmental ideas by sociopolitical players traditionally involved with the development of social justice in a broader sense. This process of redefining the environmental question is, in fact, associated with a reorganization of the arenas in which social struggles about the shaping of our possible futures take place. The environment is being increasingly held up in these arenas as a core issue that cannot be dissociated from the age-old social issues of jobs and income.

To put the new meaning attached to the environmental question into context, it is worth briefly looking back at the senses attributed to it in recent history. Right from the start, the environment has been invested with two contrasting meanings, one countercultural, the other utilitarian. The first has informed a movement questioning the lifestyle that has justified the dominant system of appropriation of the material world— so-called Fordist consumerism,[12] the industrialization of agriculture through chemicals and mechanization, etc. The second, utilitarian meaning was initially propounded by the Club of Rome,[13] which, after 30 years of economic growth in the core capitalist countries, was concerned to guarantee the continuance of capital accumulation by economizing on raw materials and energy.

The heterodox economist[14] Georgescu Roegen then entered the debate to warn that economizing on materials and energy would just postpone the problem. It was not enough just to economize on resources, but we should ask ourselves why we appropriate materials and energy. Ecology, he said, was not just a matter of scarcity, but of the quality of the social relations that underlay the social uses of the planet. In his view, that was the basic ecological question: should we use the planet's resources to produce plowshares or guns?

Right from the start, therefore, a utilitarian model and a cultural model have been fighting for the environmental arena. For the dominant utilitarian model, the environment is seen as a single whole composed entirely of material resources, with no specific or differentiated sociocultural content; it is expressed through quantities; it permits questions about the means by which society appropriates the planet's resources, but not the ends; it presupposes one single, instrumental environmental risk—a breakdown in the supply of raw materials and energy to the capitalist economy and thus a breakdown in the material conditions for capitalist urban society, i.e. the risk that the productive city will become increasingly uninhabitable because of pollution, congestion and other such problems. As a result of this view of the environment as a single whole that is instrumental to the accumulation of wealth, pollution is regarded as "democratic" and as unable to make class distinctions.

The cultural model, however, questions the ends for which people appropriate the planet's resources; the environment is multiple in its sociocultural qualities; there is no environment without a subjective viewpoint—in other words, its meaning and the way it is used will vary from one society or culture to another. From this angle, environmental risks are differentiated and unequally distributed, because of the various social groups' different abilities to escape the effects of the factors generating the risks. This unequal sharing of environmental risks and the multiple meanings that societies can attribute to their material bases may lead to the unwelcome realization that the environment of certain social actors prevails over that of others, giving rise to what has been termed "environmental conflicts." The environment thus becomes an issue relating to the culture of rights—at first they are the hypothetical rights of future generations, constituting an equally hypothetical conflict between the living and those yet to be born, and then, looking beyond this hypothetical intergenerational conflict, there comes the realization that environmental conflicts are actually occurring now between living actors. The living protagonists of these environmental conflicts are those who protest environmental inequality: the disproportionate exposure of the most socially deprived to the risks generated by the technological productive systems that create wealth, or their environmental dispossession through the concentration of development benefits in the hands of the few. From this viewpoint, pollution is not necessarily "democratic," because it can affect the various social groups in different ways.

The two approaches outlined here correspond to two models of strategic action. The utilitarian approach has led to the so-called ecological modernization strategy, with its emphasis on the market, technical progress and political consensus. Its aim is the "ownership society" propounded by neoconservatism: an efficiency revolution is evoked to save the planet by putting a price on what has no price. In contrast, the cultural approach has given rise to protest action seeking to overturn the unfair distribution of environmental benefits and harm. Since social injustice and environmental degradation have the same origin, there is therefore a need to change the way in which power over environmental resources is distributed—unfairly—and to take away from those in power the ability to transfer the environmental costs of development to the most dispossessed. This view states that social groups' unequal exposure to risks is due to their different mobility: the rich can escape the risks whereas the poor are trapped in a circuit of risk. Hence the resulting action to combat environmental inequality and to give all social and ethnic groups the same environmental protection.

The result, as has been increasingly apparent since the 1990s, has been a clash of two agendas, with differing discourses, concepts, institutions and practices. Ecological modernization rejects political regulation; it proposes to put a price on what has no price; it raises the argument of interests against the argument of rights; it tends to equate the environment with the idea of private property—the "tragedy of the commons"[15] is the paradigm that sees the privatization of communal assets as the solution for their economic use (contrary to the successes of such movements as the *babaçu* nut breakers in Maranhão or the *arumã* gatherers of the Lower Rio Negro, which confirm that other territorial and legal systems work); the "environment" is seen as a "business opportunity" (see the prevailing ideas in successive Multi-Annual Investment Plans drawn up by Brazilian governments); environment and sustainability become important categories for competition between regions or towns; in order to attract capital, "ecology" and "sustainability" may become mere symbols, like brands designed to appeal.

According to the strategy rooted in the notion of environmental justice, however, unequal exposure to risks is the result of a system by which wealth is accumulated through the environmental penalization of the poor. This system is considered to work through the operation of the land market, the "coordinating effect" of which means that harmful practices are located in devalued areas, and through the absence of policies to limit this effect. Such socio-territorial segmentation has been exacerbated by market globalization and the opening-up of trade, which have led to greater freedom of movement and delocation of capital,[16] a lowering of relocation costs, and an increase in the power of businesses to exert "locational blackmail"—using the threat of job losses and reduced tax revenues to force acceptance of polluting activities and cutbacks in social rights. Protesting such mechanisms and building organizational capacity and the ability to resist locational blackmail will therefore be a way to redefine the social and technical practices for appropriating the environment, planning land use, and redistributing power over environmental resources.

What is effectively at stake in this conflict? Everything suggests that it is the way in which the material conditions for production and social reproduction are organized[17]—more specifically, how different social forms of environmental resource appropriation are arranged in biophysical space, and how the permanence of an activity over time is affected by the operation of other spatial practices within this arrangement. For instance, it is how the expansion of eucalyptus monocultures means that *quilombo* inhabitants lose their lands and water; how the expansion of genetically modified soybean cultivation destroys the livelihoods of small organic farmers; how the production of cheap energy for aluminum multinationals means that the fishermen and riverside communities along the Tocantins can no longer catch fish; and how petrochemical production permanently ruins workers' health by contaminating them with persistent organic pollutants.

Environmental Justice is therefore an emerging notion that incorporates the historical subjective development of a culture of rights within a movement seeking to expand the meaning of human, social, economic, cultural and environmental rights. In Brazil, Environmental Justice arose in recent times from the strategic creativity of social movements. It has altered the composition of the social forces involved in environmental struggles and, in certain circumstances, brought about changes in the State-controlled regulatory apparatus in charge of environmental protection.

In the United States, the Environmental Justice Movement arose in the mid 1980s, protesting the socio-territorial system that generates inequality in the social conditions in which rights are exercised. Far from having a "not in my back yard" attitude, the actors who began to unite behind this movement were fighting for the politicization of environmental racism and inequality, denouncing the perceived predominant attitude of "always in the poor people's backyard" (Bullard 2002; Acselrad 2004). Representatives from a number of US Environmental Justice Movement networks visited Brazil in 1998 to disseminate their experience and establish relationships with local organizations willing to form alliances to resist the "exportation of environmental injustice."[18] They also developed contacts with non-governmental organizations and university groups, which subsequently led to the joint organization of workshops at several World Social Forums in Porto Alegre. Brazilian groups first came to re-evaluate the US experience when material for discussion was prepared and published by the NGO IBASE (the Brazilian Institute for Social and Economic Analysis), representatives of the Rio de Janeiro trade union federation CUT, and research groups from IPPUR/UFRJ, the Rio de Janeiro Federal University Institute of Urban and Regional Research and Planning. The three volumes in the series "Sindicalismo e Justiça Ambiental" (Unionism and Environmental Justice) (IBASE/CUT-RJ/IPPUR 2000) were limited in their circulation and impact, but stimulated others in academia, the nongovernmental world, and unionism to explore the threads of that debate. That led to the organization of the International Conference on Environmental Justice and Citizenship, held in Niterói in 2001, which brought together representatives of various social movements, NGOs, and researchers from different parts of Brazil, as well as a number of researchers and representatives of the US Environmental Justice movement, including Robert Bullard.

The Brazilian Environmental Justice Network was created at the conference in September 2001; after the debates, it drew up a manifesto in which it expanded the scope of its actions beyond the issue of environmental racism in the siting of toxic waste dumps, which had been the starting point for the US organization that had grown out of the Black movement there. The definition of environmental justice was broadened to cover those principles and practices that "a) ensure that no social group, whether based on ethnicity, race or class, suffers a disproportionate part of the adverse environmental consequences arising from economic operations, from the decisions made in federal, state or local policies and programs, or from the absence or omission of such policies; b) ensure fair and equitable direct and indirect access to the country's environmental resources; c) ensure ample access to relevant information on environmental resource use, waste disposal, and the location of sources of environmental risks, as well as on democratic processes for participation in the drafting of policies, plans, programs and projects that affect them; d) favor the establishment of collective entities with rights, social movements and people's organizations, so as to promote the construction of alternative development models that ensure that access to environmental resources is democratic and the use thereof is sustainable" (Declaração 2004).

Between 2001 and 2004, the Brazilian Environmental Justice Network established itself essentially as a vehicle for its 100 or so member bodies to exchange experiences and report problems electronically. At the Network's first Conference, held in 2004, the actors and social movements that it represented met face to face for the first time to clarify their lines of engagement with a development model designed to "make money at all costs." In the Amazon region, they denounced the injustices associated with primitive mechanisms of wealth accumulation, characterized by the successive phases of land grabbing, logging, clear cutting, extensive grazing, and high-tech soybean cultivation—a kind of land-use "platypus," to borrow the term used by the sociologist Francisco de

Oliveira (2003) to denote such an odd combination of modern, globalized production methods with primitive forms of labor exploitation and wealth extraction.

In reaction to the incorporation of the Amazon into the mercantilist model, with the exclusion or subordination of its local populations, alternative paths are emerging that integrate local forms of production with the domestic market on a regional basis, without destructive submission to powerful players on the world market. Such local, land-based struggles politicize the environmental issue and encourage debate about the development model that interconnects the various spatial practices. The aims of the actors in these struggles are to resist locational investment blackmail and to discuss the conditions under which local populations are to be integrated into the market. Collective bodies are thus formed that demand full access to relevant information on environmental resource use and seek fair and equitable access to the country's environment resources, setting an example of how the notion of environmental justice has developed in Brazil in recent years.

In a broad sense, as reinterpreted by the social actors in the country, the groups opposing the creation of environmental inequalities include the following:

• victims of pollution in locations that are not immediately productive, such as the areas around major risk-producing undertakings and city outskirts where environmentally undesirable facilities are located (garbage dumps, toxic waste dumps, etc.). Inequality in such cases would result from the fact that the inhabitants of these areas are less able to make themselves heard by decision makers, or even from the fact that they consent in the hope of gaining some local benefit from such undertakings, given the lack of jobs, income, public health and education services there

• victims of production-linked pollution within industrial and agricultural working environments, whereby economic interests would profit from the damage done to workers' health, via misinformation, counterinformation, withholding of information and job blackmail (Mallerba 2004)

• victims of the dispossession of environmental resources—including soil fertility, water, genetic resources, and land essential for the reproduction of community and sociocultural group identities—by major infrastructure projects and productive undertakings that destabilize traditional populations' spatial practices.

The struggles for environmental justice that occur in Brazil may be grouped as follows: struggles in defense of rights to culturally specific environments, such as those of traditional communities at the front-line of expanding capitalist and market activities; struggles in defense of rights to equitable environmental protection against market-led socio-territorial segregation and environmental inequality; struggles in defense of rights to equitable access to environmental resources and against the concentration of fertile land, water resources and safe ground in the hands of powerful market interests; and also struggles in defense of the rights of future populations. How do the movement's representatives make a logical connection between present struggles and future rights? By proposing to freeze the mechanisms that shift the environmental costs of development onto the poorest sectors of society. What these movements are trying to show is that the overall pressure on the environment will continue so long as environmental evils can be transferred to the poor. In that way they make a link between general talk about the future and the concrete, historical conditions in the present that are shaping the future. This marks the strategic interface between social justice and environmental protection: to stop the destructive pressures on the environment that belongs to us all, we must start by protecting the weak.

Under today's prevailing free-market conditions, locational investment blackmail is the main mechanism by which environmental and employment risks are imposed on deprived populations: in the absence of environmental policies for the licensing and control of appropriate activities, and in the absence of sound social and employment policies, the poorest and least organized groups will tend to give in to promises of work, whatever the cost. The dynamic of these movements suggests, therefore, that the deprived state of certain social groups is an important factor in making investment in polluting and hazardous operations profitable. That is why, in the eyes of the more organized sectors of the population, there is an increasingly clear fusion between environmental risk and social insecurity—core elements in the reproduction of inequalities at times of economic liberalization. There is also a growing realization that environmental protection is not just an urban middle-class cause but an integral part of the social struggles fought by the majority. It is through careful argument and innovative kinds of struggle that the social actors whose practices are analyzed here have sought to make the environment in Brazil an arena for creating justice and not merely for implementing the utilitarian rules of the market.

Acknowledgment

This chapter was translated from the original Portuguese by Cristopher Tribe.

Notes

1. Federal Decree n. 91305, 3/6/1985. See Acselrad 1996, p. 5, n. 6.

2. The campaign against the proposed revision of the Forestry Code put forward by the ruralist benches in Congress in 2001 was aimed at reducing the areas of rural properties in the Legal Amazon Region that had to be kept as reserves by law from 80% to 20%.

3. "NGOs have lost the ability to organize themselves and to propose public policy. Conema, FECAM, etc. are paper tigers, in which the representative NGOs merely legitimize government decisions," declared an environmentalist interviewed by Loureiro (2000, p. 221).

4. This is the title of a World Bank report for Brazil (Garrison 2000).

5. "Squeezed by the lack of channels for participation caused by the succession of authoritarian governments, the environmentalist movement sought new forms of organization and action that went beyond the political sphere, in the strict, standard interpretation of the term. Having become politicized amid the crisis of the left and as a reaction to authoritarianism, the environmentalist movement brought with it the negation of paternalism, populism and Marxist mechanicism and of the enlightened avant-garde." (Moura 1988, p. 3) The contentious environmentalist movement of the 1980s couched the utopian prospect of overthrowing capitalism in a new language. Félix Guattari had a significant influence in formulating the connections between politics and subjectivity in the ecological discourse of the time, valuing molecular experiences as producing new subjectivities in opposition to the dominant forms of subjectivization; see Carvalho 2000, p. 11.

6. A. W. de Almeida and A. C. S. Diegues have systematically analyzed local movements aiming at controlling access to natural resources, preventing the expulsion of "community members" from protected natural areas, and promoting alternative forms of social organization, such as extractivist reserves and the remaining *quilombos*, communities founded by runaway slaves. See Almeida 1994.

7. A survey of 182 representatives of Brazilian NGO Forum member organizations, out of its 935 members in 1992, revealed a greater percentage of positions indifferent to the Malthusian question of population increase. See Herculano 1996, pp. 91–126.

8. According to Ferreira (1997, p. 42), "inequality acted as a factor isolating the environmentalist discourse, since the rhetoric in defense of the excluded makes use of the justification for programs to stimulate economic growth, based on the argument of the unlimited expansion of the economically active sector of the population and the extension of the equally unlimited benefits of the Welfare State to the universe of the workers. This, perhaps, has been the most difficult problem for environmentalism to solve in recent years."

9. "With the 'Diretas Já' ('Direct Elections Now') campaign in 1984, most activists in the movement joined the political fight. A new consensus developed in the movement: environmental protection is directly linked to problems of the organization of power and property in society as a whole." (Moura 1988, p. 4) See also Viola 1987, pp. 63–110.

10. "In a highly interdependent world, it is also necessary to consider the differences between nationalists and globalists. Environmentalism entails globalism, and environmentalist forces that identify with nationalist positions end up being inconsistent." (Leis 1994, p. 37)

11. Ecological modernization is the process by which political institutions adopt ecological concerns with the aim of reconciling economic growth with solutions to environmental problems, with emphasis on technological adaptation, the exaltation of the market economy, and a belief in collaboration and consensus. See Blowers 1997, pp. 853–854.

12. Fordism is the name given to the combination of production standards, consumption patterns and regulatory bodies that ensured the ongoing growth of Western economies for the 30 years after World War II. Its basic features include mass production and consumption, together with intensive use of fossil fuels.

13. The Club of Rome is the body that commissioned the research report "Limits to Growth," which in the early 1970s simulated the future of the world economy and pointed to a major crisis of capitalism due to a shortage of raw materials and energy.

14. By "economic heterodoxy" I mean the efforts to question dominant neoclassical economic thinking by introducing political and cultural variables that might somehow alter the standard economic behavior of instrumental rationality, as assumed by orthodox economists, thus doubting the ability of the market alone to promote growth and wealth distribution.

15. The "Tragedy of the Commons" is the parable through which the conservative ecologist Garret Hardin sought to represent the problem of ecology as a shortage resulting from the fact that resources such as air, water and biodiversity are for communal use and thus not subject to private ownership (Hardin 1968).

16. Delocation is the removal of particular businesses from their current sites and their relocation to another place, region or country where the political and

institutional conditions are more favorable for wealth accumulation, e.g. laxer environmental legislation, curtailed social rights, and more flexible planning laws.

17. "Social reproduction" is used here to mean the mechanism by which any society reproduces its basic social relations in time; in the case of the capitalist society, it is the procedures that reproduce the condition of capital as capital and of workers as workers.

18. In the academic field, the notion of environmental justice and the issues surrounding it had already been addressed by the demographer Haroldo Torres (1997, 2000).

References

Acselrad, Henri. 1996. Política Ambiental e Discurso Democrático—o caso do Conselho Nacional de Meio Ambiente. Paper presented at XX Encontro Anual da ANPOCS, Caxambu.

Acselrad, Henri. 2004. Justiça Ambiental—ação coletiva e estratégias argumentativas. In *Justiça Ambiental e Cidadania*, ed. H. Acselrad et al. Relume Dumará.

Acselrad, Henri. 2005. Novas articulações em prol da justiça ambiental. *Democracia Viva* 27, June–July: 42–47.

Acselrad, Henri, and Cecilia A. Mello. 2002. Conflito social e risco ambiental— o caso de um vazamento de óleo na Baía de Guanabara. In *Ecologia Política— Naturaleza, Sociedad y Utopia*, ed. H. Alimonda. CLACSO.

Almeida, Alfredo W. 1994. Universalização e localismo, movimentos sociais e crise dos padrões yradicionais de relações políticas na Amazônia. *CESE Debate* 3, May: 43–60.

Boehmer-Christensen, Sonja. 1994. Politics and environmental management. *Journal of Environmental Planning and Management* 37, no. 1: 69–85.

Blowers, Andrew. 1997. Environmental Policy: Ecological Modernization or the Risk Society. *Urban Studies* 34, no. 5–6: 845–871.

Bullard, Robert. D. 2002. Environmental Justice: Strategies for building healthy and sustainable communities. Paper presented at the II World Social Forum, February, in Porto Alegre, Brazil.

Carvalho, Isabel. 2002. As transformações na cultura política e ao campo educativo: um olhar sobre a educação ambiental, mimeo., Porto Alegre, Brazil.

CIMA. 1991. *O Desafio do Desenvolvimento Sustentável*. Brasília, Brazil.

Diegues, A. C. S. 1994. *O Mito da Natureza Intocada*. São Paulo: NUPAUB/ USP.

Fabiani, Jean L. 1985. Science des ecosystèmes et protection de la nature. In *Protection de la Nature—Histoire et Ideologie*, ed. A. Cadoret. L'Harmattan.

Ferreira, Lucia C. 1997. Confronto e Legitimação. In *Ambientalismo no Brasil— passado, presente e futuro*. ISA.

Ferreira, Lucia C. 1999. Conflitos sociais contemporâneos: considerações sobre o ambientalismo brasileiro. *Ambiente & Sociedade* II (5, 2nd semester): 35–54.

Garrison, John W. 2000. Do confronto à colaboração—relação entre a sociedade civil, o governo e o banco mundial no Brasil. Brasília, Brazil.

Hardin, Garrett. 1968. The tragedy of the commons. *Science* 162: 1243–1248.

Herculano, Selene C. 1996. O campo do ecologismo no Brasil: o fórum das ONGs." In *Política e cultura—visões do passado e perspectivas contemporâneas*, ed. E. Reis et al. Hucitec-Anpocs.

IBASE/ CUT-RJ/IPPUR-UFRJ. 2003. *Sindicalismo e Justiça Ambiental*, series in three parts. Rio de Janeiro: IBASE/ CUT-RJ/IPPUR (Brazilian Institute for Social and Economic Analysis, Rio de Janeiro Trade Union Federation, Rio de Janeiro Federal University Institute of Urban and Regional Research and Planning).

Leis, Hector. 1994. Sociedade civil e meio ambiente. In *Comissão de Defesa do Consumidor, Meio Ambiente e Minorias da Câmara dos Deputados, Diretrizes de Ação para o Meio Ambiente no Brasil* Brasília: Relatório Final.

Loureiro, Carlos F. 2000. A assembléia permanente de entidades de defesa do meio ambiente-RJ e o pensamento de esquerda: análise crítica do coletivo organizado a partir do depoimento de suas históricas lideranças históricas estaduais. Ph.D. dissertation, Escola de Serviço Social.

Mallerba, Julianna. 2004. Meio Ambiente, classe e trabalho no capitalismo global: uma análise das novas formas de resistência a partir da experiência da ACPO. In Encontro da ANPPAS, mimeo, Indaiatuba, Brazil.

Moura, Paulo G. M. 1988. O PT e o movimento ecológico, mimeo., São Paulo, Brazil.

Oliveira, Francisco. 2003. *Crítica à razão dualista/O ornitorrinco*. São Paulo: Boitempo.

Torres, Haroldo G. 1997. Desigualdade ambiental na cidade de São Paulo. Ph.D. dissertation, IFCH/UNICAMP.

Torres, Haroldo G. 2000. A demografia do risco ambiental. In *População e Meio Ambiente. Debates e Desafios População e Meio Ambiente. Debates e Desafios*, ed. H. Torres and H. Costa. Editora SENAC.

Urban, Tereza. 2001. *Missão (quase) impossível—aventuras e desventuras do movimento ambientalista no Brasil*. Rio de Janeiro: Editora Petrópolis e Fundação SOS Mata Atlântica.

Viola, Eduardo. 1987. O Movimento ecológico no Brasil (1974–1986): do ambientalismo à ecopolítica. In *Ecologia & Política no Brasil Ecologia & Política no Brasil*, ed. J. Pádua. IUPERJ/Espaço & Tempo.

Viola, Eduardo, and S. Boeira. 1990. A emergência do ambientalismo complexo-multissetorial no Brasil nos anos 80. Paper presented at the IV Seminário sobre Universidade e Meio Ambiente, Florianópolis, Brazil.

II

Industrial Development and Environmental Justice

4

Environmental Conflicts and Environmental Justice in Argentina

Carlos Reboratti

The population of Argentina is only somewhat interested in environmental matters. Surveys consistently find that environmental problems are not considered among the ten most important issues. This does not mean that environmental issues do not exist in Argentina, but rather that many factors mediate between society and environmental problems, so it comes to the surface only sporadically and in connection with very specific issues. This separation between society and environmental issues has generated a gap between people's awareness of their environmental rights and the operation of a notion of justice that would protect them. Because the notion of a formal "environmental justice" is not entrenched in Argentine society, people more typically address environmental concerns with a discourse of "environmental conflict," which constitutes an "informal" environmental justice. Thus, in recent years there have been an increasing number of cases in which different sectors of society have joined forces to vindicate their rights in matters that are clearly rooted in environmental problems. This chapter is intended to embrace these conflicts within the idea of a quest for environmental justice that goes beyond the legal aspect and has to do with a social process of learning about rights and how to sustain them.

It is evident for many that it is not possible to transfer the idea of environmental justice as such to Latin America. According to Walker and Bulkeley, the term "environmental justice" refers to "a response to perceived injustice, as judged through observations of unreasonable inequality in outcome and lack of fair treatment" (2006, p. 656). However, it is not necessarily true that it applies exclusively to "people and social groups that are already marginalized and disadvantaged" (ibid., p. 656). That is to say, in Latin America the idea of environmental justice does not necessarily target the problems of racially or economically defined minorities; it tends to identify groups that are defined territorially rather than characterized socially. It is most typically not a problem of poor distribution of natural resources and their use but instead a problem of maldistribution of the negative effects arising from the use of the environment. Perhaps, as Williams and Mawdsley state (2006), the problem is that the contexts and circumstances in the developed countries and in the Third World are so different that their channels to access environmental justice are also necessarily different. These contexts determine that, in fact, environmental justice is the search for reparation for the injuries resulting from "environmental injustice" that arise from distortions generated in the distribution of income and decision-making capacities by the world economy in the poorest countries (Acselrad 2005).

This search for environmental justice comes from malfunctions in the political, economic, and judicial systems, which leads the population to feel that it is not given consideration in the decisions about actions that could have environmental impact, even in cases where there are regulations in place that should solve these problems. This becomes more evident in the planning of large investments whose environmental impact may be limited from a territorial viewpoint but whose benefits are not deemed worthy by the local population that would have to suffer it.

The solution adopted, what we can call a methodology for the quest for environmental justice, is to explicitly state a conflict through social action. Ultimately, the goal is for informal justice to become formal justice through the activation of the available means in the legal and political system. But many times, a system of responsibility levels is unveiled that is increasingly further away from the population, has its own dynamics, and is very difficult to adjust to the needs and desires of the population.

In general, in Latin America, this informal environmental justice is achieved (or at least sought) through ad hoc organizations that differ from place to place as to their organization, constitution and dynamics. In some cases, they are ephemeral institutions, which disappear once their objective has been fulfilled; in other cases they lead to the creation of formal institutions and institutional networks. Sometimes they comprise the low-income sector, other times they comprise the middle-income sectors; sometimes they are rural, other times they are urban and deal with very different problems that range from deforestation to industrial pollution.

In this chapter I analyze three cases of environmental conflict that developed in the last fifteen years in Argentina. By 2005 there were at least 20 social movements related with environmental issues in Argentina (Giarracca 2006), but I will focus on the three most important cases, which reveal both the diversity of possibilities and, at the same time, a surprising similarity in their objectives, characteristics, and development. But first it will be necessary to briefly establish the general context of environmental politics in Argentina.

Argentine Society and the Environment

For several reasons, Argentina has not been especially open to the ideas of environmentalism. Although this is a common trait in less developed countries, in this case it is somewhat contradictory, because the environmental discourse is more rooted in Argentina's highly developed urban middle class, and the middle class has been an important player and driver in other social, economic, and political issues. It cannot be said that this lack of awareness is due to the fact that Argentina is a country where there are no environmental problems; they exist and are many. In a long list of problems, we could include deforestation, water pollution, erosion, indiscriminate fishing, over-grazing, mining impacts, and urban flooding as the most pressing issues (Di Pace 1992; Morello et al. 1997). However, until relatively recently, this list has not been sufficient to cause a reaction by society.

Successive presidential administrations have taken a very passive attitude toward environmental matters. The Secretaría de Medio Ambiente (Department of the Environment), created in 1973, was lethargic until the early 1990s, when Carlos Menem's neoliberal administration reactivated it. However, Menem's government was more concerned with the economic use of the environment than with its preservation. To head the department, the administration appointed a person who was much more interested in business deals and a high public profile than in building a serious environmental policy. This person's subsequent prosecution and imprisonment for embezzlement of public monies only managed to tinge the environmental issue with frivolity, futility, and corruption. In view of this public image, subsequent administrations hid the Secretaría de Medio Ambiente behind a tangled bureaucracy from which it has yet to escape.

From a legislative standpoint, a large number of environmental protection laws were passed, beginning with the Argentine Constitution which, after its 1994 amendment, guarantees the right to a "healthy environment" and the right to petition the authorities where this right is violated. By the late 1980s, below constitutional law, there were already more than 4,000 national and provincial provisions related to the preservation of nature broadly speaking, to which others were added later about issues as diverse as nuclear energy, fisheries, formation of different levels of environmental authorities, and transportation of toxic materials (Bertonati and Corcuera 2002). But very few of those legal provisions were effective, either because of the absence of any specific regulation or because of the government's incapacity to enforce compliance.

Argentina did not tend to generate environmental movements with the capacity to affect society as a whole. The general trend accompanied that of Latin America in terms of the creation of this kind of institution (Christen et al. 1998; Roberts 2000; Price 1994), but it was more focused on what Bryant and Bailey (1997) call "professional non-governmental organizations." The two most important ones, Fundación Vida Silvestre and Fundación Argentina de Recursos Naturales, though well established, have purposes that are very narrow in scope. One of these foundations, the Fundación Vida Silvestre, is engaged in the protection of endangered species; the other one, the Fundación Argentina de Recursos Naturales, addresses the environmental legislation problem. Though both have a long tradition, they have had relatively little impact beyond their limited area of focus. The non-governmental environmental organization that has had the most significance has been the Argentine branch of an international NGO: Greenpeace. Although its flamboyant actions attract much public notice, Greenpeace's relatively short and sporadic campaigns have earned it only a modest degree of awareness among the population at large. In truth, perhaps because of the country's social structure, Greenpeace gains its support mainly from the urban middle class of Buenos Aires. With this political context in place, I now turn to the justice dimensions of some of Argentina's most important recent environmental conflicts.

A High-Voltage Line in the Quebrada de Humahuaca

The Quebrada de Humahuaca is deep valley, approximately 120 kilometers long, located in the Altiplano at altitudes of 1,200–3,000 meters above sea level. It connects the temperate agricultural valleys of the Southern Andes with the Argentina-Bolivia border. The Quebrada has a distinct landscape and cultural value, and in the late 1990s the Argentine province of Jujuy presented it before UNESCO to be declared a World Heritage site, a recognition achieved two years later. The Quebrada de Humahuaca is an icon of national and international tourism, emblematic of Argentina much as the Grand Canyon is of the United States. Approximately 29,000 people live there, half of whom are located in three main urban centers of under 8,000 residents, with the rest in rural areas. Demographic density is high, however, as the valley floor is only between 200 and 2,000 meters wide, and most of it is taken up by the Río Grande or covered with the crops that are the main source of employment in the region other than tourism and public administration. It is here where we can trace the first environmental conflict related to a spontaneous social action. This search for "environmental justice" started in 2000 as a result of the attempt by the province of Jujuy to build a high-voltage line through the Quebrada. It was a project of great importance for local standards since 400 large high-voltage towers (22 meters high) would be set up, every 300 meters throughout the Quebrada. These would be very conspicuous in such a restricted territory.

The idea of building a high-voltage line to connect the towns close to the Bolivian border with the interconnected power-supply network in Argentina was not a new one; the call for bids to build it went back to 1994. For various reasons, it was not until 1999 that the province awarded the project on the basis of an environmental impact assessment conducted by the construction company. When the study was disclosed to the public at large, it was proven to be extremely poor and evidently targeted at merely justifying the project, which is not unusual in these cases. (For example, the environmental impact assessment stated that the high-voltage line could be installed on the West end of the Quebrada, as the tourists "mainly focus their attention on the Eastern slope.") The news about the project went relatively unnoticed initially, but the presence of the construction company in July the following year and the beginning of the works (apparently before the province granted an explicit permit) gave rise to a quick reaction from the local community.

The residents of the Quebrada de Humahuaca are largely of indigenous origin and, in some towns, immigrants attracted by the local culture, the landscape, tourism, and the peaceful lifestyle. The native population was undergoing a euphoric process of recreating their indigenous identity, in line with occurrences in much of the country after the 1994 constitutional reform, which had included the rights of aboriginal peoples among its articles (Briones 2005).

The social mobilization in the Quebrada to oppose the construction of the high-voltage line was an odd mixture; these two social sectors came together to build a dense communications network that included articles published in regional and national newspapers and TV shows. Neighborhood centers, professional associations in the provincial capital (for example, the association of architects), and, finally, with some reluctance, the municipal governments, joined in the movement. The protests were sparked by the intention of the construction company to begin setting up boundary stones in the southern end of the Quebrada, where the high-voltage line would enter toward the north. A group of locals removed a boundary stone in an indigenous ceremony; setting the boundary stone in the ground without ceremonially requesting permission from the Pacha Mama, the regional indigenous deity that represents nature, was considered an intrusion. Although that was an activity that attracted a lot of attention, the movement took advantage of a legal weakness in the construction process: according to the provincial legislation, prior to the award of the contract, any work that could have an impact on society's cultural or environmental heritage had to be submitted for consideration at a public hearing where the public could express their views. However, in this case, the hearing was scheduled by the provincial authorities for a date that was after commencement of the works. This clumsy maneuver was thwarted by an avalanche of letters from people wishing to participate in such hearings and by the resonance the issue had with the public. By mid August, the governor ordered that any activity related to the high-voltage line be suspended. A few months later, an official decree indicated that the works were to be suspended until the issue could be thoroughly examined. The subsequent declaration of the Quebrada de Humahuaca as a World Heritage Site ruled out the possibility of any similar work, and there was no further attempt to revive it.

The informal quest for environmental justice was conducted without a great physical mobilization. The largest public protest included only a few hundred people, and involved the removal of the boundary stone that the construction company had placed at the site. However, there are two very important elements in that action. One is that it included diverse segments of society, which indicates a certain capacity of the local identity to bring together sectors that usually develop separate means of expression, organizations and representations. The other is that it brought to light the formal legal system's flaws in protecting citizens from environmental impact; in this case it was a large infrastructure project. Although from a legal perspective the province had the necessary mechanisms in place to conduct a serious analysis of the possible impact of building a high-voltage line, it chose, possibly driven by the corruption of the provincial administration, to avoid these mechanisms, even going as far as scheduling the public hearing after the works were already awarded, approved, and in progress. None of the branches of government seemed to want to participate. The executive was evidently willing to have the work performed. The provincial legislature approved a project that was contradictory to another parallel initiative on which it was working at the same time (i.e., the petition to have the Quebrada de Humahuaca declared a World Heritage Site). The judiciary was inaccessible to the spontaneous social movements because of its attachment to the bureaucratic channels. In light of the fact that the access routes to formal environmental justice were blocked, the local society, without violence, opted for a parallel path of action that ended up forcing the government to reverse its decisions.

We could say that this was the first spontaneous environmental social movement in Argentina. It was small in scale, owing to the limited number of residents involved, the size of the project, and the size of the construction company (a local one). It was quick and efficient in its creation and development, but did not lead to any subsequent institutionalization and dissolved after the initial objective was fulfilled. Subsequent environmental conflicts and movements would be different.

Esquel's Gold Mine

In 1994, Argentina passed a law to promote mining, granting interested companies a series of advantages for mineral prospecting and exploitation. This triggered massive investments, particularly in western Argentina. The growth of mining activity and its environmental impacts brought about a series of conflicts involving legal, political, and economic issues. One of the earliest conflicts, and the one with the most widespread coverage at the time, was in the Patagonian Andes, specifically in Esquel, in the west of the province of Chubut. Esquel is a small town with a population of 28,000. Its origin goes back to the process of populating western Patagonia that started in the late nineteenth century (although there is no foundation date, the year 1906 is accepted as such), after the indigenous peoples had been pushed to live in marginal areas. The weather is cold and wet, and the area is at the limit of the Patagonian cold forests, which have great timber and landscape value. Also of great landscape value are the beautiful Andes lakes. The first important resource activity in Esquel was timber production, but this activity declined when most of the bordering forests were declared national parks. However, this created a new activity: tourism, which is the most important local economic activity together with low-intensity cattle raising. The original population was the result of European immigration, whose descendants proudly refer to themselves as "NYC" (a Spanish acronym that stands for "nacidos y criados," meaning "born and raised"). Over time there was additional immigration from the rest of the country, as is so frequently the case in Patagonia.

The mountains of Esquel, at the base of which the city is located, were subject to a mining prospecting survey since 2000, and in November 2001 a consulting firm prepared an investment project for gold mining in a deposit located 5 kilometers away from the city for Meridian Gold, a Canadian company. The project stated that, with an investment of a little more than $130 million and a large benefit afterward, the deposit could be exploited for 10 years, with an annual production of 500,000 ounces of gold. To reach that figure, almost 20 million tons of rock had to be removed, and 2 million metric tons of ore had to be ground to extract gold and subsidiary silver, first by gravity and then by cyanide leaching. The project included the use of large quantities of water (it was calculated that approximately a quarter of the quantity used by the entire city of Esquel was needed), which was apparently going to be obtained mainly from the underground aquifers and secondarily from local brooks. Additionally, the project would employ about 340 workers. The company recognized that it would be necessary to be "sensitive to present and future community needs" and that, although some contamination and environmental impact were expected, after the closure of the mine, the necessary actions would be taken for "returning the site to a forested and grazing land use, similar to the existing site conditions" (Brancote Holding PLC 2001). The area directly affected would be approximately 130 hectares, as it was an open-pit gold mine. The mining company had already directly or indirectly appropriated 200,000 hectares in the area, within which the gold deposit was located.

At first, the project did not cause major unrest among the population, particularly in view of the promise of creating jobs. Note that Argentina was at that point falling into one of its worst socio-economic crises in history, which reached its peak with the massive demonstrations throughout the country in December 2001 and the resignation of the President. However, the visit and public conferences of an expert from Dupont (the firm that was going to provide cyanide to the mine) in July 2002 generated anxiety among the population. This anxiety started to take shape when a group of professors of the University of Patagonia based in Esquel began questioning the desirability of the project and made their concerns public, particularly in connection with cyanide pollution, dust from the explosions, the movement of heavy machinery, and the use of large quantities of water. By the time the company submitted its environmental impact assessment to the provincial authorities in

October that same year, the issue had become public and the people, spontaneously, began taking to the streets.

The first demonstration was organized in November. A month later, two presentations were made before the local courts requesting an injunctive measure prohibiting the company from changing the state of affairs until an intensive study of the environmental impact of the proposed gold mine site was conducted and a public hearing was held. In February 2003, the court ordered that the works be suspended, and this decision was ratified at several jurisdictional stages, including the Argentine Supreme Court.

The most striking event was that in March, the municipal administration (which had previously had an unclear attitude) held a non-binding referendum among the local citizens. Eighty-one percent of voters voted against the proposed gold mine in Esquel. Despite its continued battle before the courts, in view of this outcome the company decided to suspend the project and commission a consulting firm to make a plan to convince the population of the advantages of the project. But this project has not yet been resumed.

Meanwhile, the local residents continued with informal gatherings, eventually organizing a formal institution, the Asociación de Vecinos Autoconvocados (Association of Self-Convened Residents). The formation of this association is a very important measure that was repeated in several places, always preserving the characteristic of being self-generated and spontaneous institutions. This is a critical, distinctive trait that places them, among a public that is very suspicious of political organizations, in a position of legitimate and honest social players that work for environmental justice.

Additionally, the association was very successful in reaching the mass media, promoting the mining issue to the level of national interest. In this, the expansion of the Internet was crucial. Formal environmental institutions such as the Fundación Argentina de Recursos Naturales provided critical support to the Asociacíon de Vecinos. Strangely, Greenpeace, usually highly visible, was never an integral part of the movement in Esquel and was only marginally involved.

In a situation similar to the Humahuaca case, the provincial government was first a strong promoter of the project, but as the people's opposition increased, the government changed its attitude and ultimately ordered that the activities should cease until a more in depth study was conducted. The local municipal administration had a similar attitude, even though right from the beginning other municipal governments in the region had joined the protest. As regards the legal aspect, we can see that, in view of a greater degree of organization, the presentations before the formal judicial system were effective and the judiciary responded positively at all levels.

Uruguay River Pulp Mills

The next environmental conflict arose in central eastern Argentina, on the border with Uruguay. This border is formed by the Uruguay River, a tributary of the Río de la Plata. A series of cities have developed along both sides of the river. Since the late 1980s, Uruguay had developed a very active pine and eucalyptus tree forestation policy (more than 600,000 hectares were planted) intended for industrialization of timber for furniture, construction and, especially, pulp manufacturing, although it was only in 2001 that discussion about setting up pulp mills began. In Argentina there were already more than 20 such plants and—although they were strong contaminants—no conflict with the population had occurred until then.

The construction of paper mills generated several environmental conflicts during the 1990s, particularly because of their large contamination potential (Sonnenfeld 2002). However, in Argentina, the issue only became public knowledge in 2002. At that time, a movement emerged in Gualeguaychú, a city of approximately 80,000 located on the Argentine side of the Uruguay River. Some residents of Fray Bentos, a smaller city (23,000) located across the Uruguay River, had gone to Gualeguaychú and were concerned because an investment plan to set up two pulp mills close to that city materialized. The two cities have always enjoyed very close relations since they are connected by a bridge—the most widely used land route access between Argentina and Uruguay, because it is the closest one to Buenos Aires.

The concern of the Uruguayan citizens was based on the possibility that these industries might pollute the river, which was a very important resource for both cities, since they both had an incipient development of tourism. It should be noted that the entire region, on both sides of the river, up until that time relied economically on cattle raising and agriculture, with little industrial development.

Two companies, one Spanish and one Finnish, were preparing an investment plan to set up two pulp-manufacturing plants near Fray Bentos, with a total investment of $1.8 billion, intended to produce 1.5 million tons of paste annually. This was going to be done based on the output of 150,000 hectares of eucalyptus that these companies had been planting for several years. As usual, these mills promised to create jobs and to apply the Elemental Chlorine Free technology to their industrial processes, which is the method that is most widely used in the world and that at least in theory had made progress until reaching levels of almost no contamination.

Some residents of Gualeguaychú took very seriously the possibility that these industries could create pollution and started to organize, like in Esquel, a self-generated institution, in this case called the Movimiento Ambientalista de Gualeguaychú (Gualeguaychú Environmental Movement). During that year, there were several demonstrations against the proposed paper mills, which already contained the seeds of a problem that would become magnified: the motto was "Say no to paper mills," but these paper mills were going to be built in another country. The residents alleged that the pulp mills would pollute the Uruguay River with chlorine and other elements, thus causing the death of the fish, and also that the contaminant elements included dioxins, which are carcinogenic substances. Additionally, another complaint was that the mills were going to produce nauseating odors, which are so characteristic of the pulp mills in Argentina and other parts of the world.

In view of the general apathy of the Argentine government and court system, the citizens decided to implement a more radical methodology: in September 2003 they blocked the international bridge for a few hours. In the eyes of the public, the protests of the environmentalists in Entre Ríos could be lumped in with the demonstrations organized by the Piquetero movement, which was formed by groups of unemployed people that blocked the roads in Argentina as a means to protest against their situation. This methodology had grown since its appearance by the mid 1990s as a result of the closure of the oil refineries in Northern

Patagonia, which were privatized by the government. This manner of protesting had grown, boosted by the 2001 crisis, and in the big cities— particularly Buenos Aires—it had had much impact. After initially having significant popular support, support for the movement started to decline after the roads were blocked more and more frequently, causing transportation problems that adversely affected the entire population.

In 2003 the Argentine government began to worry about the issue, as it concerned a river shared by two countries and as social unrest was increasing. However, the Uruguayan government continued its policy of promotion for the mills, and in October, it officially authorized the setup of the first one, implicitly accepting their environmental impact assessment. Over time, popular protest and blockages of the bridge grew more frequent. Despite the fact that the two governments had met several times in an attempt to find a solution to the problem, the Uruguayan government approved the setup of the second mill in February 2004.

The environmentalists' response was conclusive: in April the Assembly of residents organized a demonstration of more than 40,000 people, a considerable number taking into account the size of the city. The issue adopted unprecedented characteristics due to the resonance in the mass media and the action capacity shown by the Assembly of residents. This group was horizontally organized; there was no management structure and everything was solved through open meetings and deliberations. The only institution it created was an NGO that would allow it to bring legal actions and administer the funds from the numerous donations they received.

The formation of a Joint Commission between the two countries proved to be a failure, and both companies started building the plants, which were growing visibly while a deaf ear was turned to the environmentalists' claims. Finally, in February 2006, the Assembly decided to block the international bridge indefinitely.

The decision and the wide scope of the action triggered a strange effect: the Argentine government, in the absence of a specific environmental policy, adopted in the facts the extreme environmentalist discourse of the Assembly and started putting pressure on Uruguay by instituting proceedings before the International Court of Justice, which has its seat in The Hague, claiming that Uruguay had breached international treaties.

In view of this presentation, in early May the Assembly opened the international bridge after organizing an enormous demonstration of 100,000 people. This was clearly the largest gathering of people ever witnessed in connection to an environmental issue in Argentina's history, and was in fact much larger than most of the gatherings that any political parties have managed to achieve. The Assembly, after this demonstration of force, is waiting expectantly, while the Argentine government generates abundant environmental rhetoric.

Compared to the previous cases mentioned, in this case, the players in the conflict have a different scale and different characteristics. On the one hand, the Assembly of residents appears as a characteristic movement of urban middle-class people and this is reaffirmed when on several occasions they refuse to be labeled Piqueteros, distancing themselves from other social movements organized by the lower-income classes. Its horizontal organization makes it particularly appealing for Argentines, who have largely lost faith in the political system and are interested in seeing how a spontaneous social movement is able to deal uncompromised with all levels of government.

Institutionalized environmental organizations have had an expectant attitude. Some, including Greenpeace, have tried to participate in the issue. (Greenpeace has been unsuccessful, as the Assembly distrusts it as much as it distrusts politicians.) Also, this NGO has adopted a more moderate position: it opposes industrial pollution but not the setup of factories.

The municipal government was committed to supporting the Assembly from the very beginning, while the provincial government had an ambivalent attitude. When it analyzed the magnitude of the social movement it expressed support, but when the economic and political effects of the prolonged blockage became apparent (Uruguay alleges that the blockage caused a loss of more than $500 million, particularly due to the resulting slowdown in the flow of Argentine tourists to Uruguay, which is a very significant source of revenue), it tried to convince the members of the Assembly to drop the issue.

At the beginning, the national government tried to handle the issue with a very low profile, presumably in the belief that it would be solved through simple negotiations. But the growth of the Assembly, and particularly their great success with blocking the bridge, put the government in a very uncomfortable position: it could not force the release of the bridge (just as it has never had a confrontation policy with the Piquetero movement) and it did not plan to become an out-and-out defender of the environment. The weakness in this position was evident, as the topic had never been a priority. It finally opted for what was possibly the worst of solutions: it resorted to an international court, trusting that this action would demobilize the Assembly, which strained relations with Uruguay and jeopardized the possibility of forming a bi-national commission that could control the pollution from the mills.

By mid 2006, the situation is that of a tense wait, where the government has convinced the Assembly—for the time being—to free up the bridge, but in the absence of that element of mobilization and cohesion, the Assembly is planning other actions, such as demonstrations in Buenos Aires. Nobody is sure how this conflict can be solved, but the construction of paper mills continues and the relations between Uruguay and Argentina have been practically interrupted.

Conclusion

As can be seen from the three examples, in recent years conflicts in search of environmental justice have increased in scale, frequency, and complexity. It is evident that the development of each one has been a step forward in the organizational methods used by these spontaneous movements. Regardless of whether or not they obtained the desired result, it would seem that the search for environmental justice has brought a new player into the country, in the form of spontaneous environmental social movements. In the Argentine case, incipient environmental justice movements are not about the "environmentalism of the poor" (Martinez Alier 1992). Although that situation could occur in the future or in other contexts, at present the urban middle class plays a fundamental role.

On the other hand, in the origin of these movements there are two elements that are very important: the local identity and the value attributed to nature as a source of landscape and tourist resources; those "ecological processes and human values that are impossible to be reduced to the market standard of measurement" mentioned by Leff (2000,

p. 51). It is true that in some cases—as illustrated in the pulp-mill conflict—this leads the social movements to adopt very extreme positions from which it is difficult to negotiate solutions that do not have repercussions at other levels; the absence of a broader vision could be negative for the movements themselves in the long term. But what is undeniable, particularly in a country like Argentina with very limited environmental awareness, is the role played by movements that seek environmental justice in raising that awareness.

Another notable aspect is the near incapacity of political parties to become involved in the issues, partly because they do not know how to deal with spontaneous social movements and partly because these movements are a result of the bad practice conducted by the political parties themselves, clearly evidenced in the fact that the most common motto in the worst of the crisis was "throw them all out."

These spontaneous social movements, which are horizontal, noisy, and politically unapproachable, are growing day by day in Argentina, learning from the old movements the methodologies of pressure and demonstration that are increasingly stronger and, clearly, increasingly more effective. That these actions really generate a change in the way environmental politics are conducted is a challenge for the future.

References

Acselrad, Henry. 2005. Cuatro tesis sobre políticas ambientales ante las coacciones de la globalización. www.nuso.org.

Belli, Elena, Ricardo Slavutsky, and Cristina Argañaraz. 2001. De cada mojón, una apacheta. In Estudios Sociales del NOA. Instituto Interdsiciplinario de Tilcara.

Bertonatti, Claudio, and Jorge Corcuera. 2002. Situación ambiental de la Argentina 2000. Fundación Vida Silvestre Argentina.

Brancote Holdings. 2001. Esquel Gold Project. Pre-feasibility Study.

Briones, Claudia. 2005. Formaciones de alteridad: contextos globales, procesos nacionales y provinciales. In Cartografías Argentinas, políticas indigenistas y formaciones provinciales de alteridad, ed. C. Briones. Editorial Antropofagia.

Bryant, Robert, and Simon Bailey. 1997. Third World Political Ecology. Routledge.

Christen, Catherine et al. 1998. Latin American Environmentalism: Comparative views. Studies in Comparative International Development 33, no. 2: 58–86.

Di Pace, Maria, ed. 1992. *Las utopías del medio ambiente. Desarrollo sustentable en la Argentina.* Centro Editor de America Latina.

Di Pace, Maria, et al. 1992. *Medio ambiente urbano en la Argentina.* Centro Editor de America Latina.

Giarracca, Norma. 2006, Territorios en disputa: Los bienes naturales en el centro de la escena. *Realidad económica* 217: 41–56.

Leff, Enrique. 2000. *Saber ambiental. Sustentabilidad, racionalidad, complejidad, poder.* Siglo XXI.

Martínez Alier, Joan. 1992. *De la economía ecológica al ecologismo popular.* Icaria.

Montenegro, Ricardo. 2003. Estudio sobre el impacto ambiental y sanitario de minas de oro. El caso Cordón Esquel. www.greenpeace.org.

Morello, Jorge et al. 2002. *El ajuste estructural Argentino y los cuatro jinetes del apocalípsis ambiental.* Centro Editor de America Latina.

Price, Marie. 1994. Ecopolitics and environmental nongovernmental organizations in Latin America. *Geographical Review* 84, no. 1: 42–58.

Roberts, J. Timmons. 2000. Global restructuring and the environment in Latin America. In *Latin America in the World Economy*, ed. R. Korzenewicz and W. Smith. Praeger.

Sonnenfeld, David. 2002. Social movements and ecological modernization: The transformation of pulp and paper manufacturing. *Development and Change* 33: 2–27.

Walker, Gordon, and Harriet Bulkeley. 2006. Geographies of environmental justice. *Geoforum* 37, no. 5: 655–659.

Williams, Glen, and Emma Nawdsley. 2006. Postcolonial environmental justice: Government and governance in India. *Geoforum* 37, no. 5: 660–670.

5

Waste Practices and Politics: The Case of Oaxaca, Mexico

Sarah A. Moore

While much attention has been paid to the "garbage crisis" (Melosi 1993; Miller 2000; Melosi 2000; Rathje and Murphy 2001) in Northern countries, especially the United States, less attention has been paid to the "politics of garbage" in the global South. While Northern countries are dealing with the aftermath of decades of siting problems and costly and environmentally suspect municipal solid waste (MSW) technologies, Mexico is trying to import these very same practices in an effort to "modernize" (Aguilar 2001). These trends have led to a multi-billion-dollar market in waste-management equipment and services. As table 5.1 shows, waste-management equipment and services constitute a significant proportion of the total global environmental market. While the world-wide technology trade expands, though, garbage problems persist (OECD 2004).

These problems persist, in part, because while countries in the global South are attempting to modernize waste management through the importation of technologies, they are also confronted with significant changes in the quantities and qualities of the waste they have to manage. As consumption-based development projects proceed in these areas, per-capita waste production increases. In the case of Mexico, for example, this means that people today produce twice as much garbage as they did 40 years ago (SEMARNAT 2003). At the same time the ratio of organic to inorganic waste has gone down (SEMARNAT 2003). This means that the waste stream contains a smaller proportion of items that will decompose and more materials that will be a continuing burden on the disposal system because they do not break down naturally.

Table 5.1
The global environmental market ($US billion). Source: OECD 2004.

	US/Canada	Western Europe	Aus/NZ	Africa/Latin America	Eastern Europe	World 1996	World 1998
Equipment							
Total	47.7	29	20.5	10.1	1.7	108.9	114.1
Waste management	11.5	9.1	9	2	0.4	32	32.6
Services							
Total	93	69.6	49.5	14	2.6	228.6	246.9
Solid waste	34.9	29.5	31	5.8	1.1	102.3	105.4
Hazardous	6.3	5.2	4	0.9	0.3	16.7	16.4

The changing nature and quantity of waste produced in the global South presents challenges beyond the sphere of waste management. The municipalities dealing with waste face a crisis of legitimacy if they are not able to keep their city clean. On the other hand, the need to eliminate waste from the city raises the question of disposal, a question that is very difficult in many parts of the world. The negative environmental and public-health effects produced by the open-air dumping common to the global South are distributed unevenly. This uneven distribution often becomes a point of contention between state agencies and local populations and is the starting point for any discussion of environmental justice in Latin America.

Beyond these difficulties, though, there is also the fact that many waste-related problems cannot be addressed by collection and disposal technologies alone. That is to say that garbage and its management are also social, economic, and political issues (Hawkins and Muecke 2003; Stallybrass and White 1986; Stam 1999; Strasser 1999). In this chapter, I consider waste-management practices and politics in Oaxaca, Mexico by examining the context in which a particular *colonia* (neighborhood)— Guillermo González Guardado—uses its proximity to the municipal dump to meet its development goals. The residents of this *colonia* create garbage crises (figure 5.1) by blocking the city's access to the dump, thereby causing garbage to pile up in the central city. In response, the city negotiates with the *colonia* making these garbage crises a very effective form of social protest. The effectiveness of this tactic, I argue, has its roots in the context of modernization that equates cleanliness with modernity in contemporary urban spaces and in the inability of modern waste collection and disposal systems to fully eliminate garbage from the city.

The remainder of this chapter is divided into three sections. First, I discuss the historical links between modernity and cleanliness and contemporary waste-management practices in Oaxaca. Next, I discuss public perceptions of the city's waste-management practices and the cleanliness of the city. Finally, I conclude with a discussion of the success of the *colonia*'s tactic of creating garbage crises and its implications for environmental justice.

Figure 5.1
Garbage in the streets during a garbage crisis.

A Clean City Is a Beautiful City: Urban Development and Garbage

The practical purpose of sanitation is to efficiently remove waste; that was its modernist promise. Here was a technology that would purify urban space, that would allow populations physical and moral escape from the unacceptable; that would render shit secret. Transport it away from the body and home . . . out of sight, out of mind.
—Hawkins 2003, p. 40

[T]he director of municipal services expressed the fight for a clean city, as in no other entity of the country is 24-hour service offered, as it is here. . . . The current municipal government is looking to preserve and reinforce the cleaning of the city, as more than just being an obligation, this situates (Oaxaca) as one of the cleanest in all of the republic.
—Torres 1988, p. 14

In *The Sanitary City*, Martin Melosi notes that there has long been a connection between cleanliness, beauty, and order and that the desire for these in urban areas has been a contributing factor in the development of urban infrastructure (Melosi 2000). Similarly, in *History of Shit*, Dominique Laporte argues that the articulation of such concepts goes back as far as Rome's sewer system, which was considered not only a technological achievement, but also the height of civilization (Laporte 2000). Though Laporte is speaking more specifically of human feces, the same argument can be made for garbage. While these two books deal specifically with the history of sanitation in the global North (Melosi's in the United States, Laporte's in France), Beatriz González Stephan (2003) has made a similar, compelling argument for Latin America:

The modern era was intimately linked to hygienization policies for individuals, languages, and territories . . . imposing pure and non-polluted categories. . . . The *asepsis* and *cleanliness* of streets, language, body and habits appeared as the panaceas of progress and materialization in a modern nation. . . . Bodies were not the only things that should be disinfected. The modern city plan redesigned Latin American cities by redistributing buildings into discreet units, removing waste and the "vulgar" bustle of social life from the urban centers.

In this spirit, Oaxaca, the capital of the southern Mexican state of Oaxaca and now home to more than half a million people, started a campaign in the 1985 called "Una Ciudad Limpia es una Ciudad Bonita" ("A clean city is a beautiful city"). This campaign was enacted to preserve the image of the city locally, but also nationally, as was noted by the head of municipal services: "One of the most serious problems in the city, without doubt, is that of garbage. One day without sweeping stains the impeccable image that Oaxaca has at the national level" (Cruz Garcia 1987). Signs were posted at each of the major entrances to the city, saying "Oaxaca welcomes you to a clean city," and, of course, "A clean city is a beautiful city"; both assertions that could only be supported by effectively hiding (that is, containing or expelling) the city's waste. To this end, Oaxaca has (though not evenly or in a linear way) tried to increase the efficiency of its collection services which includes two main components—the *barrenderos* (who use hand-made brooms of natural materials to sweep up litter in the cities streets and parks—see figure 5.2) and a fleet of garbage trucks. Collection is more frequent and there are several times as many *barrenderos* in the city's center, El Centro, where most of the tourists are, than in other areas (City of Oaxaca 2003). However, uneven collection is only one of the city's problems.

The question of disposal is a difficult one for Oaxaca, as it is for many rapidly growing medium to large cities in the global South. While some

Figure 5.2
A traditional *barrendero*.

sanitary landfills and processing plants exist in Mexico, the majority of solid waste (including hazardous, toxic, and medical) goes to open-air dumps. Compared to the United States, which produces more waste overall, Mexico both disposes of more waste in landfills (99 percent versus 57 percent) and has fewer landfills (76 versus 2,216) (OECD 2004). This means that the average amount of waste per fill in Mexico is staggering—396,840 tons (versus 54,010 in the United States). Like many Mexican cities, then, Oaxaca has only one open-air dump for the entire municipal area. Its 16 hectares are located on land in a neighboring county (Zaachila). Like many cities at the time Oaxaca decided to export its garbage to what were then its hinterlands.

However, as greater numbers of people who had been expelled from their pueblos by the modern state (through direct violence, political exclusion or more subtle threats to rural agrarian livelihoods (Murphy and Stepnick 1991; Stephen 1998) saw in the image of the modern capital city the promise of a better life, the rate of rural to urban migration outpaced official planning and development schemes (Girón Méndez 1990; Ramirez 1990). Informal squatter settlements (*colonias populares*) began to pop up on any unused land. This included the land around the dump, which was sold (often illegally) for very little (interview with Felimon Diaz, Office of the Regent for Ecology of Zaachila, October 16, 2003). By 1986, when the dump was legalized, there had already been a number of complaints from the neighborhoods of Vicente Guerrero and Emiliano Zapata, near the site, that the environment and their health had been threatened by the city of Oaxaca dumping its waste there (Bracamontes Ruiz 1991). These neighborhoods were also upset about the lack of city services in the area, a common complaint in *colonias populares*. Even those who had derived subsistence or supplemental income from the dump were asking for its removal. One garbage scavenger described it this way: "Well yes, it is true that the dump has served us in a certain way as a source of work, although with ridiculously low earnings, but it is preferable that it be moved to another area, in view of the serious health problems that it has caused us." (quoted in Bracamontes Ruiz 1991) In spite of such concerns, the municipal dump is still on the same site and has grown in size and area of contamination. Now 22 municipalities—the city of Oaxaca and its 21 contingent *municipios* (counties)—dispose of their waste there. There is still no official processing or separation of waste and only minimal attempts have been made at mitigating the contamination it causes.

While the city and state governments still have not adequately addressed the issue of disposal, they continue to expand collection service (both in area and frequency) and look for other ways to "modernize" MSW management and make the system more efficient. The Integrated System of the Management and Use of Solid Wastes (SIMARS), implemented in January 2004, is the best example of this. SIMARS is a program proposed for the *municipio* of Oaxaca by a consulting firm based in the state of Puebla. Noting that MSW management has led to high levels of dissatisfaction among the public, the firm suggested the reorganization of routes, an increase in the frequency of collection, the use of dumpsters and other transfer units, an increase in the number of mechanical *barrenderos* (figure 5.3), and especially, the implementation of recycling and composting programs at the community level. All in all, such recommendations departed very little from the initiatives undertaken by previous city administrations. The administration also declared that the

Figure 5.3
A mechanical *barrendero*.

"project of the systematic closure of the municipal dump is a real alternative with the acceptance of the people of Guillermo González Guardado and the other surrounding neighborhoods, which has gained the approval of many institutions" (City of Oaxaca 2003). While it may have become a "real alternative" the city has yet to close the dump. In the next section, I discuss how residents of the city view waste management and the cleanliness of the city. While residents in some areas view the city as relatively clean, residents in all areas still list garbage among the main ecological problems the city faces as will be discussed in the following section.

Public Perception of Waste Management and Cleanliness in Oaxaca

In a survey conducted in three areas of Oaxaca in 2004, respondents were asked their views of Oaxaca's contemporary garbage problem and current MSW management in the city. The following tables describe how citizens view the problem of MSW in Oaxaca and its management. As table 5.2 shows, all respondents, regardless of location, ranked garbage as the top ecological problem in the city. This was the first question in order to prevent influencing the response unduly with questions focused on garbage.

Forty percent of respondents listed garbage alone as the primary environmental problem in the *municipio* of Oaxaca. An additional 24 percent listed it in the top two environmental problems (WS + G; S + G). Thirteen percent of respondents listed garbage as one of the top three environmental problems (All). The second highest percentage of responses fell to water shortages, which was listed as the primary environmental problem by 11 percent of respondents. Sewage was the third most named response, with 6 percent. The prevalence of the garbage problem belies the municipality's inability to erase waste entirely from the city. Both waste and expectations of cleanliness, though, are uneven distributed through the metropolitan area. When this data is stratified by location (table 5.3), it reveals that residents of Zaachila (including Guillermo Gonzalez Guardado), are more concerned about garbage than residents of other areas. What is more surprising though, is that a larger percentage of residents of the center city listed garbage compared to residents of the outer city, despite the fact that collection is more frequent in the center.

Several of the survey questions concerned contemporary MSW management practices and how they affected different locations and

Table 5.2
What is Oaxaca's main environmental problem?

	Count	Percent
Garbage (G)	145	40.17
G and S	47	13.02
Water Shortage (WS)	40	11.08
WS and G	37	10.25
All of these	36	9.97
Sewage (S)	23	6.37
Other (O)	21	5.82
Other combinations	9	<1.00
Missing	3	0.83

Table 5.3
What is Oaxaca's main environmental problem? (Percentages do not add to 100 because of the possibility of combined answers.)

Main problem	Central city %	Outer city %	Zaachila %
Water shortage	41.58	25.15	37.11
Garbage	72.27	66.87	91.75
Sewage	20.79	22.09	55.67
Other	5.94	111	1.03

Table 5.4
How often do garbage trucks come through your neighborhood?

	Citywide	Central city	Outer city	Zaachila
<1 time/week	37.12	27.72	56.44	16.50
1–3 times/week	488	275	40.49	73.20
>3 times/week	140	39.60	0.61	9.28
Missing	3.60	7.92	2.45	1.03

populations within the metropolitan area. Table 5.4 shows responses about the frequency of garbage collection in the surveyed *colonias*. In 38 percent of the total cases, the respondent said that garbage trucks pass less frequently than one time per week. Approximately 45 percent of respondents said that the trucks pass between one and three times per week and 14 percent said that garbage was collected in their area more than three times a week. This would be true mostly in El Centro, where the garbage trucks pass some areas four times a week, including Sundays. About 40 percent of people in the center said that trucks pass more than three times per week, compared to less than 1 percent in the periphery of the city and less than 10 percent in Zaachila. The majority of respondents in the outer city said that the trucks pass less than one time per week while the majority of respondents in Zaachila (73 percent) said that the trucks pass between one and three times per week.

Respondents from all areas were more consistent in the amount of garbage that they estimated that their household produced per week (table 5.5). This holds across different survey sites. Most of those surveyed (64 percent) thought that their household produced between 3 and 7 kilograms of garbage per week. Thirty-one percent of respondents estimated amounts exceeding 7 kilograms per week (table 5.5.) According to the survey, there was always someone home when the garbage trucks passed in 67 percent of cases (table 5.6). This is important in Oaxaca, in that garbage is usually taken directly from the house to the truck. It is against local regulations to leave garbage in the street for later collection. Only 4 percent of respondents said that there was never anyone at home when the trucks passed, while 27 percent said that there was sometimes someone at home. Table 5.7 reveals a related practice: 89 percent of respondents answered that they disposed of garbage in the garbage trucks, rather than the street or another location. Again, this was true across the survey sites.

Three survey questions were aimed at people's perceptions of garbage and the cleanliness of Oaxaca City. Table 5.8 shows that 35 percent of respondents thought their neighbors produced more garbage than they

Table 5.5
How much garbage does your household produce each week?

	Percent	Central city	Outer city	Zaachila
1–2 kg	3.05	5.94	2.45	1.03
3–5 kg	32.69	48.52	29.45	21.65
5–7 kg	31.30	33.66	33.74	274
7–10 kg	17.73	5.94	20.25	25.77
>10 kg	196	95	111	26.80
Missing	0.28	0.99	0	0

Table 5.6
Is someone home when the garbage trucks pass? (Percent of responses.)

	Citywide	Central city	Outer city	Zaachila
Always	67.31	55.44	65.64	82.47
Sometimes	26.59	33.66	29.45	143
Never	16	9.99	2.45	1.03
They don't pass	0.55	0.99	0.61	0
Missing	1.39	0	1.84	2.06

Table 5.7
Where does your household dispose of your garbage?

	Citywide	Central city	Outer city	Zaachila
Trucks	89.20	80.20	92.02	93.81
Street	16	10.89	1.84	1.03
Other	6.09	6.93	6.13	12
Missing	0.55	1.98	0	1.03

Table 5.8
How much garbage do your neighbors produce a week?

	Citywide	Central city	Outer city	Zaachila
More than we do	35.46	38.61	32.51	37.11
Less than we do	12.47	11.88	15.95	7.21
Equal to us	39.61	46.54	28.83	50.51
Missing	12.47	2.97	22.70	5.15

Table 5.9
How much garbage does your household produce now, compared to the past?

	Citywide	Central city	Outer city	Zaachila
Less	7.20	6.93	9.82	3.09
More	57.06	58.41	52.76	62.89
Same amount	35.18	365	36.20	302
Missing	0.55	0	0	0

did. Only 13 percent thought their neighbors produced less garbage than they did, and 40 percent said the amounts were equal. Similar trends are apparent in all three locations where very few people were willing to say that they produced more garbage than their neighbors. When asked if their household produced more garbage than in the past (table 5.9), the majority of respondents (57 percent) said they produced the same amount as before, while another 35 percent claimed that their household produced more garbage than before. This trend held across areas, but respondents in Zaachila were relatively more likely to answer that their household's garbage production had increased.

Table 5.10
Is Oaxaca a clean city?

	Citywide	Central city	Outer city	Zaachila
No	58.17	32.67	73.00	59.80
Yes	41.00	636	26.99	40.20
Missing	0.83	2.97	0	0

When asked if Oaxaca was a clean city (table 5.10), the majority (58 percent) said it was not, while 41 percent said it could be considered a clean city. Differences can be seen in this variable between the outer-city and the central city. Central city respondents were more likely to claim that the city was clean, than were residents of outer areas of the city. Zaachila residents were more closely divided, but still tended toward claiming the city was not clean. These responses can be compared with how respondents in each area ranked garbage as an environmental problem. In the case of the outer city residents, the proportion that ranked garbage as one of the biggest environmental problems (67 percent) is fairly similar to the number of respondents who answered that Oaxaca was not a clean city (73 percent). This is not true for the other areas. Respondents from Zaachila listed garbage as the main environmental problem at a much higher rate (92 percent) than they said that the city was not clean (60 percent). On the other hand, even though the majority of respondents in the center said that Oaxaca was a clean city (65 percent), a majority (72 percent) still listed garbage among Oaxaca's main environmental problems. This apparent contradiction can be directly related to the mismatch between the production of the image of a clean and modern city, and the inadequacy of waste management to match those expectations. It is this same mismatch the *colonia* Guillermo González Guardado exploits when it creates garbage crises.

Garbage Crises as Protests

Since the year 2000, there have been a series of blockades in which people from Guillermo González Guardado have closed off access to the dump, leaving the municipal area of Oaxaca with no way of disposing of its trash. During these blockades the city suspends collection and usually asks residents to keep the trash in their houses, though this request often goes unheeded by the public.

As garbage piles up in the city center, particularly around markets (figure 5.4), and begins to smell and get in the way, the city is forced into negotiating with the *colonia* to end the blockade. Because of the nature of public space and political protest in Oaxaca (it is perfectly legal to block roads, occupy parks, etc.), the city does not have recourse to remove the protesters. The public in Oaxaca is fairly tolerant of, or at least accustomed to, their streets being filled with protesters. However, the presence of garbage in the streets is considered a crisis that demands immediate attention.

To date, these blockades have resulted mostly in promises by the city to find a new location for a dump, to reforest, or to provide facilities or services for the *colonia* (interview with Arquitecto Cutberto, January 31, 2004). Through these efforts, though, the *colonia* has gotten a meeting center and a basketball court (2001) a medical center (2003), and electricity in some areas (2003).

[handwritten margin note: but no action taken?]

Figure 5.4
Waste piles up around a popular market during a garbage crisis.

When garbage crises occur, the 800 tons of garbage that Oaxaca and its suburbs produce per day can no longer be ignored. The "public secret" of waste (Hawkins 2003) is thereby revealed. Despite the fact that the city's cleanliness ordinances prohibit the leaving of garbage in the street (Ciudad de Oaxaca, 1993, chapter 2, article 23), this is often ignored. According to the Secretary of Ecology of Oaxaca City, this is an act of protest against the city for not fulfilling one of its important obligations to the citizenry (interview with Jacqueline Mariana Escamilla Villanueva, September 29, 2004).

By blocking the flow of trash, the people of the *colonia* are able to make the usually hidden product of development, garbage, visible, revealing the "public secret" (Hawkins and Muecke 2003) of waste. By forcing the citizens of the center to live with their own garbage, they reverse their relationship to waste, and claim their "rights to the city" (Mitchell 2001) by demanding official recognition, services, and municipal responsibility for the health of the *colonia*'s residents. In this way, one marginalized *colonia* is able to take their struggle for environmental justice to the center of the city, while at the same time highlighting the precariousness of the divide between clean and dirty and between empowered and marginalized.

As Cresswell (1996) argues, the notion of normativity is directly related to that of transgression. The action of transgressing the boundaries of what is acceptable in a particular space/time is enabled by the very rules that establish those boundaries in the first place. This is also significant in terms of environmental justice: "If we can grasp the system of extremes which encode the body, the social order, psychic form and spatial location, we thereby lay bare a major framework of discourse within which any further 'redress of balance' or judicious qualification must take place." (Cresswell 1996) In terms of garbage and the city, then, the desire for clean and modern environments means that garbage and those associated with it must be erased from the landscape. However, as this process of purifying the city is never complete, remnants threaten the integrity of the (social) body. The residents of Guillermo González Guardado are able, for this reason, to use waste and their proximity to it as a political resource.

References

Aguilar, Silvia. 2001. La basura, problema social, económico, y de salud. *Las Noticias*, Oaxaca, January 25.

Bracamontes Ruíz, Reynaldo.1991. Miseria y explotación brutal sufren cientos de pepenadores. *Las Noticias*, Oaxaca, November 8.

City of Oaxaca. 2003. Report on SIMARS.

Cresswell, Tim. 1996. *In Place/ Out of Place: Geography, Ideology and Transgression*. University of Minnesota Press.

Cruz Garcia, Abraham. 1987. Basura, problema grave en la ciudad. *El Imparcial*, Oaxaca: August 11.

Girón Méndez, Mario. 1990. Difícil inicio de año para amplios sectores desprotegidos. *Las Noticias*, Oaxaca, February 2.

González Stephan, Beatriz. 2003. On citizenship: The grammatology of the body-politic. In *Latin American Philosophy*, ed. E. Mendieta. Indiana University Press.

Hawkins, Gay. 2003. Down the drain: Shit and the politics of disturbance. In *Culture and Waste*, ed. G. Hawkins and S. Muecke. Rowman and Littlefield.

Hawkins, Gay, and Stephen Muecke. 2003. Introduction: Cultural economies of waste. In *Culture and Waste*, ed. G. Hawkins and S. Muecke. Rowman and Littlefield.

Laporte, Dominique. 2000. *History of Shit*. MIT Press.

Melosi, Martin V. 1993. Down in the dumps: Is there a garbage crisis in America? In *Urban Public Policy*, ed. M. Melosi. Pennsylvania State University Press.

Melosi, Martin V. 2000. *The Sanitary City: Urban Infrastructure*. Johns Hopkins University Press.

Miller, Benjamin. 2000. *Fat of the Land: Garbage in New York*. Four Walls Eight Windows.

Mitchell, Don. 2003. *The Right to the City*. Guilford

Murphy, Arthur, and Alex Stepnick. 1991. *Social Inequality in Oaxaca: A History of Resistance and Change*. Temple University Press.

OECD (Organization for Economic Cooperation and Development). 2004. *Addressing the Economics of Waste*.

Ramirez, Luis. 1990. Irresponsibilidad oficial en el case de asentamientos humanos. *Las Noticias*, Oaxaca, March 9.

Rathje, William, and Cullen Murphy. 2001. *Rubbish: The Archaeology of Garbage*. University of Arizona Press.

SEMARNAT (Secretaria de Medio Ambiente y Recursos Naturales, Mexico City). 2003. Cruzada Nacional por un México Limpio.

Stallybrass, Peter, and Allon White. 1986. *The Politics and Poetics of Transgression*. Methuen.

Stam, Robert. 1999. Palimpsestic aesthetics: A meditation on hybridity and garbage. In *Performing Hybridity*, ed. J. May and J. Fink. University of Minnesota Press.

Stephen, Lynn. 1998. Between NAFTA and Zapata: Responses to restructuring the commons in Chiapas and Oaxaca. In *Privatizing Nature*, ed. M. Goldman. Rutgers University Press.

Strasser, Susan. 1999. *Waste and Want: A Social History of Trash*. Metropolitan Books.

Torres, Humberto. 1988. La ciudad que fue limpia en peligro de ser la más sucia. *El Imparcial*, Oaxaca, February 22.

Valencia, Paulina. 2004. Maestros dejan 120 toneladas de basura. *El Imparcial*, Oaxaca, June 2.

6

Where Local Meets Global: Environmental Justice on the US-Mexico Border

David V. Carruthers

The US-Mexico border is an enigmatic place where the local and the global collide. It is at once prosperous and poor, urban and rural, Anglo American and Latin American, First World and Third World. In few places do we see in such· stark terms the unevenness with which the modern global economy parcels out costs and benefits. Border residents feel the environmental and social contradictions of global development, North and South, with great intensity. "We live with this every day. We know that there are many things that we have to put up with on this border—the *maquiladoras*,[1] the contamination from the *maquiladoras*, the fact that all of the things that we assemble, that we build, that we sew together, are not even for us—[this] is very clear in everybody's minds." (García Zendejas 2005). Likewise, on the border we find multiple and sophisticated efforts to confront and exploit those contradictions, including the emergence of local and cross-border movements for environmental justice.

While we must be cautious about the generalizability of lessons learned in this peculiar region, the border does present a telling microcosm of North-South relations, revealing the forms, consequences, and tensions of global economic and cultural integration. The border is likewise the paradigm case for transnational citizen activism on environmental and social justice issues (Brooks and Fox 2002; Hogenboom, Cohen, and Antal 2003). With this intensified representation of global tensions, it offers especially fertile terrain to assess the international dimensions of environmental justice in Latin America.

This chapter explores a set of cases from northern Mexico in which community resistance and cross-border collaboration are generating a uniquely binational conception of environmental justice. The first section looks at a community's efforts to confront the notorious industrial waste hazards of the region's export assembly plants. The second section explores the politics of energy in the border region, focusing on Baja California's emerging role as an export platform for electricity and lique-fied natural gas to meet US demand.

Industrial Hazardous Waste

Many academic studies and journalistic accounts have chronicled the varying successes and shortcomings of a series of environmental justice struggles over chemical hazards in and around the industrial parks and factories that dominate the landscape of the northern Mexican border. Debates about the capacity of the North American Free Trade Agreement's "side agreement" institutions to protect communities and workers propelled several local cases into international prominence. Scholars, policymakers, and journalists have focused attention on scandalously high clusters of neural-tube birth defects (such as spina bifida and anen-cephaly) in border communities, acute chemical toxicity in Mexicali's New River, and lead smelters, battery recycling facilities, and other uncontrolled hazardous wastes or chemical releases that have tarnished the reputations of Stepan Chemical, Alco Pacífico, Chemical Waste Management, Hyundai, and many other international companies.[2]

Even with that inglorious background, one of the most visible symbols of NAFTA's institutional failure to protect the environmental health of a community is Metales y Derivados, my focus here. Metales stands at the edge of Tijuana's Otay Mesa industrial park, 150 yards above the canyon in which the community of Colonia Chilpancingo houses more than 10,000 residents. Owned by San Diego-based New Frontier Trading Corporation, the Metales plant began smelting in 1972 to recover refined lead and copper from automobile batteries and other sources.

For more than 20 years Chilpancingo residents expressed concerns to local and national officials about possible threats to public health and the environment. One 1990 Mexican study of the river below found lead levels 3,000 times higher than US standards, and cadmium 1,000 times higher (Sullivan 2003). In 1987 and again in 1989, Mexican authorities ordered cleanups and imposed fines; however, the factory owners did not respond, and no enforcement was forthcoming (Fritsch 2002). The facility remained in operation until March 1994, when the federal environmental enforcement agency (PROFEPA) finally ordered its closure for violating Mexico's environmental laws.[3] Since its closure, approximately 24,000 tons of mixed hazardous waste, including more than 7,000 tons of lead slag, remained exposed to the elements. With only a crumbling retaining wall and the tattered remnants of plastic tarps to contain the wastes, the plant continued to leach arsenic, cadmium, antimony, and other hazardous metals into the soils and waters of the community below for more than 10 years (EHC 2004).

The Metales case was thrust onto the international stage in October 1998, when San Diego's Environmental Health Coalition (EHC) and residents of Colonia Chilpancingo (the Comité Prorestauración del Cañón del Padre/Canyon Restoration Committee) filed a petition with the North American Commission for Environmental Cooperation (NACEC), the main institution of the NAFTA environmental side agreement. Over the next few years Chilpancingo's parents and activists held news conferences, organized vigils and protests, and launched the kinds of letter writing and direct action campaigns that would be familiar to environmental justice activists everywhere. Not surprisingly, Metales gained a high profile in the ongoing debates over the failures of NAFTA and the potential lessons for the proposed Free Trade Agreement of the Americas (Fritsch 2002).

In February 2002, the NACEC released its factual record on the case. The report confirmed the community's claim that the site presented a grave risk to human health, and called for remediation (NACEC 2002a). The NACEC ruling offered vindication and a great symbolic achievement, but was a frustratingly hollow victory, given that the Commission has no enforcement authority or budget.

With no cleanup forthcoming, Chilpancingo homemakers, mothers, and activists formed a new citizens' organization, the Colectivo Chilpancingo Pro Justicia Ambiental (Chilpancingo Pro Environmental Justice Collective) in April 2002, to keep up the pressure for a cleanup. The new organization was rooted in gender empowerment, composed of working-class women concerned about threats to their households and children, and propelled into action "because we were looking at a case of injustice, because of Metales y Derivados. . . . We're working on cleaning up the environment here. . . . We're looking for justice, and the government and the companies are not giving it to us." (Lujan 2002) The women of the Colectivo, collaborating with their EHC allies, continued pressuring the PROFEPA (EHC 2002). In May 2003, the Colectivo and the EHC turned up the pressure by presenting a cleanup plan of their own, and challenging officials on both sides of the border to seek implementation (Colectivo Chilpancingo 2003). In February 2004, the US EPA and the Mexican counterpart agency responded to the challenge, and began to seek funding for a cleanup strategy (Cantlupe and Wilkie 2004). In March 2004, EHC and Colectivo members met with US, Mexican, and Baja California officials to establish a working group to carry out the cleanup.

On June 24, 2004, the women of the Colectivo achieved the community's long-sought victory. The Colectivo and the Mexican government signed an agreement to achieve a comprehensive cleanup of the Metales y Derivados site within 5 years. The first stages of a site restoration that is ultimately expected to cost $5–10 million were initiated immediately, with the Mexican federal and Baja governments providing $500,000 and the US EPA contributing an initial $85,000 (Cantlupe 2004; Dibble 2004; EHC 2004). The first step in the remediation plan called for 2,500 tons of lead slag to be removed and transported to Kettleman Hills, California (EHC 2004).[4] By the end of 2005, most of the above-ground hazardous waste had been removed from the site (nearly 2,000 tons), and the EHC and the Colectivo had succeeded in archiving all the waste-removal manifests.

Energy and Environmental Justice

While cross-border organizing has focused on *maquiladora* waste for a number of years, environmental health and social justice concerns have recently been finding new expressions in the area of binational energy development. The story begins north of the border, in the wake of California's costly and humiliating rolling electricity blackouts of 2000–2001. Energy production and distribution in the California–

Baja California region features high levels of interdependence across the border and high dependence on outside sources of energy. Baja California's power grid is not connected to the main transmission system in Mexico; Mexico's mainland gas pipeline system also does not reach the peninsula (CEC 2005a, p. 27). San Diego and Imperial counties are likewise more dependent on imported power than the state as a whole (SCERP 2003, p. 92).

After 2001, major energy producers played on fears of future blackouts, proposing a vastly expanded binational energy system to meet anticipated regional demand. Recognizing from the outset the strong community resistance that has long slowed new installations in California, the companies set their sights on northern Baja California, which they see as an ideal production platform to meet future energy needs. Energy companies rushed to present dozens of proposals for the construction of thermoelectric power plants, receiving terminals and regasification facilities for liquefied natural gas (LNG), new gas pipelines, and new electricity distribution systems across the region. This section explores contestation over two categories of energy development: electricity generation and LNG regasification.

Power Plants and Transmission Lines

While energy companies have proposed 17 power plants for the Mexican border as a whole, I focus attention here on two new gas turbine, combined-cycle thermoelectric plants near Mexicali, the state capital of Baja California. Proposed immediately after the crisis and constructed without delays, both plants have been exporting power to Southern California via the Imperial Valley substation since mid 2003. The first is Sempra Energy's 650-megawatt Termoeléctrica de Mexicali (TDM). The second is InterGen Services' 1060-megawatt La Rosita Power Complex.

Environmental groups on both sides of the border raised early alarms about potentially adverse impacts on air and water quality. Electric power plants are the single largest source of toxic air pollution in North America, accounting for nearly half of all industrial air emissions (NACEC 2002b). The Mexicali Valley–Salton Sea binational airshed is already seriously polluted, with high incidence of pulmonary disease; it regularly violates established ambient air quality standards for ozone, particulate matter, and on the Mexicali side, carbon monoxide (Powers 2005a; CEC 2005b, pp. 7–14). In a fiercely hot and arid region, the plants' wet cooling systems could reduce stream flows, increase salinity, and contaminate surface or groundwater, negatively affecting the Salton Sea and the New River, already among the most polluted waterways in the hemisphere (CEC 2005b, pp. 32–35). Many Mexicali residents opposed the plants, as did Imperial county officials and residents concerned about cross-border emissions (Lindquist 2005a). However, Mexican federal and Baja state officials promoted the projects on the basis of job creation and economic growth. Localized opposition did not develop into organized resistance. While there was nationalistic resentment on the street, especially a sense that Mexico was going to be "used," by and large "people didn't think you could stop it" (Powers 2005b).

As energy companies started to reveal their ambitious plans for the region, energy consultants and environmental activists on both sides of the border began to collaborate to formulate a community response. In May 2001, a US air quality engineering group, Mexico's Grupo Yeuani (an environmental law organization), Mexico's Proyecto Fronterizo de Educación Ambiental (see appendix below), the Border Ecology Project, and others formed the Border Power Plant Working Group, an advocacy network dedicated to the promotion of environmentally sustainable energy for the US-Mexico border region.

With the plants granted quick approvals by Mexican agencies, the Working Group concluded that opposition in Mexico was futile (Powers 2005b). However, transmission lines to carry the electricity into the United States presented an opportunity. In early 2001, the companies applied for permits for two parallel 230-kilovolt lines to transmit the new electricity across BLM (US Bureau of Land Management) land to the Imperial Valley substation for distribution on the Southern California electric energy grid. The US Department of Energy and the BLM prepared an abbreviated environmental assessment (EA) outlining the impacts of the power plants and transmission lines. Eager to expedite the development of new power plants, the DOE ruled two Findings of No Significant Impact (FONSIs) in December 2001, and the US Energy Secretary issued the federal permits (CEC 2005b, pp. 87–88).

In March 2002, the Working Group teamed with Earth Justice and Wild Earth Advocates to file a lawsuit against the DOE and the BLM in the US District Court, alleging that the EAs, FONSIs, and presidential permits violated US environmental law by not adequately evaluating plant emission impacts on Imperial Valley air quality, or liquid cooling impacts on the Salton Sea (Lindquist 2003; CEC 2005b, pp. 87–88). On May 2, 2003, the District Court agreed, ruling that the DOE had acted illegally by not requiring a more thorough environmental review. The victory was short-lived; a few months later the same judge ruled that the companies could bring the plants online and proceed with electricity export during the year the court allotted the DOE to come up with a more thorough environmental impact study. The companies completed the lines and started exporting electricity in June 2003. Not until November 2006 did the DOE and BLM finally complete the long-overdue environmental review, which received the court's final approval (Lindquist 2006).

Another important dimension of this story involves technological differences between the United States and Mexico. While the plants were still in the planning stages, the Working Group identified two concerns. Ironically, while Mexico is a world leader in air-cooled plant technology, its officials had permitted these plants with environmentally damaging water-cooled technology, inviting serious water quality problems (Powers 2005a). A second issue has to do with the nitrogen oxide scrubbers that would be required to comply with California air quality standards. Sempra agreed to install selective catalytic reduction equipment (SCRs) on the TDM plant, but InterGen offered no such guarantee.

These issues gave environmental justice advocates new political traction, as they went public with the charge that the companies were deliberately installing dirty plant technology in Mexico to evade higher US environmental and community health standards. Senator Dianne Feinstein and Representative Duncan Hunter (both from California) responded with a proposal to ban electricity imports if the plants were not brought into compliance with California standards. Under Congressional pressure, in January 2003 InterGen announced a commitment to install SCRs on the export turbines at La Rosita; Feinstein and Hunter shelved their legislation.[5]

Amazingly, the company did not follow through with this promise, only installing SCRs on one of the smaller turbines. Only the determined vigilance of the Working Group revealed their duplicity, in late 2003, after tons of additional pollutants had been released into the airshed. The exposure was a major embarrassment to plant advocates and public officials on both sides of the border, especially the Mexican regulatory agencies and the DOE, who failed to catch the company's flagrant non-compliance. In January 2004, under a DOE threat to revoke the export permit, InterGen finally shut down the export turbine (Lindquist 2004a). The following year the company attempted to secure Mexican govern-ment funding to cover the cost of the SCRs, but the Mexican electricity agency responded that it does not require them; the turbine complies with Mexican law without them (Lindquist 2005a).

From a social and environmental justice standpoint, the Mexicali thermoelectric plants manifest important parallels with the *maquiladora* sector—located in Mexico to take advantage of a streamlined permitting process, limited political space for popular resistance, lower wages and land costs, and a more favorable political and investment climate. Like the export factories, they are oriented to serve external consumer demand, with few local benefits or linkages. Most glaringly, Sempra's TDM is not even connected to the Baja California electricity distribution grid—its entire generating capacity is transmitted directly across the border. Two of the InterGen plant's turbines are likewise transmitting more than half of their capacity northward (560 MW of the plant's total 1,060 MW) (CEC 2005b, pp. 46–47). The inequitable distribution of burdens and benefits could not be clearer: adverse air and water impacts are born principally by Mexicans, while Californians enjoy consumption of an increased energy supply. Notably, in terms of global greenhouse gases, Mexico is also shouldering part of the carbon burden for US consump-tion (Moreno 2005). "The CO_2 quotas generated are not added to the US's emissions account but to Mexico's. We are in fact laundering carbon for our neighbors up north, whose energy policy is absolutely unacceptable and deadly for the planet." (Greenpeace 2002, p. 1)

Liquefied Natural Gas
Another set of environmental inequities appears in the conflicts that have erupted over company plans to install a string of liquefied natural gas

receiving terminals, regasification facilities, storage tanks, and new gas pipelines along Baja's Pacific coastline. Mexico is one of the world's major energy producers, with its own substantial natural gas supply and infrastructure. Nonetheless, US energy companies see growth opportunities for imported LNG, given the limited exploration and development capacity of the state-owned Petroleos Mexicanos (PEMEX), Baja California's distance from the mainland system, and expectations of increased US demand for gas in coming years. Mexican energy planners expect to build as many as 11 Pacific coast LNG terminals to receive gas imported from Australia, Indonesia, Russia, Bolivia, and other countries (Lindquist 2005b).

Cooled to minus 259 degrees Fahrenheit, natural gas becomes a clear, odorless liquid that occupies one six-hundredth of its gaseous volume, enabling economical transport between continents in special, double-hulled tankers (CEC 2006a). Natural gas is the preferred fuel for new power plants, and US demand is expected to exceed the domestic US gas supply. Even with the technical complexity and expense of liquefaction and cold shipment, regasified LNG costs less than half the price of oil in terms of comparable energy yield, and emits fewer greenhouse gases. There are currently only four LNG terminals in the United States, but companies have plans for as many as 40 (Romero 2005). However, LNG is difficult to work with, highly unstable, and potentially dangerous. When spilled, it warms into an extremely combustible vapor cloud that can travel for miles over water or land. Given the possibilities of leaks, accidents, or terrorist attacks, US safety standards emphasize the need for remote siting, typically requiring a one-mile buffer zone directly around a plant, and prohibiting LNG plants within 6 miles of population centers. At this point, Mexico has clarified no such restrictions (Moreno 2005).

No LNG facilities currently exist on the west coast of the United States. Energy companies have longer-term plans to install three in Oregon, one in Washington, one in Northern California, two in Ventura County, and one in Long Beach (CEC 2006b). However, company officials recognize the political barriers to siting dangerous, controversial, and unsightly industrial facilities in US coastal communities, where they rightly anticipate that lengthy, deliberative policy processes and well-organized opposition will derail some projects and delay construction of

"not in my backyard!"

others for years. Sharing the expectation that Mexico offers faster, streamlined government permitting processes, limited public resistance, lower land and construction costs, and fewer barriers to entry, the companies turned to Baja California in the race to bring imported LNG supplies more quickly to market. After the California crisis, companies proposed six initial projects; two have withdrawn, two were defeated, and two are currently proceeding. Their stories are instructive.

The earliest projects out of the gate were first to fail, due to heightened local perceptions of environmental injustice and determined street-level opposition. In early 2002, El Paso Corporation teamed with Conoco Phillips Petroleum to purchase a 74-acre plot near an existing power plant in the picturesque tourist town of Rosarito Beach, about 25 miles south of the border, unveiling plans to construct a regasification facility for gas imported from Australia (Niller 2002). The companies apparently did not anticipate local resistance, assuming the community would welcome facility modernization, job creation, and growth opportunities (García Zendejas 2005; Powers 2005b). However, the citizens of Rosarito have a healthy distrust of the energy industry, after a long history of pipeline and tank leaks and air pollution problems with CFE (Federal Electricity Commission) and PEMEX facilities there. A local citizens group, the Comité de Planeación y Saneamiento (Planning and Sanitation Committee), along with nearly a dozen other community activist groups, mobilized hundreds of students, teachers, parents, and residents in a series of protests that captured the attention of the local media and government officials, including the mayor, who turned vocally against the project (Lindquist 2002a; Treat 2002). In the face of mounting public and local government opposition, and especially when it appeared that the local land use permit was not forthcoming, the companies withdrew the plan in 2003.

Also in February 2002, Houston-based Marathon Oil announced plans for a massive LNG complex less than 15 miles south of the border, on the southern outskirts of a coastal residential neighborhood, Playas de Tijuana. Marathon proposed an onshore receiving terminal for tankers from Indonesia, along with a regasification plant, thermal storage tanks, new gas pipelines to ship the gas north to the United States, a 400-MW power plant, and to make the project more attractive to residents of the community, a wastewater treatment facility and desalination plant (Treat 2002).

Once again, company planners underestimated the mobilizational power of perceived injustice and the passion of community opposition. Playas de Tijuana has experience confronting environmental threats, including one of the border region's earliest environmental justice victories, when a neighborhood homemakers association (Amas de Casa de Playas de Tijuana) halted the construction of a chemical waste incinerator in the neighborhood in 1991. This time, the grassroots Comité Ciudadano Estatal (State Citizen's Committee) spearheaded the opposition to Marathon's project, utilizing the direct-action strategies on which so much environmental justice activism has been based: community workshops, blockades, public marches, protests, publicity, press conferences, networking with allied groups (including those across the border), and calling political leaders to account (García Zendejas 2005). Claims for environmental justice obtain close to home: "Why don't they put these plants on the other side? . . . I'm concerned about what will happen to my family, my kids." (Lindquist 2002b) When company spokespersons lauded the benefits of water treatment and desalination, one resident quipped: "We don't even want to hear about the benefits. . . . I don't think the residents of La Jolla or Coronado [upscale San Diego neighborhoods] would want to hear about the benefits either, if this kind of project were being built there." (Lindquist 2002b)

In spite of the fury of protest on the street, the federal government welcomed Marathon's LNG proposal, granting permits from the Energy Regulatory Commission (CRE) in May 2003 (Lindquist and Dibble 2004). However, the protests captured national attention, increasing community pressure on public officials (García Zendejas 2005). In June, the controversy appeared in Mexico City's main newsmagazine, Proceso, widening the scope of opposition (Salinas 2003). On January 20, 2004, a deadly explosion at an LNG facility at the Algerian port of Skikda killed 27 people and injured more than 70. The accident shattered industry claims about safety, reignited debates about risks, and deepened community opposition in Playas de Tijuana, which would experience many deaths in a similar incident (Lindquist 2004b). Hostility to the project mounted throughout the summer (Mier 2004). During an LNG workshop hosted by the Comité Ciudadano, one invited senator went so far as to call support for Baja LNG projects "treason," claiming the agreements violate the Mexican Constitution. He spoke directly to the inequity manifest in the projects: "This state government is not interested in the people it represents. Why doesn't the United States put the gas plants there? Because the North American population won't let them." (Rea Torres and Osuna Murillo 2004)

As with El Paso/Conoco, the Marathon proposal was inherently provocative to environmental justice activism. The plan was overly ambitious, too industrial for the location, too close to too many people, and politically mismanaged. For the local political establishment the costs of support became too high, and the payoffs became too elusive. In the face of sustained popular resistance, officials finally turned against the project. In February 2004, the state government expropriated the site, claiming overlapping property titles and jurisdictional confusion over ownership. Though Marathon had not yet applied for environmental and land use permits, state officials indicated municipal plans would prohibit industrial use on the site in any event. On March 1, 2004, the company bitterly announced the project's cancellation (Lindquist and Dibble 2004).

The other energy companies have since attempted to remain agile and to learn from their early competitors' mistakes. Of the three remaining projects, Energía Costa Azul is the most ambitious and the farthest advanced in construction. Costa Azul is the only remaining onshore LNG project, but unlike its ill-fated predecessors, it is not located in a residential neighborhood. Instead, it occupies 400 acres of unpopulated coastal plain about 15 miles north of Ensenada.[6] Costa Azul is a partnership between the owner, Sempra Energy, and Shell Oil. Shell initially had its own proposal nearby (one of the original six), but withdrew those plans and signed an agreement to share plant capacity with Sempra instead. Costa Azul holds a solid lead in the race to bring LNG to market. The Sempra-Shell partnership has signed agreements for LNG supplies from Australia, Indonesia, and Russia's Sakhalin Island, holds contracts to provide gas to Mexico's CFE, and was the first LNG facility to obtain all required local and federal permits (Calbreath 2005; Lindquist 2005c, 2007).[7] The imposing facility has reconfigured the coastline with an immense stone jetty and two 180-foot insulated storage towers. It is expected to be operational in early 2008.

Chevron Texaco's Terminal GNL Mar Adentro de Baja California was the first proposal for a facility to be sited offshore, in order to avoid the controversies associated with the land-based sites. Announced in October 2003, Mar Adentro proposed a regasification terminal 6 miles off the coast of Playas de Tijuana, consisting of a 1,000-foot concrete island, with docking facilities for tankers to bring LNG from Australia, a regasification plant, storage tanks, a heliport, and an underwater pipeline to carry the gas to Baja California's existing pipeline system. The Mar Adentro project invited immediate and heated protest from conservation groups, because it was proposed for the heart of the rugged, uninhabited Coronado Islands National Marine Protected Area, and designed to use the southern island as a breakwater. Protest notwithstanding, SEMARNAT (Secretariat of Environment and Natural Resources) granted the project its environmental permit in August 2004; the other permits followed.[8] Outraged by SEMARNAT's approval, on May 3, 2005, a coalition of seven Mexican and US environmental groups filed a petition with NAFTA's NACEC, charging that the agency had failed to adequately consider negative impacts on plant, sea, and bird life, including the largest coastal nesting colony of the endangered Xantus murrelet, whose breeding would be disrupted by the facility (Enciso 2005; Rodriguez 2005a).[9] The NACEC panel agreed to review the complaint. Before the NACEC report was completed, however, Chevron stunned and delighted their opponents with the March 12, 2007 announcement that the company had withdrawn the permits and suspended plans for constructing the facility. In spite of its controversial legacy, company officials asserted that "the decision was based on business needs," presumably market competition from Costa Azul (Lindquist 2007).

And in 2005, Moss-Maritime teamed with TAMMSA (Terminales y Almacenes Maritimos de México, S.A.) to propose a floating storage and regasification unit 5 miles off the coast of Rosarito Beach. This unit, relatively modest in scale, would consist of an LNG ship and an undersea pipeline connected to existing PEMEX facilities in Rosarito. It would be much less costly (US $55 million, versus $800 million for Costa Azul and $650 million for Mar Adentro), technologically simpler, and poses significantly lower environmental impact (Lindquist 2005e). In January 2005, Moss-TAMMSA applied for the required environmental permits from SEMARNAT, receiving approval in April. Other required permits are pending (CEC 2006b, p. 23).

These three projects suggest that company planners learned a critical lesson from the missteps of the early entrants, a lesson familiar to environmental justice experiences everywhere: siting hazardous industrial facilities in residential neighborhoods invites opposition. People will mobilize against perceived threats to their households, families, and workplaces. By proposing subsequent facilities in isolated locations, the companies have displaced the problems away from people and onto coastal and marine habitats, where advocacy groups have been less successful at achieving the same level of popular resonance. This problem of threat displacement is familiar to environmental justice advocates. While industrial developers typically refer to local resistance as NIMBY (not in my back yard) syndrome, environmental justice activists promote the idea of NIABY (not in anyone's back yard) to challenge the legitimacy of hazard sources altogether. In this case, opponents to Baja's energy projects have worked to defy industry assertions of high expected energy demand. Movement leaders have sought to delegitimize the rationale for the facilities by presenting data in support of an alternative energy program that could satisfy binational needs with a greatly reduced role for LNG, emphasizing new conservation measures and an assortment of less threatening energy sources and technologies.[10]

So far, Moss-TAMMSA's relatively small footprint proposal has drawn little protest. In spite of its advanced construction, even Costa Azul still faces at least fifteen different legal challenges in Mexican state and federal courts, many brought by the owner of a nearby golf resort community, Bajamar, which would be within the blast zone of an accident (Lindquist 2004b). Sustained popular resistance has percolated upward to the state legislature, which has launched an official inquiry, and has considering placing a referendum on the ballot that could halt LNG development in the state altogether (Lindquist 2005f). According to Bill Powers of the Border Power Plant Working Group, "they might have the project under construction, but that doesn't mean it's going to get built" (Lindquist 2005g).

As of this writing, only two of the original six proposals remain active, and only one is under construction. A binational environmental justice movement has consolidated around LNG issues, consisting of grassroots groups, national associations, activists, attorneys, parents, teachers, scientists, and engineers. The movement employs an array of direct action, legal, advocacy, and political strategies, and works at all levels of government (Gortazar 2005; Ovalle 2005). There are at least 35 networked US and Mexican organizations currently opposing LNG developments in Baja California.[11] Their campaigns have catapulted LNG into the national limelight, tapping into public resentment about Mexican national territory serving foreign energy demand (Rodriguez 2005a, 2005b; Naumann 2005). An image capturing exactly this sentiment appeared in a major national newspaper, featuring protestors in Ensenada carrying a banner reading "Mexico: hay quien te quiere y hay quien te USA" ("Mexico: there are those who love you, and those who use you," with the Spanish verb for "use" spelled out as the abbreviation for "United States of America").[12] "We're very aware of the fact that they want to put this here because they don't want it there," said one activist. "There is absolutely no doubt in anyone's mind about that . . . they're going to put this on our side of the border and all the benefits are going to go to the other side. That is ingrained in people's minds as border inhabitants. The fact that we're open minded about it, that we can live with it day to day, is a result of living on a border." (García Zendejas 2005)

Borderland Environmental Justice

These accounts demonstrate the peculiar character of environmental justice on the US-Mexico border. Growing out of a strong tradition of cross-border social movement collaboration, local conceptions of environmental justice are firmly rooted in Baja California communities, infused with Mexican national political culture, yet unmistakably binational in character. Environmental and social justice concerns have come together in unique ways that capture both local and global dimensions of identity and protest.

As with many stories of environmental justice activism from around the world, the lessons in these accounts are mixed, including both discouraging and encouraging elements. At the neighborhood level, environmental justice has demonstrated some success. Whether it can affect the bigger picture—the inequitable distribution of environmental burdens North and South—remains to be seen. While the victory at Metales is surely significant for the women of the Colectivo and the community of Chilpancingo, the threats of industrial hazards remain omnipresent, with hundreds of contaminated sites dotting the length of the border. While the Mexicali plants were largely brought into compliance with California air quality standards, they still stand as monuments to an economic model that parcels benefits in one direction and costs in another. While the most threatening LNG plants have been derailed or withdrawn, the companies remain determined to identify new opportunities and sites for development.

These limitations notwithstanding, environmental justice has clearly emerged as a force for change on the Mexican border. Local victories have fueled a sense of community power. Borderland environmental justice has developed with its own language, logic, and flavor, and cross-border collaborations have raised its profile as both slogan and strategy. "And that does change things, I think. It does empower you because you say 'this is environmental racism. This is an environmental injustice.' . . . [It's] putting a name on what we know, putting a name on something that you've always lived but didn't know what it was called, or what people call it somewhere else in the world." (García Zendejas 2005) "This is a very new concept. For most people in Mexico, the environment means forests, species. We're breaking away from that. We want to focus on human beings. . . . If we think of the world as neighborhoods, then it's obvious—the poor countries pay the environmental costs. Mexico is a poor neighborhood." (Cerda 2002)

Border activists are linking local struggles for a safer environment to global claims for justice. Not only are they pushing the boundaries of Mexico's political opening, they are fueling popular demands for increased participation on both sides of the border, as well as transnationally, via the NAFTA bodies. These efforts demonstrate the potential of what Margaret Keck and Kathryn Sikkink (1998) call the "boomerang strategy," by which advocacy networks reach above the state to lever external pressures onto recalcitrant governments to resolve claims of injustice. With Metales y Derivados, the citizens of Colonia Chilpancingo and their allies at the EHC brought the case into the larger debates about NAFTA and economic integration. In energy politics, local groups and their international partners have framed their struggles in terms of corporate power and government accountability, promoting a larger dialogue about environmental and social injustices in the North American energy economy and in NAFTA's institutions. On the US-Mexico border, environmental justice is indeed linking the local with the global, uniting activists, scholars, and professionals, and enhancing their prospects for future successes.

Appendix: Environmental Justice Organizations in the Borderlands

This appendix provides only an illustrative list, selected from the dozens of organizations and networks involved in environmental justice work along the US-Mexico border. For more thorough accounts, see Bandy 1997; Interhemispheric Resource Center 1997; Bejarano 2002; Kelly 2002; Alfie Cohen 2003; Antal 2003.

Regional Environmental Justice Advocacy Organizations and Networks

Arizona Toxics Information (ATI)
Border Ecology Project (BEP)
Fundación Ecológica Mexicana (Mexican Ecological Foundation)
Greenpeace Mexico
Interhemispheric Resource Center (IRC)
Red Fronterizo de Salud y Medio Ambiente (Border Health and Environment Network)
Southwest Network for Environmental and Economic Justice (SNEEJ)
INCITRA Project (Información Ciudadana Transfronteriza/Cross-border Citizen Information)[13]

Environmental Law and Justice Organizations

Center for International Environmental Law
Centro Mexicano de Derecho Ambiental (CEMDA, Mexican Environmental Law Center)
Comité Cívico de Divulgación Ecológica (Civic Committee for Ecological Disclosure)
EarthJustice Legal Defense Fund
E-LAW Mexico

Labor, Trade, and Workplace Health and Safety Organizations and Networks

Coalition for Justice in the Maquiladoras (CJM)
Comité de Apoyo Fronterizo Obrero Regional (Regional Border Worker Support Committee)
Frente Auténtico del Trabajo (FAT, Authentic Labor Front)
Red Mexicana de Acción Frente al Libre Comercio (RMALC, Mexican Action Network on Free Trade)

Community Organizations, East

Comité Chihuahua de Solidaridad y Defensa de los Derechos Humanos (Chihuahua Solidarity Committee for the Defense of Human Rights)
Comunidad Ecológica de Matamoros (Matamoros Ecological Community, which works with CJM on *maquiladora* toxics issues)
Northeast Environmental Rights Center[14]
Texas Natural Resources Conservation Commission[15]
The Border Commission against Radioactive Waste
The Texas Center for Policy Studies (works with base organizations in Coahuila and Tamaulipas

Community Organizations, Central (Ciudad Juarez/El Paso)

Grupo Ecologista y Participación Ciudadana
Alianza Internacional Ecologista del Bravo
Comité Ecológico de Ciudad Juárez
Enlace Ecológico (Ecological Linkage, Agua Prieta, Sonora)

Community Organizations, West (Baja California/San Diego)

Border Power Plant Working Group/Grupo de Trabajo de Termoeléctricas Fronterizas
Colectivo Chilpancingo Pro Justicia Ambiental (Chilpancingo Pro Environmental Justice Collective)
Comité Ciudadano Estatal (State Citizen's Committee)
Comité de Planeación y Saneamiento (Planning and Sanitation Committee)
ECO-SOL
Environmental Health Coalition (EHC)[16]
Foro Ecologista de Baja California (Baja California Ecologist Forum)
Grupo Ecologista Gaviotas ("Seagull" Ecology Group)
Grupo Factor X/CITTAC (Centro de Información Para Trabajadoras y Trabajadores/Workers Information Center)[17]
Grupo Yeuani[18]
Movimiento Ecologista Mexicano en Baja California (MEBAC, Mexican Ecology Movement in Baja California)

Proyecto Fronterizo de Educación Ambiental (Border Environmental Education Project)

Acknowledgments

Portions of this chapter draw on Carruthers 2007. I am grateful to San Diego State University for the support that allowed me to complete this project, and to the experts, organizations, and individuals who generously shared their wisdom and experience.

Notes

1. *Maquiladoras* are "in-bond" assembly plants in Mexico's export processing zones.

2. For more complete treatment of these cases and related issues see Bandy 1997; Alfie Cohen and Méndez 2000; Bejarano 2002; Kelly2002; Kopinak and Barajas 2002; Alfie Cohen 2003; Antal 2003; Kopinak 2004.

3. PROFEPA (Procuraduría Federal de Protección al Ambiente/Federal Ministry for Environmental Protection) is the enforcement branch of Mexico's environmental protection ministry, the SEMARNAT (Secretariat of the Environment and Natural Resources).

4. Ironically, Kettleman City is familiar to US environmental justice advocates as the site of a victory for low-income Latino residents who defeated a hazardous waste incinerator (Kay 1994).

5. Note that even with the SCRs there is still a cost advantage of locating in Mexico over California, where producers must purchase emissions credits to offset emission increases; Mexico does not require offsets (CEC 2005b, p. 14).

6. Costa Azul occupies what was the last contiguous stretch of undeveloped native habitat between the border and Ensenada (Powers 2005b).

7. In April 2003, Costa Azul received the environmental permit from SEMAR-NAT. In August 2003, they received both the permit from the federal CRE (the Energy Regulatory Committee) and the land use permit from the Municipality of Ensenada (CEC 2006b, p. 26).

8. In January 2005, Mar Adentro received CRE approval and a third permit from the Secretariat of Communication and Transportation (SCT). No municipal land use permit was required for an offshore terminal; approval of pipeline right of way was pending when the project was suspended (CEC 2006b; Lindquist 2005d, 2007).

9. The petition (SEM-05-002) was presented by the Center for Biological Diversity, Greenpeace Mexico, American Bird Conservancy, Los Angeles Audubon

Society, the Pacific Environment and Resources Center, Conservación de las Islas, and Wildcoast.

10. Multiple reports detailing the viability of an alternative energy future for the California–Baja California region can be found on the websites of the leading advocacy groups, including Greenpeace Mexico's comprehensive report on LNG (Greenpeace 2004). See www.greenpeace.org/mexico. For reports from the Border Power Plant Working Group and the RACE coalition (Ratepayers for Affordable Clean Energy), see www.borderpowerplants.org; www.local.org/fercrace.html; www.lngwatch.com.

11. Leading organizations active on LNG include the Border Power Plant Working Group, Comité Ciudadano Estatal, Conservación de Las Islas, Grupo Ecologista Gaviotas, Wildcoast, RACE coalition (Ratepayers for Affordable Clean Energy), Greenpeace Mexico, Amazon Watch, and the Comité Estatal Contra la Instalación de las Plantas Regasificadoras (State Committee Against the Installation of Regasification Plants).

12. *La Jornada* (Mexico City), March 21, 2005.

13. INCINTRA is a collaborative effort involving the Red Fronterizo, BEP, and IRC.

14. Works with the Comité Chihuahua on forests, watersheds, and hazardous waste incineration.

15. The Texas Natural Resources Conservation Commission and The Border Commission against Radioactive Waste assisted local organizations in the defeat of the Sierra Blanca radioactive waste facility and a Chemical Waste Management site in southern Texas.

16. EHC is a San Diego environmental justice group affiliated regionally with the SNEEJ and nationally with the CHEJ (Center for Health, Environment, and Justice). It sponsors the "Border Environmental Justice Campaign" focused on maquiladora hazardous waste, and works closely with the Colectivo Chilpancingo Pro Justicia Ambiental in Tijuana.

17. Grupo Factor X/CITTAC works with CJM, RMALC, Yeuani and others on workplace health, safety, and gender issues.

18. Yeuani works in the area of environmental law, coordinating its efforts with CEMDA.

References

Alfie Cohen, Miriam. 2003. The rise and fall of environmental NGOs along the US-Mexico border. In *Cross-Border Activism and Its Limits*, ed. B. Hogenboom et al. Center for Latin American Research and Documentation.

Alfie Cohen, Miriam, and Luis H. Méndez. 2000. *Maquila y movimientos ambientalistas: Examen de un riesgo compartido*. Grupo Editorial Eon.

Antal, Edit. 2003. Cross-border relations of Mexican environmental NGOs in Tijuana-San Diego. In *Cross-Border Activism and Its Limits*, ed. B. Hogenboom et al. Center for Latin American Research and Documentation.

Bandy, Joe. 1997. Reterritorializing borders: Transnational environmental justice movements on the US-Mexico Border. *Race, Gender, and Class* 5, no. 1: 80–103.

Bejarano, Fernando. 2002. Mexico-US environmental partnerships. In *Cross-Border Dialogues*, ed. D. Brooks and J. Fox. Center for US-Mexico Studies, University of California, San Diego.

Brooks, David, and Jonathan Fox, eds. 2002. *Cross-Border Dialogues: US-Mexico Social Movement Networking*. Center for US-Mexico Studies, University of California, San Diego.

Calbreath, Dean. 2005. Baja LNG terminal gets first contract. *San Diego Union Tribune*, April 12.

Cantlupe, Joe. 2004. Abandoned smelter gets near to cleanup. *San Diego Union Tribune*, June 23.

Cantlupe, Joe, and Dana Wilkie. 2004. Cleanup slated at toxic plant: US-Mexico plan targets closed facility in Tijuana. *San Diego Union Tribune*, June 25.

Carruthers, David V. 2007. Environmental justice and the politics of energy on the US-Mexico border. *Environmental Politics* 16, no. 3: 394–413.

CEC (California Electricity Commission). 2005a. Energy Supply and Demand Assessment for the Border Region. CEC-600-2005-023 (May).

CEC. 2005b. Environmental Issues and Opportunities in the California-Mexico Border Region. CEC-600-2005-022 (May).

CEC. 2006a. Frequently asked questions about LNG. www.energy.ca.gov.

CEC. 2006b. West Coast LNG projects and proposals. www.energy.ca.gov.

Cerda, Magdalena (Coordinator, Colectivo Chilpancingo Pro Justicia Ambiental). 2002. Interview by author, September 27, Tijuana.

Colectivo Chilpancingo Pro Justicia Ambiental y Coalición de Salud Ambiental. 2003. Plan de saneamiento del sitio de Metales y Derivados in Tijuana, Baja California, Mexico.

Dellios, Hugh. 2004. Access law spurs culture shift: Mexicans make use of open information. *San Diego Union Tribune*, February 8.

Dibble, Sandra. 2004. US, Mexico get set for cleanup of abandoned toxic plant. *San Diego Union Tribune*, (June 25).

EHC (Environmental Health Coalition). 2002. Community celebrates opening of new Tijuana Office. *Toxinformer* 21, no. 3: 3–5.

EHC. 2004. Victory at last! Community celebrates Metales y Derivados cleanup agreement. *Toxinformer* 23, no. 3: 3–5.

Enciso, Angelica. 2005. De nuevo, piden revisar proyecto de regasificadora en islas Coronado. *La Jornada* (Mexico City), July 30.

Fritsch, Peter. 2002. Mexican toxic waste case shows Nafta's limits. *Wall Street Journal*, January 16.

García Zendejas, Carla. 2005. Border Power Plant Working Group. Interview by author, October 10, Tijuana.

Gortazar, Iciar. 2005. Foro internacional de lucha contra el gas natural licuado. *El Vigia en Linea*, Ensenada, February 15.

Greenpeace. 2002. Terra Sempra: A report on plans to develop the California/ Baja California border region as a dirty energy export zone. San Francisco.

Greenpeace Mexico. 2004. Gas natural licuado: El fin de la independencia energética. Mexico City.

Hogenboom, Barbara, Alfie Cohen, and Edit Antal, eds. 2003. *Cross-Border Activism and Its Limits*. Center for Latin American Research and Documentation.

Interhemispheric Resource Center. 1997. Cross-border links 1997: A directory of organizations in Canada, Mexico, and the United States. Albuquerque.

Kay, Jane. 1994. California's endangered communities. In *Unequal Protection*, ed. R. Bullard. Sierra Club Books.

Keck, Margaret, and Kathryn Sikkink. 1998. Activists beyond borders: Advocacy networks in international politics. Cornell University Press.

Kelly, Mary E. 2002. Cross border work on the environment. In *Cross-Border Dialogues*, ed. D. Brooks and J. Fox. Center for US-Mexico Studies, University of California, San Diego.

Kopinak, Kathryn, ed. 2004. *The Social Costs of Industrial Growth in Northern Mexico*. Center for US-Mexico Studies, University of California, San Diego.

Kopinak, Kathryn, and Maria Del Rocio Barajas. 2002. Too close for comfort? The proximity of industrial hazardous waste to local populations in Tijuana Mexico. *Journal of Environment and Development* 11, no. 3: 215–247.

Lindquist, Diane. 2002a. Proposed plants fuel passions. *San Diego Union Tribune*, March 4.

Lindquist, Diane. 2002b. Energy plants face Baja backlash. *San Diego Union Tribune*, November 29.

Lindquist, Diane. 2003. Court hears suit against power lines from Mexico. *San Diego Union Tribune*, April 19.

Lindquist, Diane. 2004a. InterGen gives in, unplugs turbine. *San Diego Union Tribune*, January 17.

Lindquist, Diane. 2004b. Mexican agency warns of potential for LNG disaster. *San Diego Union Tribune*, January 23.

Lindquist, Diane. 2005a. Power plant billing could go to tribunal in Paris. *San Diego Union Tribune*, March 11.

Lindquist, Diane. 2005b. Mexico pushes forward with LNG plans. *San Diego Union Tribune*, February 27.

Lindquist, Diane. 2005c. Sempra LNG gets contract to supply Mexico's power agency. *San Diego Union Tribune*, January 12.

Lindquist, Diane. 2005d. Oil firm's LNG plan gets OK of Mexico. *San Diego Union Tribune*, January 7.

Lindquist, Diane. 2005e. Another entry in the LNG stakes. *San Diego Union Tribune*, February 3.

Lindquist, Diane. 2005f. Legal hurdles await Baja LNG project. *San Diego Union Tribune*, September 8.

Lindquist, Diane. 2005g. Sempra's gas venture gathering steam at Baja site. *San Diego Union Tribune*, October 24.

Lindquist, Diane. 2006. Permits on 2 power plants in Mexico OK. *San Diego Union Tribune*, December 1.

Lindquist, Diane. 2007. Chevron gives up on building LNG plant. *San Diego Union Tribune*, March 13.

Lindquist, Diane, and Sandra Dibble. 2004. Plans for Baja fuel plant are dropped. *San Diego Union Tribune*, March 2.

Lujan, Lourdes. 2002. Promotora, Colectivo Chilpancingo Pro Justicia Ambiental. Interview by author, September 27, Tijuana.

Mier, Fidel. 2004. No se establecerán regasificadoras en BC. *El Sol de Tijuana*, August 17.

Moreno, Arturo. 2005. Greenpeace Mexico. Interview by author, June 2, Mexico City.

NACEC (North America Commission for Environmental Cooperation). 2002a. Citizen Submissions on Enforcement Matters: Metales y Derivados, Submission SEM-98-007.

NACEC (North America Commission for Environmental Cooperation). 2002b. Environmental Challenges and Opportunities of the Evolving North American Electricity Market.

Naumann, Talli. 2005. Courage, fortitude evident in confrontation over Baja Peninsula gas plans. *The Herald Mexico: El Universal*, May 23.

Niller, Eric. 2002. LNG terminal plans proliferate in Baja California. IR/PS in the news: Eoamericas. Graduate School of International Relations and Pacific Studies, University of California, San Diego.

Ovalle, Fausto. 2005. Anuncian marchas contra plantas de gas. *La Frontera*, Tijuana, February 20.

Powers, Bill. 2005a. Energy, the environment, and the California-Baja California border region. *Electricity Journal* 6, no. 6: 77–84.

Powers, Bill. 2005b. Border Power Plant Working Group. Interview by author, September 20, San Diego.

Rea Torres, Hugo, and Conrado Osuna Murillo. 2004. Autorizar gaseras, tración a la patria. *El Mexicano*, Ensenada, August 17.

Rodriguez, Israel. 2005a. Arriesga el ecosistema la planta de regasificación en Tijuana. *La Jornada* (Mexico City), March 7.

Rodriguez, Israel. 2005b. Manifestaciones en Ensenada y Tijuana contra regasificadoras. *La Jornada* (Mexico City), March 21.

Salinas, Juan Arturo. 2003. La batalla de Chevron y Marathon oil en Tijuana. *Proceso* (Mexico City), June 21.

SCERP (Southwest Center for Environmental Research and Policy). 2003. *The US-Mexican Border Environment: Trade, Energy, and the Environment.* San Diego State University Press.

Sullivan, Kevin. 2003. A toxic legacy on the Mexican border: Abandoned US-owned smelter in Tijuana blamed for birth defects, health ailments. *Washington Post*, February 16.

Treat, Jonathan. 2002. Baja Energy and Environment Update. Americas Program, Interhemispheric Resource Center.

7

Environmental Justice in Mexico: The Peñoles Case

Jordi Díez and Reyes Rodríguez

The environmental consequences of Mexico's postwar industrialization became apparent by the 1980s. Despite the adoption of environmental legislation in 1971, rapid state-led industrialization resulted in serious environmental damage as air pollution and deforestation levels increased significantly, water resources became seriously degraded and soil erosion reached unprecedented levels.[1] Growing awareness of the country's environmental degradation during the 1980s coincided with the rise of large-scale social mobilization in the country as socio-economic conditions deteriorated. The debt crisis and the adoption of a market-friendly economic model encouraged many sectors of Mexican society to pull out of corporatist structures and place their demands directly upon the state. Against this backdrop of increased environmental awareness and growing social mobilization, Mexico's environmental movement strengthened, gained national visibility, and became an important actor in national politics. The 1990s witnessed strong environmental activism and a rather marked proliferation of environmental non-governmental organizations (ENGOs), which resulted in a number of salient policy triumphs for Mexico's green movement as well as a noticeable and unprecedented effect on the formulation of environmental legislation.[2]

As advocacy for environmental justice took root in the United States during the 1980s, and as American ENGOs increasingly transferred resources and expertise to their Mexican counterparts,[3] one could have expected Mexico's green movement to have espoused the concept of environmental justice. However, despite growing mobilization and the achievement of several important victories by Mexico's green movement, environmental mobilization in Mexico has not generally adopted a discourse based on environmental justice. Even though some mobilization has taken place in some cases under the banner of environmental justice (see chapter 6 of this volume), several social, legal, and institutional factors help explain why the concept of environmental justice has not been adopted by Mexican social movements. In this chapter we advance the argument that several social and legal restrictions are important disincentives for the formation of a culture, and mobilization, of environmental justice as well as obstacles to collective action. To advance our argument, we look at the Peñoles Case, a case in which hundreds of children in the Northern Mexican city of Torreón, Coahuila, were poisoned by the release of high levels of lead by an ore smelter, causing changes in metabolism and in the psychometrical and neurological systems and a decrease in IQ.

The question that we address in this chapter is the following: Why has a prototypical case for environmental justice in Mexico, such as the Peñoles case, not generated a social movement advocating environmental justice? In the first section we provide a description of the case study. In the second section we analyze the reaction and mobilization by the citizenry before the contamination problem. In the third section we delve into the legal and institutional obstacles that, we argue, pose significant obstacles for the development of a culture of environmental justice in Mexico.

The "Children of Lead"

Met-Mex Peñoles is the largest producer of silver in the world and the largest producer of gold, lead, and zinc in Latin America. This ore smelter, located in the city of Torreón of the northern Mexican state of Coahuila, is one of the most important economic actors in the area. It employs more than 2,200 people, it spends more than $85 million (US) in the city in the form of wages and purchases of local products, and it has average yearly sales of $875 million. Founded in 1887, the company was taken over by the American Metal Company in 1917 and eventually nationalized in 1971 by President Luis Echeverría Álvarez (1970–1976). The company expanded significantly after its nationalization when it established a refinery for lead and silver. As employment increased, it attracted hundreds of people to its surrounding area who settled illegally and established an extensive barrio. Weeks before leaving office, President Echeverría granted the settlers legal entitlement to their land, thereby officially establishing the Luis Echeverría neighborhood, which became one of the largest in the city.

Complaints against pollution from the plant can be traced back to 1937, but it was not until 1961 that workers filed a formal complaint with the federal Ministry of Health. The ministry conducted a series of tests to determine whether pollution in the area could be attributed to the plant, and even though the studies found high levels of arsenic, lead, and sulfur dioxide in the area, it stated that it was not possible to establish the firm as the source of these particles (Viniegra et al. 1964). In 1976, a toxicologist, Dr. Lila América Albert, conducted the first test on children in the area. Looking at samples of hair from children in five Mexican cities, it found that children from Torreón exhibited the highest levels of lead out of the five cities under study: an average of 55 micrograms (μg) of lead per gram of hair, with a maximum of 220 μg/g. The findings were published in 1978 (Albert 1978), but no action was taken by either the plant or the government despite the serious health risks lead poses to children's health; the exposure of children to high levels of lead has an effect on their neurological development and can cause mental retardation, behavioral problems, anemia, permanent liver and kidney damage, hearing loss, and, in some cases, death (Rosen 1992a). Studies have found a direct relationship between lead levels in children's blood and their IQs. One study identified a drop of 5.8 points in children's IQ for every 10 μg of lead per deciliter of blood (Rosen 1992b). Children under the age of 6 are more susceptible to the exposure of lead because they are still in the early stages of their neurological development (ATSDR 1998).

Following up on the 1978 study, and in an effort to determine whether exposure to lead was having effects on the health of the children, a group of researchers found that children who lived within a kilometer of the Peñoles plant showed an average of 21.64 μg of lead per deciliter of blood (Calderón-Salinas et al. 1996a). According to the US Center for Disease Control and Prevention, amounts exceeding 10 μg/dl of lead pose serious health risks for children (CDC 1991). In an additional study, the researchers found a correlation between lead levels in the children's blood and their IQ (Calderón-Salinas et al. 1996b). Several subsequent studies corroborated these findings. A 1998 study found that some of the children that attended the school closest to the plant had amounts of up to 50 µg/dl in their blood systems. They also found a direct relationship between levels of lead particles in the air and in the streets and the proximity to the plant (Rubio Andrade et al. 1998). Moreover, in samples from children living close to the plant, 92.1 percent of them were found to have levels of more than 15 µg/dl. A study undertaken by the Medical School of Dartmouth University in 1997 also found that the levels of cadmium in the area around the plant were the highest ever found in the world: from 787 to 13,231 µg per gram of dust, and from 11 to 11,497 µg of arsenic per gram of dust (Benin et al. 1999). In the United States, the maximum levels allowed are 500 and 20, respectively.

Based on the results of some of these studies, a number of academics, scientists and some locally based ENGOs demanded action from the local authorities in the late 1980 and early 1990s, but no action was taken (Valdés and Cabrera 1999). An agreement was eventually reached in 1989 between the municipal government of Torreón and the firm's management to reduce the emissions of heavy metals into the air, but it was never implemented (Albert 2004, p. 7). However, in 1994, the recently established Procuraduría Federal De Protección al Ambiente (PROFEPA), ordered Peñoles to conduct an environmental audit. The inspection took place between early 1994 and mid 1995 and, upon its conclusion, the environmental institution ordered the firm to implement 113 "immediate measures" to reduce emissions. In 1996 the Environmental Protection Office reached an agreement with the firm through which a timetable to implement the various measures was developed (PROFEPA 2000).

Pollution, however, continued. In July 1998, a local physician, José Velasco, noticed that one of his patients, a year-old baby, exhibited symptoms of anemia and, after conducting tests, found that the infant had 45 µg/dl of lead in his blood. The physician carried out blood tests on 50 children under his care and found that nine of the children had levels between 10 and 14 µg/dl, three children had between 15 and 19 µg/dl, eight had between 20 and 44, and four had between 45 and 69. Dr. Velasco presented the results of his analyses to city councillors, but similar to what had occurred in the past, no action was taken (Valdés and Cabrera 1999, p. 16). Given the local government's inaction, a respected toxicologist from Juárez University, in the state of Durango, Dr. Gonzalo García Vargas, conducted a two-year study of 398 children in the area and found that 98 of them showed levels higher that $25\,\mu g/dl$ and that 10 showed signs of lead poisoning (García Vargas et al. 1999). At the end of January 1998, García approached local officials with his study results, but the municipal Director of Ecology declared that the levels of lead found in the children were not a threat to their health (*La Opinión*, January 20 and February 7, 1998). After the results of García's study were dismissed by city officials, Velasco decided to take further action by presenting the results of the study to the state and federal ministries of health and to several media outlets between December 1998 and January 1999.[4] It is at this point that we see the emergence of social mobilization in defense of what some activists referred to as "the children of lead."

Social Mobilization and Government Reaction

The Emergence of a Movement

Velasco's actions unleashed a locally based social movement in defense of the affected children. In January 1999, Velasco approached the state legislature with the results of the study and convinced one legislator, Salvador Hernández Vélez, to take up the case and present it to the legislature. The legislature agreed to act immediately and launched a series of public consultations. At these consultations, Hernández demanded that the federal Minister of Health, the Environmental Protection Office, and the Ministry of the Environment investigate the case. Several other state legislators, from different political parties, joined Hernández's effort and became active in denouncing the high levels of lead emissions and demanded that a government-sponsored inquiry be launched. At around the same time, the results of the study conducted by Dartmouth University, referred to above, were released, providing Hernández with additional proof to force the federal government to act. His efforts were soon thereafter joined by some local non-governmental organizations (NGOs), such as In Defense of the Environment (En Defensa del Ambiente, A.C.) and Citizens of the Lagoon Region in Defense of Human Rights (Ciudadanía Lagunera por los Derechos Humanos, A.C.). These NGOs took up the case and demanded action from the state and federal governments, mostly through the media, and were responsible for publicizing the case at the national level. At the local level, the mothers of the affected children mobilized. In February 1999, a group of mothers wrote a letter to the Minister of the Environment demanding her to intervene, and began, under the leadership of María Dolores Guillén—a mother of three from the Luis Echeverría neighborhood—a series of demonstrations through 1999 in front of the Torreón city hall and the state legislature. They demanded that "Peñoles recognize its culpability, that the authorities act, and that the plant be closed" (*La Jornada*, June 6, 1999).

The denunciations made by the NGOs and the demonstrations held by the mothers of the "children of lead" attracted national attention to the case thereby increasing pressure on the government to act. While at the beginning government reaction was slow and confusing—the state government, for example, arbitrarily established that the acceptable level of lead poisoning was 25 $\mu g/dl$ when the international standard is 10—the state government commissioned further studies and, in early 1999, the federal Ministry of Health officially admitted that Peñoles was the source of hazardous emissions of lead (*La Jornada*, July 7, 1999). In March 1999, the State government declared that at least 700 children had levels higher than 10 $\mu g/dl$ of lead in their blood. As a result, the Environmental Protection Office ordered Peñoles to implement 80 contingency measures to reduce the concentration of lead in the area, such as a reduction of emissions and the "vacuuming" of dust in neighboring areas (PROFEPA 2000, p. 7). Twenty-four additional measures were announced the following month, and in May 1999 the Environmental Protection Office ordered the plant to reduce production by 50 percent. Moreover, the federal institution, in conjunction with the State government, ordered Peñoles to hospitalize 13 children who showed symptoms of lead poisoning, to relocate 393 families from the Luis Echeverría neighborhood, and to establish a 60-million-peso health fund to provide medical care to the affected children (*Reforma*, May 6, 1999). The plant was fined $80,000 in January 2000 for not having complied with all the contingency measures ordered by the Environmental Protection Office (*Excelsior*, January 26, 2000), but the following month it was allowed to resume production at full capacity (Ugalde 2006, p. 387).

Resonances of Environmental Justice Mobilization

The lead poisoning of hundreds of children by the firm Met-Mex Peñoles in Mexico, as the foregoing description of events suggests, represents an archetypical case in which a struggle under the banner of environmental justice can emerge; a highly vulnerable group—children of a working-class neighborhood—is severely and disproportionately affected by pollution created by an industrial facility. Such pollution was the result of years of neglect by the firm's management and by various levels of government. It appears that the citizens' reaction to the poisoning of children in fact exhibits several important characteristics similar to discourses based on the concept of environmental justice.

First, people affected by the pollution, the mothers of the poisoned children, mobilized and demanded that both the firm and the government act to reduce lead emissions from the plant. Starting in December 1998, when the first demonstration was held in front of the plant, a group of mothers held protests throughout 1999 and 2000 demanding that the plant provide their children with medical care and, in some instances, that it be shut down. While protests originally took place around the plant, they were subsequently held in front of the city hall and the state legislature in the state's capital of Saltillo. The movement eventually weakened, partly as a result of internal divisions and disagreements on objectives,[5] but mobilization in the defense of the affected children did take place.

Second, a call for the rendition of "justice" was advanced by the mobilized mothers, a call that went far beyond the restoration of the damaged environment and the provision of health care to the children. Indeed, an integral part of the mothers' demand was that the government take action against Peñoles so as to bring about justice to case. Guillén, one of the movement's most prominent leaders, encapsulated this demand by declaring: "I am not a leader of a party. I am simply the mother of a girl that has more than 70 micrograms of lead in her blood, who is disabled for life. I only want justice and the truth for a common good [para un fin común]." (*La Jornada*, June 7, 1999)

The demand for justice became an important element in the discourse adopted by the movement. Moreover, unlike several other environmental mobilizations that took place in Mexico during the 1990s (Umlas 1998; Díez 2006), the movement was made up of actors that did not strictly have an environmental focus. For example, one the most active and influential NGOs within the movement was Citizens of the Lagoon Region in Defense of Human Rights, which is primarily a human rights organization. In effect, this NGO argued that the issue was one of the children's human rights and hence inherently one of justice. Finally, and certainly more important, soon after the state and federal governments ordered Peñoles to establish the health fund and to relocate the 393 families, a group of 28 parents filed a civil law suit against the firm demanding compensation (indemnización) for damages caused to their children (*Reforma*, May 12, 1999). Legally advised by a prominent lawyer, the plaintiffs demanded indemnity equivalent to four times the highest regional minimum wage, multiplied by 1095—an amount calculated according to the federal Civil Code and the Labor Law ($43,000 US per child). The argument advanced by their lawyer was that the children had been permanently, and completely, disabled (*Reforma*, May 12, 1999). In a country in which the notion of class-action suits is not part of legal proceedings, the submission of a collective civil suit not only represents an important, and rather novel, development, but it resembles a strategy that is very commonly used by movements that call for the bestowal of environmental justice. What we have, then, is an example of social environmental mobilization that exhibited many characteristics of environmental justice mobilization.

The Limits to Environmental Justice

Despite these common characteristics, several factors explain why this particular social mobilization was not framed around a call for environmental justice. Unlike struggles that are based on environmental justice, the affected children in the Peñoles case were not deliberately targeted by the polluting firm. For example, as David Carruthers notes in the introduction to this volume, one of the central tenets of environmental justice movements in the United States has been that the sitting of industrial hazards has disproportionately taken place in poor communities, which, in the United States tend to be Hispanic, Afro-American, or Native American. As he points out, analysts in the United States have been able to impose spatial maps of environmental hazards over demographic data to confirm environmental racism. In our case, however, the establishment of the plant preceded the formation of the neighborhood most affected by the plant's emissions. As may be recalled, the firm's employment opportunities attracted the individuals to settle in the areas adjacent to the plant. The plant, then, was not deliberately established in an underprivileged neighborhood. It was therefore simply not possible for the local movement to mobilize around the notion of discrimination. The main argument used by the mothers was that of neglect by the plant's management and the government in the face of growing evidence pointing to high levels of toxicity in the area. In effect, one of the most important challenges facing the movement in framing their demands was the limited range of justifications to demand compensation as the firm was not in violation of any legal provisions since there in fact were not any legal provisions controlling the release of lead particles (Ugalde 2006, p. 389).

More importantly, the affected people did not mobilize around the concept of racial identity to demand action from both the plant and the government and, subsequently, to demand compensation. Identity has been at the core of environmental justice mobilization in the United States, however. As Carruthers also observes in his introductory chapter, US environmental justice movements first appeared not as an outgrowth of popular environmentalism, but as an extension of the civil rights movement. In many ways, this has been possible because of the long history of civil rights mobilization in that country which has been largely the result of the rather prominent racial divisions that are salient features of contemporary US society. These distinctions allow groups to mobilize around identities based on racial divisions. In the case of Mexico, however, mobilization based on race is more difficult given the relative racial homogeneity of its social makeup. This is not to say that Mexico has not had identity-based social mobilization. Indeed, some of the most visible social movements in contemporary Mexico have been those which have developed around identities, such as gender. But unlike other Latin American and Caribbean countries whose societies are composed of distinct ethnic groups, such as peoples of African descent, mobilization around race and ethnicity in Mexico has been almost entirely restricted to indigenous movements. This explains the fact that environmental mobilizations that have taken on an identity component have been those in which alliances have been forged with indigenous groups. Indeed, several rather successful environmental campaigns in Mexico have been the ones that have forged alliances with indigenous movements and have, to one extent or another, relied upon indigenous identities to frame their discourses. This was clearly the case of the successful mobilization to stop the construction of a golf course in the city of Tepoztlán in the mid 1990s (Díez 2006, pp. 86–87). Because a racial component did not exist in the Peñoles case, however, the mobilization could not adopt an identity discourse based on identity. Given that the affected sector of the population belonged to a working-class neighborhood, mobilization could have unfolded around discourse based on social class. However, in this case, the social movement does not deploy a class-based discourse.

It is partly because of these reasons that the concept of environmental justice has not been embraced by the most prominent national ENGOs in Mexico. With the exception of alliances formed with indigenous movements in some instances, the most prominent, and resourceful, ENGOs in Mexico are those which have concentrated on issues regarding the "green agenda." That is, they have primarily focused on conservation efforts and in the protection of biodiversity (Díez 2006, pp. 34–37). This is primarily because the funding these organizations have been able to secure from international donors tends to place an emphasis on issues that form part of the green agenda. Because the issue pursued by the Peñoles mobilization—compensation for damages caused by industrial pollution—has not been an important focus of the most established national ENGOs in Mexico, the movement did not forge alliances with them. Unlike many other sustained, and ultimately successful, environmental movements, which have relied very heavily on the formation of alliances, the Peñoles movement remained local and weakened over time.

Institutional and Legal Obstacles to the Adoption of Environmental Justice

One of the most important reasons for the weakening of the Peñoles mobilization was its inability to achieve the compensation it had sought through the lawsuit some of the mothers launched, a failure that is explained by the rather significant legal and institutional obstacles that individuals and groups have in Mexico to attain compensation for environmental damages incurred. It is these obstacles that we analyze more closely in this section.

The Legal Case

As mentioned, a representative of some of the families filed a civil suit demanding compensation for damages caused to their children. The case was taken to the courts as a typical case of civil responsibility and had the particularity that the party which caused the damage was directly responsible for the degradation of the environment. As a result, the plaintiffs filed the suit demanding compensation for the damages caused to their children, without requesting the judge to stop the activity that was the cause of pollution or to repair the environmental damage caused by the firm.[6] The suit filed by the parents demanded that the court establish the permanent disability of the children as a result of the damages caused to their health, which were provoked by the gases emitted by Peñoles, and, consequently, that the company pay $43,000 (US) to each child.

The response from the company's representatives, presented on May 26, 1999 to the presiding judge, indicated that the children affected did not live in close proximity and that they did not exhibit all the symptoms that were described in the lawsuit, arguing that the plaintiffs had not included medical records demonstrating that the children had shown the symptoms. It also questioned the validity of the document which showed the high levels of lead content and argued, more importantly, that there was no link between the plant's production activities and the fact that the children had high concentrations of lead in their blood. It stated that other factors could have caused the poisoning, such as car pollution, emissions released by pottery factories in the surrounding area, the use of toys and pencils, the combustion of gasoline, the consumption of canned goods, or the use of pesticides. The firm, then, did not accept that the high concentrations of lead were a direct cause of the symptomatology shown by the children. In challenging the facts presented to the judge, the firm forced the plaintiffs to provide evidence linking the plant's production and the symptoms shown by the children.

In March 2000 the case was opened to the submission of evidence, a process that lasted six months. However, during this period of time, the firm presented an appeal demanding that the judge dismiss the proof submitted by the plaintiffs on the ground that it was inconclusive. After a series of proceedings, Peñoles was successful in convincing the judge that most of the evidence submitted be dismissed. Logically, with most of the evidence dismissed, the plaintiffs lost their case and the firm was absolved of the charges. On July 10, 2001, the judge pronounced his sentence declaring that the plaintiffs had not been able to prove their case based on the evidence presented. The group of mothers, represented again by a lawyer, decided to present their case to a different authority, which they again lost. However, in February 2003 they won a writ of *amparo*[7] which brought the case back to the stage at which the evidence submitted had been annulled. The case is still in the courts at the time of writing.

The Concept of "Civil Responsibility" as a Legal Instrument for Reparations

The case advanced by the lawyer representing the families was based on the notion of "civil responsibility." In the Mexican legal system, civil responsibility refers to the legal procedure through which an individual or a company has the responsibility to compensate for damages caused to individuals (Colín et al. 1924, pp. 725–726), whether as a result of a failure to comply with a legal contract (contractual responsibility) or as a result of an activity that, without a legal agreement, causes damages or affects the interests or rights of a third party (extra-contractual responsibility) (Borja 1991, p. 456).

In the Peñoles case, the lawyer representing the children advanced their case relying on the notion of extra-contractual civil responsibility in the demand for compensation. He had to use this recourse because no contract existed between the company and the children, a contract that would have been breached and which consequently would have caused the damage. In the case, the plaintiffs attempted to establish a link between the industrial activity of the plant and the damaged incurred by the population, which at first glance would appear direct and immediate: the plant's productive activities produce lead and the children that live in the area adjacent to the plant show high levels of lead in their blood. The damages to their health are therefore caused by the plant. Based on this rationale, and through the use of extra-contractual civil responsibility, the plaintiffs sought to prove

• that Met-Mex Peñoles performed industrial activities related to the processing of lead (hazardous activity),
• that these activities resulted in the emission of gases which pollute the air, soil, and water (hazardous activity),
• that the children lived in an adjacent area, which meant that the children were directly and continually exposed to these emissions (causal link),
• that the damage caused to the children's health is a direct consequence of the exposure to the lead emissions (causal link),

and

• that the lead caused the damage.

With the objective to prove these components (activity, link, and damages), the plaintiffs presented evidence that made the link. However, as we have seen, it was not accepted by the judge and he discarded the evidence. Because a link was not established according to the evidence presented to the judge, the non-contractual civil responsibility recourse could not therefore be used and the plaintiffs consequently lost their case. Given the difficulty in establishing direct responsibility in cases of extra-contractual civil responsibility, as this case shows, they tend not to be very successful in Mexico. They are therefore a disincentive for people to seek compensation when a contract does not exist, which, in terms of environmental degradation, is always the case; industrial plants do not sign contracts with the population. Moreover, this disincentive is augmented by the high costs; given the complexity of these cases, especially in cases which are highly technical, cases tend to last long periods of time, increasing significantly the legal costs. The procurement of justice for environmental damages through this method is thus very difficult to achieve. If, as in this case, non-contractual civil responsibility cannot successfully be used in cases in which pollution is the responsible for health, a question that naturally arises is: does the Mexican environmental legal framework provide for mechanisms to achieve compensation for environmental damage? We answer this question below.

Institutional and Legal Framework of Environmental Protection and Compensation for Environmental Damages

Starting in 1971, when the first piece of legislation for environmental protection was introduced, Mexico has had several environmental laws.[8] At the national level, the main piece of legislation dealing with environmental matters is the General Law for Environmental Protection (Ley General de Equilibrio Ecológico y Protección al Ambiente, henceforth referred to as Environmental Protection Law). Mexico City and every federated state, as well as numerous municipalities, also count with environmental legislation, which have been modeled after the national Environmental Protection Law. There are also various federal institutions in charge of the formulation of environmental legislation, such as the Environmental Protection Office (PROFEPA), the Ministry of the Environment (SEMARNAT), the National Institute of Ecology (INE), and the National Water Commission. Environmental legislation in Mexico has undergone numerous reforms. In 1996, a rather significant reform of the Environmental Protection Law was undertaken and it added numerous legal provisions to increase environmental protection and to include the possibility of resolving environmental conflict through the courts. Among many things, this reform sought to introduce the possibility of litigation before civil courts, the notion of responsibility for environmental damages, and mechanisms to sanction these damages, thereby inducing their redress. The same logic was introduced to other pieces of legislation, such as the Water Law, which was enacted in 2004, and which has an entire chapter devoted to the repair of environmental damages caused by the pollution of bodies of water in the country.

The 1996 reform to the Environmental Protection Law introduced the notion of public complaints [denuncia popular], which grants every citizen the ability to right to report to the authority any violations to environmental legislation and, more particularly, to report any actions that produce, or could produce, environmental damage, According to Article 189 of this legislation:

Every individual, social group, non-governmental organization and associations can report before the Environmental Protection Office [PROFEPA] or before other authorities any actions, acts or omissions that have, or could have, an effect on the ecological balance or result, or could result, in environmental damage, or which contravene the stipulations of this legislation and all other legal provision that relate to environmental protection and the preservation and restoration of ecological balance. Should there not be a representative from the Environmental Protection Office in the individual's locality, the report could be presented to the municipal authority, or, should the individual so decide, to the closest offices of such institution. Should the report be presented to the municipal authority, and should the issues be of federal competence, the report will have to be sent to the Environmental Protection Office.

Public complaints for environmental damages, according to Article 195 of the Environmental Protection Law, can only result in administrative, preventive or corrective actions against an individual or in the issuance of a recommendation to federal, state or municipal institutions which are responsible for the environmental damage. These recommendations are public, but are not binding. That is, they do not force government institutions to repair the environmental damage caused. Public complaints, however, do not necessarily result in an immediate action against the individual or entity that causes, or could cause, environmental damage. An individual or a collectivity can submit the complaint to the authority but the resulting action is entirely dependent on the decision reached by the environmental institution, such as the Environmental Protection Office. The public complaint does not constitute an administrative recourse that automatically results in legal action which would force the environmental authorities to act in the restoration of environmental damage, or to take preventive measures to avoid the any potential damage.

In addition to popular complaints, the Environmental Protection Law also contains a provision which appeared to have allowed for environmental litigation through civil courts. This relates to Article 203 of the legislation, which states:

Without affecting the penal and administrative sanctions that may proceed, every person whom pollutes or damages the environment or affects natural resources or biodiversity, will be held responsible and obliged to repair the damages caused, according to the applicable legislation. The timeframe within which the request for environmental responsibility be made will be of five years from the time the act, action or omission takes place.

Based on the wording of these legal provisions, it could be surmised that environmental damages may be compensated by the civil code when an individual invokes these provisions. These provisions, however, do not stipulate anything in regard to damages caused to individuals and strictly relates to environmental damage. Similar to what occurs with the non-contractual civil responsibility, the link between environmental damage and health damage needs to be made. Moreover, according to the logic of Mexican law, as stipulated by its civil procedural code (Código Federal de Procedimientos Civiles), in order for an individual to launch a judicial proceeding to demand compensation for damages incurred, it must be demonstrated that a right, specifically established in a legal provision, has been violated and that there is an obligation on behalf of the authority or individual to respect it. Because damages to the individual for environmental damage are not included in Mexico's environmental legislation, individuals are simply not able to demand compensation based on it. It is precisely because of this that, in the Peñoles case, the plaintiffs could not invoke Mexico's environmental legislation to demand compensation. Given that the environmental framework does not provide recourse to demand compensation for personal or health damages, individuals must therefore use the civil responsibility route, which, as we seen, is also problematic.

The Unfeasibility of Legal Class Action in Mexico

One of the most significant deterrents for collective action in pursuing compensation for personal damages in Mexico is that its legal system does not recognize groups of individuals as legal entities, what in Mexico is known as interés jurídico. As a result, the demand for compensation due to damages cannot be conducted through a group, unless they are recognized as such by the legal system. It is therefore not possible, according to Mexican law, to submit lawsuits as class-action suits in the same manner that they are done in the United States. In the Peñoles case, a group of individuals was represented collectively by a lawyer, but the lawyer represented each one of them individually and not as a group. In Mexico this is known as litis consorcio; a collective defense of individual rights. Each individual must prove that there was a damage done to her, and the compensation, should it be won, would be granted to each individual. Compensation, then, could be awarded to some individuals among a group and not to others. This is perhaps the most powerful disincentive for people to organize and pursue the judicial cases collectively. Whereas in other countries the possibility to launch class-action suits may well encourage people to organize and pursue legal action to demand compensation, in Mexico this incentive is not there given that the concept of class-action lawsuits is not recognized by the Mexican legal system.

As we can see, neither the Mexican legal system nor environmental legislation counts with effective provisions to demand compensations for damages done. The legal system has provisions that have "no teeth" to allow for the reparation or compensation for damages to the environment. In Mexico, then, the legal system makes is very difficult indeed to adopt the notion of "polluter pays." Indeed, on of the most important obstacles for the emergence of environmental justice mobilization is the ineffectiveness of environmental legislation. Moreover, Mexican law does not count with provisions that would allow tribunals to act as independent third parties capable of enforcing environmental legislation. In this case, it is up to environmental authorities, namely the Environmental Protection Office, to implement the law. Under these circumstances, it is very difficult for environmental legislation to function as an incentive to organize collective action in pursuit of environmental justice.

Conclusion

This volume set out to explore the promise and limits of environmental justice as a banner for grassroots resistance in Latin America, and to explore local forms of environmental justice consciousness and action. In this chapter, we attempted to contribute to this endeavor by looking at Mexico's worst case of human health damage caused by industrial pollution: the Peñoles case. We selected this case study because it presents the archetypical circumstances under which mobilization for environmental justice can emerge. Based on our analysis, we argued that, in Mexico, there exist numerous social and legal obstacles that inhibit the emergence of environmental justice activism, obstacles that are likely to limit the extent to which it will be adopted by Mexican environmentalists.

As we saw, the publication in 1998 of the results of studies conducted on children living close to the plant Met-Mex Peñoles showing very high levels of lead in their blood system prompted a reaction by state officials, NGOs, and the citizens affected. Such reaction appears to have exhibited several characteristics that are central features of environmental justice mobilization in the United States: the emergence of a social movement that demanded action from the plant's management and the government; the adoption an integration of the concept of justice into their discourse and demands; and the collective pursuit of compensation through the submission of a civil law suit. It would thus appear that environmental justice mobilization has the potential to emerge in Mexico. However, as we saw, the movement that emerged did not construct a discourse based on environmental discrimination, which has been one of the most important factors fueling the emergence of environmental justice mobilization in the United States. In the Peñoles case, the affected population, the children living in a neighborhood adjacent to the plant, were not deliberately targeted by the plant as the sitting of the plant preceded the formation of the affected neighborhood. The Peñoles case illustrates rather well the difficulty for social mobilization to adopt the notion of environmental discrimination in Mexico given that urban development does not unfold along a structured urban planning logic; the sitting of plants does not usually follow a carefully planned strategy. It is therefore difficult for social groups to base arguments against environmental discrimination on deliberate attempts to establish industrial plants in disadvantaged neighborhood.

The movement did not adopt an identity-based discourse based on race either, which has also been a salient characteristic of environmental justice discourses. Apart from indigenous mobilizations, in Mexico social mobilization around race or ethnicity is very difficult to crystallize given the relative homogeneity of its social makeup. The Peñoles case also illustrates this very well and it underscores the difficulty in the adoption of an important feature environmental justice mobilization.

More fundamental, however, are the legal obstacles that serve as powerful disincentives for the emergence of environmental justice in Mexico. As we have attempted to demonstrate, the Mexican legal system makes it very difficult for people to obtain compensation for damages done. As our case study shows, it was simply not possible for the group of people to win their case given that a clear connection could not be established between the environmental damage and their health consequences in the children. Because no contract existed between the plaintiffs and the affected population, they had to resort to a legal recourse based on "non-contractual civil responsibility" which proved challenging to win their case. Moreover, the Mexican environmental legal framework does not allow for the compensation for damages resulting from environmental degradation when the connection is not clear. Finally, the Mexican legal system does not allow for the submission of class-action law suits as groups of people are not considered legal entities. Individuals are treated on an individual basis even when their cases are collectively represented by a lawyer, as was the case in the filing of the civil suit against Peñoles. This is a very strong disincentive for people to organize and act collectively in the pursuit of compensation. The Peñoles case, then, presents the contextual setting within which environmental problems emerge in Mexico as well as the various obstacles faced by people in the pursuit of justice as a result of environmental damage and highlights the limits of the notion of environmental justice in the country.

Notes

1. The groundwater quality in most of Mexico's 24 hydrological regions has been qualified as polluted or as strongly polluted, the air quality in the major urban centers is one of the worst among OECD countries, and its deforestation rate is the third highest in the world (OECD 1998).

2. For a review of environmental mobilization in Mexico see Díez 2006, pp. 27–37. On the impact of the movement on policy see ibid., pp. 57–76, 93.

3. The increase in the number of ENGOs in Mexico in the early 1990s was helped greatly by the transfer of expertise and technology from US ENGOs (Díez 2006; Hogenboom 1998; Gilbreath 2003).

4. See "Detectan a 15 menores con envenenamiento de plomo," *El Siglo de Torreón*, December 11, 1998; "Una incógnita cómo adquirieron plomo en la sangre 18 niños contaminados," *La Opinión*, January 7, 1999.

5. One of the most important factors behind the movement's loss of strength was disagreement in regard to the demands made to the firm. While some activists primarily demanded compensation, others went further and demanded a complete closure of the plant (personal communication from Francisco Valdés-Pérezgasca, activist, April 25, 2006).

6. Another group of parents opted to pursue the case based on criminal grounds and submitted a compliant to the Federal Attorney, a suit hat was eventually rejected on the ground that the activity was not criminal as it did not violate the Criminal Code.

7. A writ of *amparo* is a form of injunction granted to an individual by a court through which constitutional provisions are waived based on the ground that a law or an administrative act has violated a constitutional right or guarantee. For excellent descriptions of *amparo*, see Burgoa 1998 and Baker 1971.

8. For an overview see Díez 2006, pp. 40–43.

References

ATSDR (Agency for Toxic Substances and Disease Registry). 1998. The Nature and Extent of Lead Poisoning in Children in the United States: A Report to Congress. US Department of Health and Human Services.

Albert, Lila, M. Martínez-Dewane, and M. García. 1978. Metales pesados I. Plomo en el cabello de niños mexicanos. *Revista Socio-Química Mexicana* 30, no. 2: 55–62.

Albert, Lila, M. Martínez-Dewane, and M. García. 2004. Met-Mex Peñoles y los niños de Torreón. *Revista de Toxicología en Línea* 4: 1–16.

Baker, Richard D. 1971. *Judicial Review in Mexico: A Study of the Amparo.* University of Texas Press.

Benin, A., J. Sargent, M. Dalton, and S. Roda.1999. High concentrations of heavy metals in neighborhoods near ore smelters in northern Mexico. *Environmental Health Perspectives* 107, no. 4: 279–284.

Borja Soriano, Manuel. 1992. *Teoría general de las obligaciones.* Porrúa.

Burgoa, Ignacio. 1998. *El juicio de amparo.* Porrúa.

Calderón-Salinas, J., B. Valdés-Anaya, M. Zúñiga-Charles, and A. Albores-Medina. 1996a. Lead exposure in a population of Mexican children. *Human and Experimental Toxicology* 15: 306–311.

Calderón-Salinas, J., C. Hernández-Luna, B. Valdés-Anaya, M. Maldonado-Vega, and A, López-Miranda. 1996b. Evolution of lead toxicity in a population of Mexican children. *Human Experimental Toxicology* 15: 376–382.

Colín, Ambroise, and Henri Capitant. 1924. *Curso elemental de derecho civil.* Reus.

Díez, Jordi. 2006. *Political Change and Environmental Policymaking in Mexico.* Routledge.

Escobar, R., M. Borja, G. Vinegra, L. Antopia, and F. Silva. 1964. Estudio epidemológico de la metalúrgica Penoles. *Salúd Pública México* 6, no., 5: 387–403.

Garcia Vargas, G., M. Rubio Andrade, L. Del razo Jiménez, V. Borja Aburto, E. Vera Aguilar, and M. Cebirán García. 1999. Lead exposure in chldren from urban areas in the Region Lagunera, Mexico. *Toxicological Sciences* 48: 329.

Hogenboom, Barabra. 1998. *Mexico and NAFTA Environment Debate: The Transitional Politics of Economic Integration.* International Books.

OECD (Organization for Economic Cooperation and Development). 1998. Environmental Performance Reviews: Mexico.

OECD. 2003. Environmental Performance Reviews: Mexico.

PROFEPA (Procuraduría Federal De Protección al Ambiente). 2000. Met-Mex Peñoles y el plomo en Torreón: Acciones de la PROFEPA de 1999 a 2000.

Rosen, John F. 1992a. Effects of low levels of lead exposure. *Science* 256, no. 17: 294.

Rosen, John F. 1992b. Health effects of lead at low exposure levels. *American Journal of Diseases of Children* 146: 1278–1281.

Rubio Andrade, M., L. del Razo, V. Borja, E. Vera, M. Cebirán, and G. García-Vegas. 1998. Evaluación de le exposición a plomo en niños residentes en el área conurbada de las ciudades de Gómez Palacios y Torreón. XVI Congreso Internacional de Investigación Bioquímica.

Ugalde, Vicente. 2006. La politique des déchets dangereux au Mexique. Thèse en droit, Université Panthéon-Assas, Paris.

Valdés, Francisco, and Victor Manuel Cabrera Morelos. 1999. La contaminación por metales pesados en Torreón, Coahuila, México. Texas Center for Policy Studies.

Viniegra, G., R. Escobar, E. Borja, and P. Caballero. 1964. La polución atmosférica e hídrica de Torreón, Coahuila. *Salúd Pública México* 6, no. 5: 405–414.

III

Land, Resources, and Environmental Justice

8

Ecotourism, Park Systems, and Environmental Justice in Latin America

Michele Zebich-Knos

As ecotourism increases around and within parks and protected areas, Honey (1999) reminds us that this growing industry is not the solution to every ill and that it must be approached with local communities and sustainability in mind. The current Latin American discourse on development surrounding parks and other protected areas, such as biosphere reserves, leads us to posit the need for inserting environmental justice into the economic and environmental equation—and to ask the question, do ecotourism businesses and national protected areas make good neighbors for local residents? The cases of the México's Monarch Butterfly Biosphere Reserve, Jeannette Kawas National Park, Toledo District, Belize, and Panama's Kuna Reserve project around Nusagandí offer insights for addressing this question and will form the basis of our inquiry.

The International Union for Conservation of Nature and Natural Resources (IUCN) defines a protected area as "an area dedicated primarily to the protection and enjoyment of natural or cultural heritage, to maintenance of biodiversity, and/or to maintenance of ecological life-support services" (Ceballos-Lascuráin 1996, p. 29). National parks come to mind first as a protected area, but protected areas also include other management classifications such as biosphere reserves which allow limited human activity within their confines (Haenn 2003). México's Monarch Butterfly Biosphere Reserve is one such example that falls within the generally accepted definition of national protected areas (Ceballos-Lascuráin 1996, pp. 29–31). While it is technically not a national park, it is an area dedicated to conservation of monarch butterflies' winter habitat.

Environmental justice can take a back seat in the policymaking process as national level policymakers often take a top-down approach to parks creation which is devoid of meaningful grassroots input. Through the cases in this chapter we will examine the extent to which national level policymakers incorporate the grassroots level into their national conservation process. The chapter will also examine the growing impact ecotourism plays as a means of local revenue generation for small towns and villages, and its relationship to a growing environmental movement aimed at expanding national and even private parks. Particular attention will be devoted to ecotourism as it relates to distribution of development revenues in areas surrounding national parks or reserves in Latin America. Few instances of grassroots ecotourism development occur without the insertion of non-governmental organizations into the mix. Thus, no examination of these issues would be complete without an understanding of the role NGOs play in communities within, or bordering, protected areas.

While there are fine examples of successful private reserves, such as Costa Rica's Monteverde Cloud Forest Reserve, this chapter focuses on the relationship between local communities and public sector protected areas (Budowski 1992). One hybrid within the public sector protected area classification is the region defined by the Study Project for the Management of the Wildlands of Kuna Yala, or PEMASKY, located in the Kuna Reserve of Panama. The reserve is home to the Kuna people and, since 1953, operates as an autonomous political government under Panamanian national law (Chapin 2000). The law provides for self-rule and a politico-legal framework within which the Kuna people can manage their own affairs, particularly their land and natural resources. This case illustrates how a hybrid protected area and an ecotourism project can unfold when initiated by indigenous rather than national policymakers. Through these cases the chapter places ecotourism within the larger context of people-centered development and also clarifies its role as catalyst for environmental conservation.

Applications for Environmental Justice

Before we begin to assess this relationship between ecotourism, protected areas and local residents we must review the conceptual basis of environmental justice which forms the framework for this investigation. Environmental impact is not equally distributed and, as a result of greater concern for what is placed in one's "backyard," a new grassroots environmentalism gained strength worldwide in the 1990s (Bullard 1994; Bullard and Clinton 1994; Faber 1998). This new environmentalism became connected to issues of social justice and the concept of environmental justice took hold.

While environmental justice often focuses on harmful environmental effects incurred by unempowered or disadvantaged groups (Steel, Clinton, and Lovrich 2003), this research takes the concept a step further and uses Taylor's paradigm to define environmental justice as "a well-developed environmental ideological framework that explicitly links ecological concerns with labor and social justice concerns" (Taylor 2000, pp. 508–580). The US Environmental Protection Agency's definition views environmental justice as the "fair treatment and meaningful involvement of all people regardless of race, color, national origin, or income with respect to the development, implementation, and enforcement of environmental laws, regulations, and policies" (US EPA 2006; Parris 2005). Both definitions combine procedural involvement in environmental decision making with substantive output-based results that recognize the needs and expectations of communities adjacent to protected areas. Actual application, however, proves to be a far cry from the theory, as most of our examples reveal.

Combining Taylor's linkage of environmental issues to labor and social justice, and blending it into the environmental policymaking process inherent to the EPA definition, we arrive at a useful framework for the study of rural areas in Latin America that are subject to park expansion into their communities. Since income disparities between urban and rural areas are significant in Latin America, communities adjacent to protected areas meet the definition of those "in need"—i.e., low-income or disadvantaged persons who may not receive fair treatment by public authorities or entrepreneurs.

While the EPA wrote its definition for US stakeholders, its conceptual applicability to developing countries is largely supported in the development literature (Desai 1998, p. 299). Many conservation organizations now acknowledge the linkage between conservation and development around protected areas, although this was not always the case. The IUCN encouraged the linkage in a report titled Can Protected Areas Contribute to Poverty Reduction? That report recommended a balanced approach between biodiversity conservation and development needs of populations living adjacent to protected areas (Scherl et al. 2004). Without using the term "environmental justice," the IUCN nevertheless encourages protected areas to "play a more significant role in addressing the needs of the rural poor by adopting socially responsible management approaches and by being fully integrated into national and international sustainable development and poverty reduction strategies" (IUCN 2004, p. 48).

Park creation or expansion becomes an important economic issue for rural inhabitants in Latin America. Subject to forces from their own national government, global conservation movements and savvy urban tourist-interests, rural dwellers are vulnerable to protected area expansion on lands that traditionally generate income from hunting, logging, or farming. The relationship between local communities, national or state-level officials, and ecotourist enterprises may thus provoke a "grassroots community reaction to external threats" (Agyeman 2005, p. 12).

A Conceptual Basis for Ecotourism in Latin America: The Responsible Tourist

Tourism means big business throughout the world and many developing countries regard it as a quick way to earn foreign currency. Tourism often overtakes traditional exports as a primary foreign currency earner as the case of Costa Rica illustrates. By 1990 tourism outranked coffee to become that nation's second largest foreign currency earner after bananas. In another example, Cuba's foreign currency strapped government pursues a policy of tourist development to assuage its convertible currency problems. In both cases, tourism is viewed with national level economic goals in mind. However, few words are written about tourism's benefits to small communities, especially those that border national or private, parks, which are often the anchor for ecotourism in a given area. It is therefore useful to examine the role of ecotourism, especially small-scale tourism, in the development process at community and village levels (Drake 1991).

The cases in this chapter examine tourism's role in small-scale development at the community level. This contrasts with large-scale beach-oriented tourism. As tourists became more sophisticated and demanding of new adventures, the formulation of a new type of tourism called "ecotourism" was touted by both the private and public sectors in developing countries and by the travel industry in developed countries. According to Héctor Ceballos-Lascuráin (1988), ecotourism involves "traveling to relatively undisturbed natural areas with the specific object of studying . . . and enjoying the scenery . . . as well as existing cultural aspects found in these areas."

The IUCN also inserts an environmental justice construct within its definition of ecotourism, which it describes as "environmentally responsible travel [that] provides for beneficially active socio-economic involvement of local populations (Ceballos-Lascuráin 1996, p. 20).

While the term 'ecotourism' is used loosely within the tourism industry, ecotourists often share the tenets of socially responsible tourism. This tourism variety is mostly small scale and seeks not only an appreciation of a locale's natural and cultural resources, but also to bring financial benefit to local people. Locals also become for the tourist more than mere fixtures surrounding a large beachfront hotel. Instead, they become purveyors of local mores and customs, and are likely to be owners of tourist necessities such as guest houses, small hotels, restaurants, and perhaps even modes of transportation such as vehicles or horses. As a result, locals acquire a new sense of empowerment that was previously reserved to higher level government officials or travel industry representatives from the big city. The responsible tourist rents rooms in modest pensions, small, locally owned hotels, or even from a family. He or she wants to see how locals live and understand their lifestyle.

Responsible tourists are sensitive to local environs, and seek to learn about local conditions rather than disrupt community life. While ecotourism presumes that some significant natural or cultural entity will attract visitors, socially responsible tourists often want to learn about, and visit, community development projects such as new clinics, irrigation projects, and schools. The advantage of responsible tourism is that it holds potential economic gain for communities located outside the generally accepted band of ecotourist attractions and has a better chance for economic success if national policymakers and private promoters accept increased community empowerment in small-scale tourist endeavors. In light of Latin America's traditional top-down policymaking process, willingness for national level actors to decentralize power becomes critical for success at the community level.[1]

Ashton offers insights that reach the core of responsible tourism which developed in a sustainable way that supports conservation, protects people's rights to choose, and provides economic opportunities in rural areas (Ashton and Ashton 1993). As a means of rural income generation, these are the tourists to attract. Unfortunately, it is difficult to know whether a visitor is actually a responsible ecotourist. For our purposes, this really does not matter since communities are concerned primarily with income generation and not affective beliefs of those who visit their area. Thus, this chapter refers to visitors to rural areas as simply ecotourists and makes the assumption that they behave as responsible tourists.

Figure 8.1 depicts the ideal management of responsible tourism as systemic interdependence among all actors involved. While hierarchies exist in the model as they do in reality, they exist as part of an integrated feedback loop which is fluid and varies depending on the individual case.

Tourism, Environment, Community: A Symbiotic Relationship?

As Latin American travel became increasingly linked to the environment, both national and local level leaders realized that there were many hardy tourists who wanted to venture into remote areas of their countries. Latin American flora and fauna thus became marketable to the tourist. Ecosystems were in need of conservation, and tourism became "the way to save 'wild' nature" through its ability to generate income both for park systems and adjacent communities, or as Zerner calls it, the "commodification of nature" (Zerner 1999, p. 3).

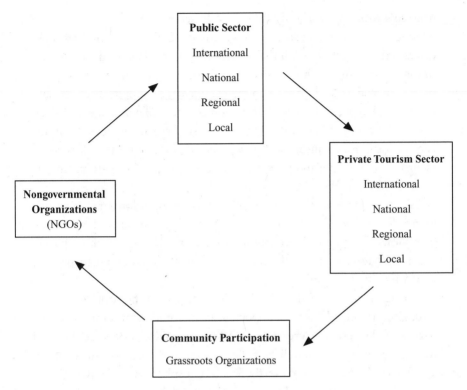

Figure 8.1
Responsible tourism management loop (interdependence model).

The development literature in recent years is replete with the words grassroots, community development, empowerment, and popular participation. Max-Neef writes of "human scale development" as a process in which the traditional paternalistic role of the Latin American state will acquiesce to "creative solutions flowing from the bottom upwards" (Max-Neef 1991, p. 8). Korten calls this "people centered development" in which local participation includes not only listening to local opinions but also "the strengthening of local resource control and ownership" (Korten 1992, p. 65). Michael Cernea reiterates this view by stating that local participation "means empowering people to mobilize their own capacities, be social actors rather than passive subjects, manage the resources, make decisions, and control the activities that affect their lives" (quoted in Lindberg and Hawkins 1993).

Mexico's Monarch Butterfly Biosphere Reserve

Nowhere is the willingness to yield greater control to communities more evident than in nature tourism planning. Brandon's study of nature tourism distinguishes this "active" participatory approach with the more passive beneficiary approach in which local communities are benefit recipients, but are not necessarily empowered to make management decisions (Brandon 1993, p. 139). Honey also studies the impact of ecotourism on local communities and recognizes that "despite the rhetoric of incorporating people and parks . . . old ways and power relationships die hard" (Honey 1999, p. 85).

As an example of the beneficiary approach Brandon cites México's "butterfly project" designed by NGOs to tap the natural migration of billions of monarch butterflies to select wintering locations within México's Monarch Butterfly Special Biosphere Reserve and to provide added income to its inhabitants.

Before understanding how various income-generating projects became wrought with problems, it is important to first understand the top down nature of the reserve's creation. In 1986 a presidential decree declared 62 square miles of monarch butterfly habitat in the states of Michoacán and México a Monarch Butterfly Special Biosphere Reserve (CONANP 2006). Tucker notes that "the reserve's establishment came as a shock to the agrarian communities, for they had not been included in the decision making process dominated by national and international conservation interests" (Tucker 2004, p. 570). The area is economically depressed and, since the reserve's inception, experienced declining agricultural productivity due to soil erosion and generally unsustainable farming practices as well as increased cattle grazing and logging in the butterfly reserves.

To aggravate matters, the reserve's rural communities retained land titles, but lost the long-held right to forest usage. To make matters worse, reserve borders were not well defined, or obvious, to local inhabitants, and included regions not even visited by the monarch butterfly population (Tucker 2004). Herein lies the problem when balancing human needs versus needs of local fauna—fauna can move around and do not necessarily respect governmental boundaries. This makes protected areas difficult to manage and it would not be improbable that, in two or three decades, the butterflies may totally move to areas outside of reserve boundaries. Such is the dilemma when dealing with nature.

The reserve is populated by descendents of the Mazahua and Otomi indigenous cultures and includes 56 *ejidos*, or communally owned lands (Camp 2003), 13 indigenous communities, and 21 small properties (WWF-México 2006). Local communities and property owners play an important role in the butterfly reserve because 82 percent of all land in both core and buffer zones is either communal or private land (Tucker 2004). This differs from a national park situation in which park land would most likely be government property. The result is a complex tug of war between Mexican government officials and local community leaders and inhabitants.

The butterfly project was initially designed by the Mexican NGOs, Alternare and Bosque Modelo, to organize local tourist infrastructure as large numbers of visitors were coming to the reserve in a relatively unorganized manner (Tucker 2004; USFWS 2006). Alternare organized visitors to the area, created a visitor center, planted trees, maintained trails, established a community booth for food/souvenir sales, and instituted a revenue sharing system in which a portion of visitor fees collected went to the local community.

While distribution of some benefits to the local community near the butterfly reserve did occur, the project was primarily coordinated by NGO managers who Barkin (2000) describes as "poorly informed businessmen." Locals became involved only after NGO experts pinpointed problems and proffered solutions. Paternalism was still at work and the result was little community identification with project success despite the fact that economic benefits could be derived from it.

Those who did benefit from the project were mainly individual entrepreneurs such as guides or food vendors. The vast majority of individuals, however, felt unconnected to the tourism project. Barkin notes that most tourist activities were subcontracted to only one of the many communities in the area (Barkin 2000, p. 161). As a result, project upkeep was poor. For example, trees planted by locals soon took sick for lack of care. Locals were paid to plant the trees, but after planting, no followup groups had a stake in overseeing their health and maintenance. Planning and community store operations were, likewise, done in a top-down fashion and, once again, locals felt uninvolved in store matters. Little community connection to the project resulted and the entire endeavor was generally thought to be of little economic impact to the area (Brandon 1993, p. 141). Yet Alternare continues to receive funds from the US Fish and Wildlife Service (USFWS) as its 2005 list of projects revealed. In 2005 the USFWS Wildlife Without Borders-Mexico Program funded Alternare's "Participatory Training for Local Communities to Restore Habitat in the Monarch Butterfly Biosphere Reserve" in the amount of $48,000 (USFWS 2005). Previous USFWS grants to Alternare totaled $309,250 (USFWS).

Only two butterfly sanctuaries are currently open to the public: Sierra Chincua in Angangueo Municipality and El Rosario in the Ocampo Municipality. This increases local ecotourism disparities (Michoacán 2006). If sanctuaries are opened and closed for ecological reasons, it is easy to see how local ecotourist initiatives can be thwarted should the Mexican government decide to close a sanctuary and reopen at a new location.

Area residents continued to degrade the forest reserve to such an extent that, by 2000, it sparked attention of the Mexican federal government and international NGOs such as the World Wildlife Fund. The WWF's main goal was for butterfly habitat protection and it completed studies that would help expand the reserve. In November 2000, the Mexican federal government expanded the reserve from 62 to 217 square miles (WWF 2006; CONANP 2000). In light of past problems that developed from a top-down administrative approach, WWF urged the Mexican government to seek community participation during the creation of the expanded reserve (WWF 2006).

WWF also created its own Monarch Butterfly Project, which facilitates continuous monitoring and also promotes tourism and environmental education in the area. WWF-México promotes ecotourist visits to the Monarch Butterfly Biosphere Reserve and provides useful information for tourists on their website. Visitors—mostly Mexican tourists, can assess the tourist infrastructure within each butterfly sanctuary that WWF lists by *ejido* and municipality (WWF-México 2006). For each location the WWF website details information on lodging, food, roads, and other amenities (WWF-México 2006).

Since the expanded biosphere reserve resulted in a new presidential decree, all prior logging permits were voided, which yielded yet another financial setback for communities adjacent to the reserve. Since logging was part of the forest degradation issue and a source of livelihood for the locals, WWF offered the Mexican government suggested solutions that address local economic concerns and would move locals from logging to sustainable alternatives. This time the newly expanded butterfly reserve would come with a financial plan to provide economic compensation for lost logging revenues.

WWF used the technique of conservation concession payments to locals in order to compensate loss of logging revenue. The conservation group's rationale is based on the premise that, if logging companies can hold a timber concession, so can they (Wolman 2004). They pay the royalty to the Mexican government and do not log the land. Instead, WWF's Monarch Butterfly Conservation Fund purchases logging permits from existing permit holders within the Butterfly Reserve at the rate of $18/cubic meter of unharvested timber. They also pay landowners without logging permits $12/hectare to conserve their lands, and pay landowners with logging permits $8/hectare (Wolman 2004, p. 880; WWF 2006). Although this partially resolves the loss of logging income, it does not address improvements to local ecotourist infrastructure—more financial support is needed for that purpose. It also does not resolve the fact that ecotourism in this reserve is seasonal. Monarch butterflies make the 2,000 mile trek south from Canada and the United States to winter in the states of Michoacán and México. This migration occurs from December through March, thereby ensuring a short visitor season and limited tourist revenues for locals. The environmental justice element in this example becomes evident as the livelihood of local residents is now inextricably connected to an international effort to save the monarch butterflies. The triangular relationship is one in which local communities, whose largely *ejido*-controlled lands mostly fall within reserve boundaries, are now increasingly depend upon NGOs and outside funding sources for reimbursement of income lost from logging. Local communities are also subject to administrative regulation by the Mexican National Commission for Protected Natural Areas, which can vary as the 2000 reserve expansion reveals (CONANP 2006; WWF-México 2006; Tucker 2004).

It is unlikely that the present state of ecotourist development can equalize lost logging revenue, which means that locals are dependent upon NGO conservation concession payments. As anyone familiar with the grant process knows, such funding can be highly erratic and variable over time. In short, the concession payment program funded by the Packard Foundation through the WWF could cease since it is grant and not market driven. If funding should cease, this would mean a major setback for affected communities.

The number of visitors increased from 25,000 in 1986 to 250,000 in 1999. Barkin (2000) is skeptical that these numbers are sufficient to support the region's 65,000 inhabitants. One solution to this NGO dependency problem is to increase the focus on building a higher quality, sustainable ecotourist infrastructure that will yield greater revenue for local communities. An improved ecotourist infrastructure especially in the form of roads, restaurants and lodging would enable locals to command higher prices and longer individual stays without the need to significantly increase the number of tourists. Human carrying capacity would be kept in check as a controlled number of tourists would pay higher prices. Barkin (2000) suggests moving beyond the region's seasonal butterfly attraction to a year-round nature and health tourism destination especially for residents of Mexico City and Guadalajara who comprise the largest number of tourists to the area. The region's geothermal springs could be provide the added attraction for sustained year-round health tourism. To meet this untapped demand, the Alianza de Ejidos, a confederation of local communities attempted to expand year-round eco and health tourism. Yet, such grassroots coordination must also confront the area's political power base that can pose a significant obstacle if its demands are not met. As an alternative to increased tourist revenue, Barkin (2000) notes that the region's watershed is a source of water for Mexico City and Guadalajara. This raises the possibility of acquiring additional reforestation and development funds for the area. A relationship of mutual need based on water could be developed between these urban areas and the monarch butterfly region. This would certainly increase this rural area's tangible power in the struggle for financial well-being.

Jeannette Kawas (Punta Sal) National Park, Honduras

The participatory approach used in the Tela Ecotourism Project on the northern coast of Honduras is an attempt to avoid the pitfalls encountered in Mexico's butterfly project. The project is sponsored by the Institute of Honduran Tourism (IHT) and focuses upon the management of tourists to, and around, Jeannette Kawas (formerly Punta Sal) National Park (JKNP). The area is home to approximately 80 percent of Honduran bird species and 60 percent of the country's flora (Travel Agent Central America 1997). The city of Tela is within proximity to the park and is known for its beaches, which makes it more attractive to tourists. Within the park's buffer zones are communities populated by *mestizos* and by Garifuna, a mixed Afro-Indigenous-Caribbean people (Buckley 2003).

Unlike the more difficult-to-maneuver websites for the Monarch Butterfly Biosphere Reserve, browsing the Internet, in both Spanish and English, for JKNP reveals a vast array of tourist amenities, tours and available means for booking a visit to the area. The ease of acquiring general information about the area may explain its successful attraction of tourists. For example, the Gray Line Tours website offers an easy to book trip to Tela from other parts of Honduras.

The park is managed by the Foundation for the Protection of Lancetilla, Punta Sal and Texiguat, or PROLANSATE after its Spanish acronym. PROLANSATE is a regional conservation organization devoted to the conservation of the Tela area's natural habitats (PROLANSATE 2006a).

To ensure park protection and encourage park tourism as a means of local revenue generation the Honduran national government developed linkages between the park and local communities. With the assistance of United Nations Development Program (UNDP) funding and consultants (Ashton 1999), a park management plan was devised. The plan discovered community needs by talking with community leaders and conducting community surveys. A park authority that includes local community leaders in the decision making aspect of park administration is the result of this process (Ashton 1993, p. 196).

Park management took a two tiered approach and utilizes a board of directors called the Jeannette Kawas (Punta Sal) National Park Authority

(JKNPA) and the JKNP Trust. This plan reflects confidence that ecotourism will generate adequate revenue for enforcement, training and other programs in the buffer zone (Ashton 1999).

The JKNPA is responsible for park conservation and for maintaining dialogue among 13 communities, the park staff, and the central government. Not only do local communities have a say in decision making, but other actors involved in tourism can provide input. JKNPA's voting members include the thirteen communities surrounding the park, the municipality of Tela, two members representing the private tourism sector, the president of PROLANSATE, directors from IHT, JKNP, the Honduran Corporation for Forest Development (COHDEFOR), and Lancetilla Botanical Gardens. COHDEFOR and IHT representatives on the Authority serve as an open channel to the central government. The park's financial aspects are managed by the JKNP trust which is comprised of the same board of directors. The trust is not only responsible for setting and collecting user fees, but it also hires the park's staff. While experts trained in park ecology and administration were initially hired for its professional staff, lower level staffers from surrounding communities could advance to professional status after acquiring adequate training and experience.

Since the JKNP is funded solely from user fees, its management has a direct interest in promoting tourism to the park. Because management and park decision making is so intimately tied to community representatives on the JKNPA and the trust, it is unlikely that tourism linked to the Punta Sal area will develop without significant community input. Already, the JKNPA called for funding projects in the surrounding communities that will enhance park conservation, facilitate tourism and benefit the communities at the same time. Immediate projects include sewage treatment and education (Ashton and Ashton 1993, p. 20). Without education, local guides cannot be adequately trained and without proper sanitary systems, a steady and larger number of tourists cannot be accommodated.

While PROLANSATE's first priority is conservation, it understands the practical need for encouraging local employment especially in the tourism sector since tourists contribute to the all-important park user fees (PROLANSATE 2006b). Its mission statement includes community development and ecotourism alongside natural resource conservation, but it is evident that the NGO is most devoted to conservation and only secondarily to community-based socio-economic issues. In 1997 it entered into partnership with US-based Ecologic to provide local assistance for agro-forestry, sustainable agriculture, and community development. However, examination of this partnership reveals no projects related to ecotourism. Projects relate solely to conservation education and sustainable agriculture (Ecologic 2006).

PROLANSATE's strong environmental emphasis might have contributed to the untimely death in February 1995 of Jeannette Kawas, the former president of PROLANSATE. It certainly contributed to tensions between peasant activists and environmentalists (Cuevas 1995). Kawas, a Tela native and avid environmentalist, was shot in her home by individuals suspected of belonging to two peasant organizations. The National Union of Farmworkers and the African Palm Agricultural Cooperative sought transfer of some park land to their organizations for the cultivation of bananas, coconuts, and other palms. The Honduran government initially sided with the peasant organizations, but, after Kawas organized protests, later rescinded its offer to transfer land. Kawas made other enemies, especially Julio Galindo, a National Party legislator who became the object of Kawas's campaign to discredit his capture of dolphins for display at his hotel (Cuevas 1995). Kawas's murder clearly reveals the tensions between environmentalists and select community representatives.

Despite some very real tensions between the park's manager, PROLANSATE, and some locals, the Tela ecotourism project sponsored by the Institute of Honduran Tourism is the type of symbiotic relationship between the environment, tourism and the community that has the makings of durability. Easy access to the park from Tela makes it an area capable of receiving 400,000 visitors annually, which as Buckley (2003) notes, will establish a "solid revenue base." In addition, the Institute of Honduran Tourism maintains an office in Coral Gables, Florida to service the US market. While its success has yet to be properly assessed, it is at least an attempt to provide more than trickle down benefits with no local decision making input.

Developing Ecotourist Initiatives

Toledo District, Belize

One success story within the Mayan region of Belize includes the communities of Toledo District.[2] Within Toledo District are three Mayan ruins—Nim Li Punit, Uxbenka, and Lubaantun, as well as Bladen Natural Reserve. Just off the coast of Punta Gorda is Sapodilla Cayes Marine Reserve. To benefit economically from the Mayan cultural and species-rich natural environment, the district's Mayan communities created their own locally managed tourism project coordinated through the Toledo Ecotourism Association (TEA). TEA was founded in 1990 by local Mayan, Garifuna and Creole residents (Beavers 1995). Initial funding by the World Wide Fund for Nature and the Nature Conservancy helped build the first five guest houses and, by 1995, the US Agency for International Development (USAID) and the Belize Ministry of Tourism and Youth funded construction of eight additional guest houses (Buckley 2003; Weizsman 2001).

Profits earned from ecotourism are divided among participating villages and portions are intended to be reinvested in further tourism development in the areas of marketing, training of local guides, and trail maintenance (Toledo Institute for Development and Environment 2006; Eco Institute 1992). To ensure that all participating communities benefit from the tourism project and do not exceed village carrying capacity, tourist stays are distributed to the various communities. This rotation system keeps conflict between villages and among residents over tourist revenues to a minimum (Beavers 1995).

Tourists are lodged in eight-person guest houses constructed by villagers. Meals are taken in villagers' homes. Regimented distribution of tourists to participating villages via radio contact with TEA means that freedom to travel in the area is restricted by the communities themselves. Tourists pay a user fee to enter the area and are literally "assigned" to visit, and stay, in a certain village (Mahler and Wotkyns 1991, p. 145). This type of restricted travel works best when tourists consider themselves "responsible" and are aware that their presence plays a definite role in the planned development of these Mayan communities. This process also ensures that ecotourism does not become the sole economic mainstay of villagers; instead it serves to supplement existing liveli-hoods—or diversify income sources (Beavers 1995).

According to Buckley (2003), villagers receive approximately US$35 per person per day from tourists. This includes payments for lodging, meals, handicrafts and dance performances. While the money is paid to the village association, 80 percent goes to TEA village members who provided the related services. The remaining 20 percent goes to the TEA headquarters in Punta Gorda and is allocated for reforestation and trail maintenance, health and education, administrative costs, advertising, and taxes with the largest share going to administrative costs (Beavers 1995, p. 3).

Based on the responsible tourism model (figure 8.1), the link between the regional (Toledo District Project) and national sector efforts becomes very real. The Belize Ministry of Tourism and Youth has established what it calls a "sustainable" tourism policy which supports community based initiatives and small businesses involved in the tourism industry (Weizsman 2001). For example, the creation of small hotels and guest houses similar to those in Toledo District communities is supported in other areas of the country through loans earmarked for this purpose. In the future, tour buses in transit through Belize, presumably on the inter-national Mundo Maya route, must utilize local guides and pay a tourism tax at the Belize border. Portions of the revenue collected through border, hotel and airport taxes contribute to Belize's overall tourism strategy in which community based tourism initiatives play a recognized role (Belize Today 1993, pp. 9–11). One setback noted by scholars studying the Toledo case pertains to the over reliance on word-of-mouth advertising, but this is easily overcome today with websites available to even the least savvy community group (Buckley 2003; Beavers 1995). The Toledo District Project continues to serve as a model of local involvement to both conservation and ecotourism efforts that translate into real benefit to participating communities.

Grassroots Tourism: Obstacles to Success in Kuna Yala, Panama

The community efforts in Toledo District, Belize are successes that make community coordination for tourist development appear facile. That is not always the case as the Kuna attempt to develop tourism illustrates.

Concern over increased colonization and deforestation of Kuna Yala, or Kuna territory, by non-Kuna Panamanians led to consultations with Panamanian and foreign forestry experts.[3] These consultations resulted in the creation by 1983 of the Study and Management Project for the Wildlands of Kuna Yala, known by the acronym PEMASKY. In 1987 the Kuna General Congress adopted the biosphere reserve model with divisions into zones for the area's management (Archibold 1992, pp. 21–33). While called a project, PEMASKY operates like an NGO, which it is not (Chapin 2000). Both Kuna leaders and US scientists were involved in the PEMASKY effort to develop a management plan for the area (Archibold 1992, p. 22). One aspect of the plan recommended not only the promotion of scientific research in Kuna Yala, but also the introduction of nature tourism in the rain forested parts of the San Blas mountain range. For added appeal, PEMASKY is referred to by many ecotourist companies as PEMASKY National Park or biological reserve. National park appeal to ecotourists is obvious and preferable to visiting a study and management project.

While the Kuna enjoy semi-autonomous legal status granted by the Panamanian government as well as their own governing structure that emphasizes community cooperation and group work, they ran into considerable problems in their plan to bring ecotourism to more remote areas of Kuna Yala (Chapin 2000).

The Kuna were aware of Costa Rica's ecotourism boom, and wanted to create their own version of tourism which they would operate on a responsible basis for the benefit of the Kuna people. Unlike Toledo District's ecotourism project, which experienced slow growth and far less funding, PEMASKY was flooded with grant monies from both local and international sources. In the 1980s the local Union of Kuna Workers (UTK) contributed US$220,000 in cash and in-kind support while the Inter-American Foundation gave US$765,000 in the period 1983–1991. The WWF donated US$159,000 from 1983–1989, the MacArthur Foundation gave US$300,000 from 1986 to 1991, and smaller donors such as Cultural Survival also funded PEMASKY. Between 1983 and 1991, Chapin (2000) estimates that PEMASKY received US$1.22 million in outside funds. At the same time the Kuna expanded the PEMASKY staff and spent heavily on salaries for its directors, technicians, carpenters, park guards and other administrators (Chapin 2000, pp. 22–23). Yet Chapin asserts that, although the Kuna made mistakes, "had the funds been managed by the Panamanian government, few if any of the Kuna priorities would have been addressed" (ibid., p. 30).

Tourism was not unknown in the region for cruise ships regularly visit Kuna coastal areas around the port of Cartí. Also, charter flights from Panama City operated since the 1960s to transport tourists to Cartí, where they were lodged in small American-owned hotels. However, Panamanian government efforts to turn the Cartí region into a tourist Mecca complete with an international airport met resistance from the Kuna. Being a "tourist attraction" for non-responsible tourists was not what they had in mind. Kuna threats of violence forced the government to retreat from its project and North American hoteliers were, in fact, driven from the area. Hotels in Cartí are today largely run by Kuna (Chapin 1990).

The PEMASKY headquarters in Nusagandí, located where the El Llano-Cartí road cuts across the San Blas range, was thought to be a suitable location for nature tourism development. The camp has a large dormitory, dining room, and offices and has hosted scientists from STRI. Expansion into the nature tourism market was the next step somewhat naively recommended by the scientists and agreed upon by the Kuna. This latter group had already produced guidelines for appropriate "foreign" behavior in Kuna territory and was not shy in enforcing such guidelines (Chapin 1990, pp. 42–45). Nusagandí's location as an ecotourism center also proved problematic as there is no community nearby to supply much needed labor (Chapin 2000; Young 2006).

Nusagandí never grew as a tourist destination for a variety of reasons some of which can be attributed to a breakdown in the responsible tourism management loop. Few solid relationships were established with travel agencies in Panama City or in the United States by the Kuna who, as a rule, lack business experience (Gündling, Korn, and Specht 2000). As a result, most ecotourist groups stay at Burbayar Lodge which lies 200 yards from the Kuna border in Panamá province, and boasts on its website that it sustains three "direct jobs" in the nearby community and several other "indirect jobs" (Burbayar Lodge 2006). The area is sparsely populated, but revenue spent within the Kuna Reserve in the form of visitor fees, for example, serves the entire Kuna population. Louise Young of Mola Tours has led ecotourist groups into the Nusagandí area since 1996 and observes that many tourists simply remain at the Burbayar Lodge to do their bird watching rather than make the difficult trek into Nusagandí's primary rainforest. This translates into a decrease in park fees paid to the Kuna (Young 2006).

While the Fundación para la Promoción del Conocimiento Indígena de Panamá helped the Kuna complete a strategic ecotourism development plan and marketing study (Eco-index 2006), the Kuna are in great need of general business skills. Since most NGOs are donor, not market, driven they are not the best source for conveying entrepreneurial spirit. This void could be filled by workshops run by business schools to impart a customer-driven model of sustained growth.

Road conditions leading to the Nusagandí camp also deter tourism. Gravel roads leading to Nusagandí from Panama City turn to mud during heavy rains and are passable only with the best four-wheel-drive vehicles. The road from Cartí to Nusagandí cannot easily feed tourists into the camp for the simple reason that it is not completely graveled and poses major driving hazards for vehicles unequipped with powerful winches (Chapin 1990). As late as 2003, travel agents in Panama City clearly specified the road problem on their websites. While offering a Nusagandí trip on their website, Condor Journeys and Adventures travel agency notes that "both the road and the field station have fallen in disrepair" (Condor Journeys and Adventures 2006).

The lack of a good road is a primary reason for the failure of tourism expansion in Nusagandí. Not only can tourists not easily reach Nusagandí, but transportation problems made further construction costly and logistically difficult. As a result, basic tourist amenities for the camp have gone unfinished—this includes toilets and electrical generators.

Roads are generally considered a public good provided by national governments. In this case, the Kuna underestimated the setback to their ecotourism enterprise presented by poor roads. At the project's inception, cultivating better links with the Panamanian government might have helped spark a nationally sponsored project to improve the 22-kilometer El Llano-Cartí road. However, the political trade-off would likely be accompanied by loss of Kuna control in Cartí, which has already been targeted by the Panamanian government as a sun-and-surf tourist attraction.

In December 2005, the Ministry of Economy and Finance approved funds for road improvements (Ministerio de Economía y Finanzas 2005). Once improved, the road would serve as the lifeline for increased nature tourism managed by the Kuna. The Kuna have also made it clear that they will patrol the land and will include two control sites—one at Nusagandí and the other at Cangandí (Quintero 2005). Fear of non-Kuna colonists is founded upon land clashes dating back to the 1970s and is one reason the lobbying for road improvements did not take place sooner (Chapin 2000). Yet, until road improvements are made, maintenance is ensured, and a market-based business model—one that is not dependent on fundraising, is put in place, regular nature tourist stays in Nusagandí will remain at a low level.

Lessons Learned: Making Environmental Justice a Reality

Responsible ecotourism has already taken hold in Belize, Honduras, Mexico, and Panama, which incorporate the concept into their national tourism strategies and as communities see greater economic benefits reaped by small-scale efforts. Responsible tourism at the community level does not require multi-million dollar Acapulco-style investments.[4] Instead, the support of national government in infrastructure creation and international marketing can contribute to a community effort modeled after that of Toledo District, Belize. Toledo District certainly benefits from the Belize Tourist Board's international media campaign. Few communities have the resources to conduct such a campaign and must, therefore, rely upon the national government for promotional marketing.

Without a coordinated working relationship between community—business—government at all levels from grassroots, regional, national to international, most residents adjacent to, or in, protected areas will find it difficult to achieve the goal of deriving significant benefit from ecotourism. NGOs can provide training and management skills needed to organize tourism infrastructure, marketing and other essentials for successfully bargaining with sophisticated outsiders. Each group, however, has its own agenda and bargaining culture in which educated stakeholders have an advantage. Bargaining equality is not likely if we consider the inherent disadvantage faced by inhabitants within the Monarch Butterfly Biosphere Reserve or the Kuna people of Panamá. Literacy rates are generally lower in these areas thus increasing bargaining disparity among relevant actors.

The Kuna have a history of dealing aggressively with the Panamanian government, and exercise a great deal of autonomy over their land, yet a lack of business skills and distrust of outsiders put them at a market disadvantage. While tourism is controlled by the Kuna General Congress, and local empowerment is not an issue, indigenous stakeholders should not underestimate the value of acquiring management and other business skills. However, it is doubtful that the Kuna will be able to build an extensive sustainable ecotourist sector as long as suspicion of outsiders within their territory remains a predominant concern (Chapin 2000; Young 2006). Threat to local culture is indeed a real issue that must be balanced with economic benefits from ecotourism.

Locally built structures are capable of housing responsible tourists who demand only a minimum of creature comforts. However, even that minimum may be lacking as Faust points out in her research on Mayan communities in Campeche, México (Faust 1991, pp. 206–210). Amenities such as bathing facilities, toilets, sanitary sewage disposal and potable water are often missing in rural villages eager to receive tourists, but unschooled in how basics can be provided.

The political situation of an area is more important than amenities in any given country. Political instability associated with Peru's Shining Path Guerrilla Movement, Mexico's Zapatista problem in the 1990s and Haiti's descent into political and socio-economic chaos, can destroy the flow of visitors to an area, and take years to recover. While responsible tourists are an adventuresome lot, they cannot be expected to brave bullets in their quest for a fulfilling vacation. Politically tranquil spots such as Costa Rica will, therefore, continue to dominate the responsible tourism market.

Lastly, diversified revenue sources independent of tourism must become part of the management strategy for local peoples whose lives are affected by protected natural areas. Sustainable agriculture and even carbon sequestration projects can contribute to a more balanced revenue generating scheme and still protect the local environment.[5] While sustainable agricultural proceeds normally go to local producers, income earned by public parks can become mired in a tug of war in which the national government reserves a final say in allocation of park-generated income.

Notes

1. For an in-depth explanation of Latin America's centralist tendencies, see Véliz 1980.

2. The Mundo Maya Sustainable Tourism Program, initiated in 1989 between Guatemala, Honduras, Belize, Mexico, and El Salvador, facilitates tourist visits to Mayan ruins. Easier border crossing, publicity, support for tourist micro-enterprises, and tourist infrastructure are all priorities of the current Mundo Maya Program, which is incorporated not only within the five national level ministries of tourism, but also in the region's Mundo Maya Organization (Organización Mundo Maya 2002; Mexican Secretariat of Tourism 2006).

3. Financial and technical assistance for the creation of PEMASKY came primarily from the Smithsonian Tropical Research Institute (STRI), the Inter-American Foundation, the US Agency for International Development, the World Wildlife Fund, the MacArthur Foundation and some Panamanian governmental assistance (Archibold 1992, p. 22).

4. Acapulco, Mexico is a classic example of national-level tourism planning which was nearly devoid of community input and went from village to beach resort in a few years. For a comprehensive examination of Acapulco's transformation, see Ramírez-Sáiz 1987.

5. Carbon sequestration is one way to meet Kyoto Protocol requirements and uses forested areas as a sink for absorbing carbon dioxide. In their untouched state, forests could become a commodity capable of generating revenue.

References

Agyeman, Julian. 2005. Where justice and sustainability meet. *Environment* 47, no. 6: 12.

Archibold, Guillermo. 1992. Pemasky in Kuna Yala: protecting Mother Earth . . . and her children. In *Toward a Green Central America*, ed. V. Barzetti and Y. Rovinski. Kumarian.

Ashton, Ray. 1993. Sustainable tourism and local communities: The need to develop a business-like approach to the problem. In Proceedings of the 1993 World Congress on Adventure Travel and Eco-Tourism. Adventure Travel Society.

Ashton, Ray. 1999. Working for a successful ecotourism story: The case of Punta Sal National Park. In *Tourism Development in Critical Environments*, ed. T. Singh and S. Singh. Cognizant.

Ashton, Ray, and Patricia Ashton. 1993. An Introduction to Sustainable Tourism (Ecotourism) in Central America. Prepared for the Paseo Pantera Ecotourism Program. Document PN-ABQ-202, US Agency for International Development.

Barkin, David. 2000. The economic impacts of ecotourism: Conflicts and solutions in highland Mexico. In *Tourism and Development in Mountain Regions*, ed. P. Godde et al. CABI.

Beavers, John. 1995. Community Based Ecotourism in the Maya Forest: A Case Study from Belize. Report prepared for Nature Conservancy–USAID/Maya Forest Project.

Belize Today. 2000. Tourism—Towards 2000.

Brandon, Katrina. 1993. Basic steps toward encouraging local participation in nature tourism projects. In *Ecotourism*, ed. K. Lindberg and D. Hawkins. Ecotourism Society.

Buckley, Ralf. 2003. *Case Studies in Ecotourism*. CABI.

Budowski, Tamara. 1992. Ecotourism Costa Rican style. In *Toward a Green Central America*, ed. V. Barzetti and Y. Rovinski. Kumarian.

Bullard, Robert D. ed. 1994. *Unequal Protection: Environmental Justice and Communities of Color*. Sierra Club Books.

Bullard, Robert D., and William J. Clinton. 1994. Overcoming racism in environmental decisionmaking. *Environment* 36, no. 4: 10–44.

Burbayar Lodge. 2006. The Lodge, committed to the community of Llano-Carti http://www.burbayar.com.

Camp, Roderic A. 2003. Politics in Mexico: The Democratic Transformation. Oxford University Press.

Ceballos-Lascuráin, Hector. 1988. The future of ecotourism. *Mexico Journal*, January: 13–14.

Ceballos-Lascuráin, Hector. 1993. Overview on ecotourism around the world: IUCN's ecotourism program. In Proceedings of the 1993 World Congress on Adventure Tourism and Eco-Tourism. Adventure Travel Society.

Ceballos-Lascuráin, Hector. 1996. Tourism, ecotourism, and protected areas: The state of nature-based tourism around the world and guidelines for its development. International Union for Conservation of Nature and Natural Resources.

Chapin, Mac. 1990. The Silent Jungle: Ecotourism Among the Kuna Indians of Panama. Cultural Survival Quarterly 14, no. 1: 42–45.

Chapin, Mac. 2000. Defending Kuna Yala. US Agency for International Development.

CONANP (Comisión Nacional de Areas Naturales Protegidas, Secretária de Medio Ambiente, Recursos Naturales y Pesca (México). 2000. Diario Oficial, November 10. http://www.conanp.gob.mx.

Condor Journeys and Adventures. 2006. Nusagandi Kuna jungle adventure. http://www.condorjourneys-adventures.com.

Cuevas, Freddy. 1995. Honduran environmentalist killed. Associated Press, February 7.

Desai, Uday. 1998. Poverty, government, and the global environment. In *Ecological Policy and Politics in Developing Countries*, ed. U. Desai. State University of New York Press.

Drake, Susan P. 1991. Local participation in ecotourism projects. In *Nature Tourism*, ed. T. Whelan. Island.

Eco-index. 2004. Program to promote indigenous alternative tourism in Panama. http://www.eco-index.org.

Eco Institute of Costa Rica. 1992. *Sustainable Tourism Newsletter* 1, no. 2: 1–8.

Ecologic Development Fund. 2006. Current projects. http://www.ecologic/org.

Faber, Daniel. 1998. The struggle for ecological democracy and environmental justice. In *The Struggle for Ecological Democracy and Environmental Justice*, ed. D. Faber. Guilford.

Faust, Betty B. 1991. Maya culture and Maya participation in the international ecotourism and resource conservation project. In *Ecotourism and Resource Conservation*, volume 1, ed. J. Kusler. Ecotourism and Resource Conservation Project.

Gündling, Lothar, Horst Kom, and Rudolf Specht, eds. 2000. Report of the International Expert Workshop: Case Studies on Sustainable Tourism and Biological Diversity *[really in English?]*. Prepared for German Federal Agency for Nature Conservation.

Haenn, Nora. 2003. Risking environmental justice: culture, conservation, and governance at Calakmul, Mexico. In *Struggles for Social Rights in Latin America*, ed. S. Eckstein and T. Wickham-Crowley. Routledge.

Honey, Martha. 1999. *Ecotourism and Sustainable Development: Who Owns Paradise?* Island.

Korten, David. 1992. People-centered development: Alternative for a world in crisis. In *Development and Democratization in the Third World*, ed. K. Bauzon. Crane Russak.

Lindberg, Kreg, and Donald E. Hawkins, eds. 1993. *Ecotourism: A Guide For Planners and Managers*. Ecotourism Society.

Mahler, Richard, and Steele Wotkyns. 1991. *Belize: A Natural Destination*. John Muir Publications.

Max-Neef, Manfred A. 1991. *Human Scale Development: Conception, Application and Further Reflections.* Apex Press.

Mexican Secretariat of Tourism. 2006. Programa Mundo Maya. http://www.sectur.gob.mx.

Michoacán State Government. 2006. Winter in Michoacán. http://www.michoacan.gob.mx.

Ministerio de Economía y Finanzas de Panamá. 2005. Consejo económico nacional—aprobaciones del Jueves, 29 de diciembre de 2005. http://www.mef.gob.pa.

Organización Mundo Maya. 2002. Componentes de la Planeación Ecoturística en el Mundo Maya. Ecotourism Summit, Québec.

Parris, Thomas M. 2005. Searching for environmental justice. *Environment* 47, no. 6: 3.

PROLANSATE. 2006a. Historial de la Fundación PROLANSATE. http://www.prolansate.org.

PROLANSATE. 2006b. Misión de la Organización. http://www.prolansate.org.

Quintero, José de León. 2005. Vía El Lano-Cartí será un paso controlado. *La Prensa*, May 13.

Ramírez-Sáiz, Juan Manuel. 1987. Turismo y medio ambiente: El caso de Acapulco. *Estudios Demográficos y Urbanos* 2: 479–512.

Scherl, Lea M., Alison Wilson, Robert Wild, Jill Blockhus, Phil Franks, Jeffrey A. McNeely, and Thomas O. McShane. 2004. *Can Protected Areas Contribute to Poverty Reduction? Opportunities and Limitations.* IUCN Publications.

Steel, Brent S., Richard L. Clinton, and Nicholas P. Lovrich. 2003. *Environmental Politics and Policy: A Comparative Approach.* McGraw-Hill.

Taylor, Dorcetta E. 2000. The rise of the environmental justice paradigm: Injustice framing and the social construction of environmental discourses. *American Behavioral Scientist* 43, no. 4: 508–580.

Toledo Institute for Development and Environment. 2006. About Tide. http://www.tidebelize.org.

Travel Agent Central America. 1997. A Taste of Honduras. Available on LexisNexis.

Tucker, Catherine M. 2004. Community institutions and forest management in Mexico's Monarch Butterfly Reserve. *Society and Natural Resources* 17: 569–587.

US Environmental Protection Agency. 2006. Definition of environmental justice. http://www.epa.gov.

US Fish and Wildlife Service, Division of International Conservation. 2005. Wildlife Without Borders—Mexico. 2005 Program Statistics and Sample Projects. http://www.fws.gov.

Véliz, Claudio. 1980. *The Centralist Tradition*. Princeton University Press.

Weizsman, Pat. 2001. Case Study: Tourism and Biodiversity (Ecotourism—A Sustainable Development Tool, A Case for Belize). Report prepared for Ministry of Tourism and Youth.

Wolman, Andrew. 2004. Review of conservation payment initiatives in Latin America: conservation concessions, conservation incentive agreements and permit retirement schemes. *William and Mary Environmental Law and Policy Review* 28, spring: 859–883.

WWF (World Wildlife Fund). 2006. The Monarch Butterfly Reserve. http://www.worldwildlife.org.

World Wildlife Fund—México. 2006. Mexican Forests. http://www.wwf.org.

Young, Louise. 2006. Interview by author, January 31.

Zerner, Charles, ed. 1999. Toward a broader vision of justice and nature conservation. In *People, Plants, and Justice*, ed. C. Zerner. Columbia University Press.

9

Environmental Justice and Agricultural Development in the Brazilian *Cerrado*

Wendy Wolford

The environmental justice movement is one of the most important social movements in the United States. Coming out of the struggle for civil rights in the 1950s and the 1960s, the discursive and analytical tools of environmental justice have been productive in both highlighting the complex connections between race, class, and environmental pollution and providing a social movement "frame" (Kurtz 2003) through which local communities are able to protest unfair exposure to environmental harm. Although the definition of environmental justice is debated, and it is variously characterized as a movement (Bullard 1990; Holifield 2001), an analytical concept (Holifield 2001), a policy rubric (Bowen et al. 1995, p. 641), a grassroots political strategy (Towers 2000), and a set of concerns about inequitable environmental risk and impacts on social welfare (Pulido, Sidawi and Vos 1996), it is now widely accepted that inequalities of class and race are tightly interwoven with uneven exposure to environmental risk.

Since the early 1980s, mobilization in pursuit of "environmental justice" has also increased rapidly throughout Brazil, although environmental justice concerns there tend to be less concerned with racial inequalities and more often framed as class-based inequalities that impede the fair distribution of natural resources.[1] With the crumbling of the military dictatorship in the 1980s, Brazilians began to organize to demand both access to resources and the right to participate in decisions over their distribution.[2] Mobilization has been accompanied by (and engendered) growing recognition among politicians and people alike that access to resources is influenced by social class, political connections, local and national forms of racialization, and cultural stereotypes.

In contrast with the United States, where environmental justice issues grew out of urban industrial development, in Brazil environmental justice issues have to be understood as agrarian problems, situated within the country's particular history of rural incorporation and modernization. Shifting the terrain of environmental justice to the Third World, when it has traditionally been firmly grounded in the US context, forces us to acknowledge diverse histories of environmental discrimination: in Brazil, environmental injustices are embedded in the ongoing practices and ideologies of colonial and imperial development that are particularly evident in unequal access to land and concomitant environmental damage. To make this case, I present the case of agricultural development in the Brazilian *cerrado*—the scrub-brush grasslands and forests of the country's Center-West. Literally translated, *cerrado* means "closed," and for centuries, little economic development has taken place in the region. Relative isolation has served to protect the high level of species diversity and endemism that make the region the biologically richest savanna in the world and a valuable ecosystem for preservation and research (Klink, Moreira, and Solbrig 1993; Stedman-Edwards 2000; WWF 2001). Since the 1970s, however, the region has been re-presented as a "wasteland" (Warnken 1999) "cluttered with scrub brush and a few small trees" (Perkins 2002) that ought to be developed for economic purposes. Government policies formulated in the context of a developing global agro-food system have combined to remake the *cerrado* into a leading agro-industrial center. New roads, bio-technology innovations, and government subsidies have encouraged agricultural commodity producers to carve out large-scale farms along rivers and roads, linking the *cerrado* frontier into sophisticated production, marketing and distribution networks world-wide. Soybeans are the major crop in the region, and Brazil has become one of the top two producers and exporters of soy products in the world, even threatening production in the United States. In recent years, farmers from the United States have moved into the *cerrado* frontier along the western edge of the state of Bahia (figure 9.1). Attracted to Brazil by high profit margins, US farmers see themselves as pioneers opening a new, wild frontier much as their ancestors did in the American Midwest. This agricultural "miracle," a yellow gold horizon of "unlimited opportunities" (AgBrazil website, August 6, 2003) necessitates a

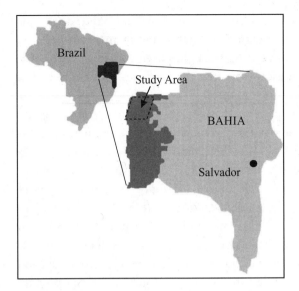

Figure 9.1
Western Bahia.

focus on the political economy of agricultural production within environmental justice. Two aspects of environmental injustice are evident in this case: distributional inequity and procedural inequity (Holifield 2001, pp. 80–81; Lake 1996).[3] "Distributional inequity" refers simply to the concentration of resources in the hands of an elite minority, whereas procedural inequity refers to the process by which inequalities are constituted and naturalized. In this chapter, I argue that both forms of inequity are present in the *cerrado*, and that they were constituted—and are maintained—through political support for large-scale, modernized agriculture producing commodities for the export market. There is a popular, even hegemonic, belief in scholarly and popular work on the *cerrado* that development occurred as it did because the ecological imperatives of the region combined with the inherent economies of scale in agricultural production to favor large-scale production (Resende 2001; EMBRAPA personnel, personal communications). Average farm size in the region is 448 hectares, more than six times the national average of 73 hectares (cited in Helfand 2003). A company based in the United States that brokers property deals for US farmers in the *cerrado* reports enthusiastically that soybean farms in western Bahia, at the edge of the *cerrado*, are typically more than 5,000 acres, and many exceed 62,000 acres. Philip Warnken, CEO of AgBrazil, has been quoted as saying that "few houses dot the landscape because the farms are so vast" (cited in Perkins 2002).

Cerrado farmers, newspaper journalists, policymakers, and academics argue that large-scale agricultural production is a natural response— indeed, the only response—to the "natural" characteristics of the *cerrado*'s environment, particularly its infertile soil that requires intensive treatment prior to planting and its flat topography that facilitates mechanization. This naturalization of large-scale production works to erase deliberate political work done at the national and international levels to promote and support large-scale, modern producers. Government policies formulated in the context of a developing global agro-food system were critical in forging the character of agro-industrial production in the *cerrado*. Public policies designed to foster agricultural productivity focused on large farms while smallholders and the rural poor were seen as sources of cheap labor and territorial colonization. At the same time, geo-political concerns over soybean market supplies pushed international research agencies and development banks to invest in the Brazilian *cerrado*: this international attention occurred in the context of the so-called Green Revolution and facilitated the adoption of input-intensive modern agriculture in the region. This deliberate work at the level of the nation-state and the world food system underlies the procedural inequities that have turned Brazil's "breadbasket" into privileged ground for a minority of agricultural producers and simultaneously threatened the ecological sustainability of production in the region.

In applying an environmental justice perspective to the problematic of agricultural development in the Brazilian *cerrado*, I argue that we are better equipped to understand the relationship between social justice, agricultural production and environmental degradation in the region. This analysis helps to explain how nature is reconstituted through productive means as a "resource" in ways that compromise the ecological and social integrity of whole regions, how elite privilege manifests itself not as intentional actions but as structural conditions for the perpetuation of destructive actions, why US farmers have been moving to the *cerrado* and planting soybeans, and why social justice claims to land distribution in regions far from the *cerrado* (e.g. in the South of Brazil) are simultaneously critiques of agro-industrial development and environmental degradation in the *cerrado*.

Environmental problems and social justice problems tend to be conceived of as "local," but they must be analyzed at the regional, national, and international levels in order to expose the material and political conditions through which they are constituted. Environmental justice claims in the United States tend to be community-oriented claims for equal access to resources and freedom from environmental risk. Beyond a transition from "not in my back yard" to environmental justice, their attention to scale tends to focus on the strategic construction of claims at various scales at the expense of thinking about the scalar and even spatial construction of the problems. Williams (1999) echoes this analysis, suggesting that the market-based explanations of environmental inequities mask a range of structural processes fostering environmental inequality, and "ignore, even de-legitimize the extra-local scales implicated in the creation of the problems" (cited in Kurtz 2003, p. 890).

In this chapter, I describe the development of the *cerrado* within the context of both the nation-state and the world food system. I then explain why this is an environmental justice problem. I see this chapter as an initial attempt to incorporate environmental justice concerns into the analysis of international agricultural development.

The Development of the Brazilian *Cerrado*

The *cerrado* lies within the center-west region of Brazil, and according to the Brazilian Agricultural Research Company (EMBRAPA), occupies approximately 204 million hectares, or 25 percent of Brazil's land area, making it the second largest of Brazil's major biomes after the Amazon basin and the most extensive woodland/savanna region in South America.[4]

The *cerrado* has a tropical climate with two distinct seasons, humid and dry. Average rainfall throughout the region is 1,500 millimeters per year, most of which falls between October and April. *Cerrado* vegetation is varied, with a mixture of grasslands and forested areas depending on soil conditions and water availability. In general, the soils of the *cerrado* are relatively toxic due to high concentrations of aluminum. The more fertile soils with regular supplies of water tend to support the denser woody vegetation while open grasslands signify less fertile growing conditions (Stedman-Edwards 2000). The topography of the *cerrado* ranges from very flat plateau to lightly rolling hills.

Low population density and limited economic development have until recently helped to maintain the integrity of the rich *cerrado* ecosystem. Researchers with the World Wildlife Fund (WWF) estimate that the *cerrado* is host to more than 4,400 endemic plant species and 117 endemic terrestrial vertebrate species. In addition, 25 percent of all Brazilian bird species can be found in the *cerrado*, 16 percent of which are believed to be endemic (Stedman-Edwards 2000). Due to the expansion of large-scale agriculture, however, habitats for many endemic species, such as jaguar, giant anteater, giant armadillo and maned wolves, are severely reduced. In 1998, Norman Myers listed the *cerrado* as one of the world's 25 "biodiversity hotspots," characterized by a high rate of endemism and low percentage of pristine vegetation.[5] Today, it is estimated that 40 percent of the *cerrado*'s original vegetation has been destroyed while another 40 percent has been degraded.

Agro-Food Development and Environmental Injustice in the Brazilian Cerrado

The *cerrado* is the face of Brazil. Overcrowded cities, slums, fields razed by machines and peopled by cows, soy, fences. Idealized as the breadbasket that would alleviate our poverty, the *cerrado* has converted itself into a grand exporter of living things.
—Marcel Bursztyn, preface to *Dilemas do Cerrado*

Investment opportunities in Brazil's *cerrado* stagger the imagination.
—Philip Warnken, CEO of AgBrazil

The *cerrado* was first targeted for development in the 1960s. Government plans for colonization and agricultural production in the region grew out of populist mobilization for land reform during the preceding decade. Demonstrations and social mobilization characterized the democratic window in national politics from 1946 to 1964: activists with the Catholic Church organized aggressive campaigns for agrarian reform, ex-communist party activists oversaw the formation of rural trade unions, and by 1964 more than 2,000 so-called Peasant Leagues had formed with the official goal of pursuing land distribution, na lei ou na marra (by law or by force) (Medeiros 1989).

Increasing popular-sector organization for land redistribution did not sit well with the powerful agrarian elite, especially as fear of a communist uprising rooted in the rural areas spilled over from the Cuban Revolution (Page 1972). On March 21, 1964, armored tanks rolled into Rio de Janeiro after President Goulart announced a radical agrarian reform, and the military seized control of government, which they would maintain for twenty-one years. Administrative technocrats within the military government soon crafted a new plan for rural development that capitalized on, rather than restructured, inequality in the countryside.

The military favored the development of large-scale industrial agriculture because exports would generate the foreign currency needed to carry out an ambitious industrial development plan (Martins 1981). Government technocrats generally agreed that agricultural modernization had to accompany industrial modernization as had happened in the more developed countries of Europe and North America. According to José de Souza Martins, "five months after the coup . . . the North American representative for the Alliance for Progress, Walt Rostow, was in São Paulo speaking animatedly with industrialists about the issue of the internal market. [He emphasized] that the industrialists should take an interest in transforming and modernizing their agriculture." (Martins 1981, p. 94)

Referred to as "conservative modernization" because it did not progressively modify the land tenure structure, the military increased inequality by providing fiscal incentives for producers who were already tied into agro-industrial input and output markets. In 1965, the government created the Sistema Nacional de Credito Rural and the distribution of credit for agricultural production increased five times in real terms between 1968 and 1978 (Goodman, Sorj, and Wilkinson 1984, p. 198). Between 1973 and 1983, high inflation rates meant that this credit actually earned a negative rate of interest. These direct and indirect production subsidies favored large-scale producers of export crops, including corn and soy (Graziano da Silva 1982; Delgado 1985). One study estimated that more than half the formal credit distributed between 1975 and 1982 went to just 3 to 4 percent of all farms (Graham et al. 1987, cited in Helfand 1999, p. 7). In Mato Grosso, the heart of the *cerrado*, agricultural producers who owned more than 10,000 hectares of land (roughly 25,000 acres) constituted only 1.88 percent of all agricultural establishments in the state, but five years after the creation of the SNCR (in 1970), these establishments were receiving 44.74 percent of all the credit disbursed to agricultural producers in the state (EMBRAPA-IBGE 1979, p. 279).[6]

Development policies constructed during the 1970s specifically targeted the *cerrado* for agricultural expansion. The Amazonian frontier was expected to absorb rural migrants who pushed for access to land, while the *cerrado* frontier would be made accessible to large farmers with the capital to engage in international commodity production. In the First National Development Plan (PND), covering the period 1972–1974, a series of measures were delineated to "give Brazilian agriculture a system of fiscal and credit support, capable of producing a technological transformation and accelerated strengthening of market agriculture, sensitive to the stimulus of prices; achieve an expansion of area, principally through the occupation of empty spaces, in the Center West (the *cerrado*), the North and in the humid valleys of the Northeast" (Executive Office, 1970, quoted in Stepman-Edwards 2000, p. 12).

The second National Development Plan (1975–1979) included a more specific set of policies called POLOCENTRO, which had three main objectives: to expand agriculture to the frontier regions, specialize for global markets, and advance the scientific and technological basis of agricultural production in order to stimulate development. Originally, the plans for POLOCENTRO included the promotion of basic food crops (Klink and Moreira 2002, p. 77) and in the 1960s, research scientists recommended that a variety of subsistence crops be planted in the region to protect local soil conditions (Recuperação 1964, pp. 148–150). After the mid 1960s, however, the military government implemented an agro-industrial modernization program in the *cerrados* that turned away from subsistence production and focused primarily on industrialized commodity crops, particularly soy, rice, and cotton.

Twelve "poles" in the *cerrado* were selected that had access to basic infrastructure such as passable roads and electricity as well as superior potential for agricultural growth (Klink n.d.). Highly experienced and capitalized farmers from around the country (and later, specifically from southern Brazil) were offered generous credit terms to buy land and finance investment in the region. Between 1970 and 1990, the average volume of public credit offered came to more than 40 percent of the production value of soybeans in the region (Warnken 1999, p. 68), and it favored large-scale producers: between 1975 and 1982, 3,373 projects were approved, 81 percent of which involved farms greater than 200 hectares (Klink and Moreira 2002, pp. 76–77). Almost 40 percent of the projects involved farms that were greater than 1,000 hectares, and these farms received a majority (60 percent) of the credit distributed. Approximately 2.5 million hectares of land were brought into development through Polocentro, and soybean coverage increased by more than 600 percent (Warnken 1999, p. 77).

Competitive agricultural production in the *cerrado* could not take place, however, until the place itself had been properly "produced" (Cunha 1994). Neither the Brazilian government nor the farmers who would colonize the region were interested in working with indigenous products or practices (Luchiezi n.d.). The intention from the beginning was to re-shape the existing ecosystem to accommodate products and practices from outside the region. In order to do this, a tropical soybean seed had to be developed. Most of the genetic material available in Brazil at that time came from the United States where soy was produced in temperate climates, and these varieties did not do well in tropical conditions. In 1976, EMBRAPA began working with new breeding programs to develop soybean cultivars suitable to the *cerrado*. Researchers from the United States collaborated with Brazilians in their efforts, and most of the research on new soybean seeds was done at or in conjunction with researchers from the Experimental Station at Stoneville, Mississippi, a US Department of Agriculture facility. By the late 1970s, a seed variety had been found that produced as well in tropical regions as traditional seed varieties did in the temperate regions.

In addition to new seeds, adequate soil also had to be found in the *cerrado*. Only seven percent of the land in the *cerrado* is considered naturally fertile. The rest is highly acidic due to the presence of aluminum. Applications of fertilizer with high quantities of limestone and water transform the area into fertile land. As the Brazilian agronomist Carlos Roberto Spehar said, "with today's technology, anyone can make soil."[7] The desire for continual soil "correction" means that input costs constitutes the largest portion of the capital required to turn one hectare of savanna land into agricultural land. One study estimates that 25 percent of the capital required to make good land out of the savanna went to the cost of land, while approximately 42.5 percent went to the purchase and application of inputs, and 17.5 percent went to the cost of opening the area for production (Goedert 1990, cited in Rezende 2002, p. 16).

Through the development of new seeds and intensive application of inputs, abundant land in the *cerrado* was created specifically for the production of agro-industrial commodities, particularly soy, rice, and cotton. In 1970, the total agricultural area was estimated to be approximately 55,000 hectares, 9,000 of which were planted at that time. In 1995–96, the total agricultural area was estimated to be approximately 75,000 hectares, 50,000 of which were planted (figures from IBGE/ Censo Agropecuario, cited in Rezende 2001, p. 2). This production of land is what makes the *cerrado* a viable economic frontier. According to one of the most important plant biologists behind the first Green Revolution, Dr. Norman Borlaug, the application of science to the *cerrado* has produced "the world's most important agricultural expansion zone for this century" (cited in Landers 2001).

Eager to encourage export production, the Brazilian government has placed few effective restrictions on the use of land or water resources. Although the *cerrado* is considered one of the most important environmental regions in South America, less than two percent of the total area was under governmental protection in 2002. Unlike the Amazon rain forest, the *cerrado* was not included for federal protection in the 1988 Constitution, and the most important environmental regulation in the region is still Brazil's Forest Code (Law No. 4.771/65), first established in 1965. The Forest Code states that landholders must set aside 20 percent of their property to maintain the original vegetation and wildlife as well as preserving certain strips of land along rivers, lakes, and natural waterways.

Until 2000, the *cerrado* area that bordered the Amazon rain forest was subject to a 50 percent legal reserve regulation, but this was lowered to 35 percent as a concession to farmers after a bitter debate with environmentalists forced the government to abandon attempts to lower the legal reserve in the Amazon from 80 percent to 50 percent (Abramovay 2000). Even with the reduction in legal reserve areas, the Forest Code is not strictly enforced in the *cerrado*. One study (Grote, Deblitz, and Stegmann 2001) estimated that if Brazil's Forest Code were actually implemented in the *cerrado*, production costs would increase by 23 percent for 500-hectare farms and by 19 percent for 1,000-hectare farms. The lack of regulation is a temporary asset for producers and further encourages large-scale, intensive, farming.[8]

Large-scale soybean production in the *cerrado* is also encouraged by low land and labor costs. In 2002, land prices in the *cerrado* were on average as much as nine times lower than in the US Corn Belt. This is one of the main reasons why soy production in the *cerrado* is competitive with other, more established grain-producing regions. (See table 9.1.) Land prices are cheaper in the *cerrado* than anywhere else in Brazil. The low cost of land is an additional incentive for large-scale production in the region (Rezende 2001). Even though production methods are very

Table 9.1
Soybean production costs ($US per hectare) in United States and Brazil. Source: Hirsch et al. 2001.

	US	Brazil
Variable costs[a]	239.7	267.4
Fixed costs	271.8	81.7
Labor	81.5	9.7
Interest rate on investment	69.2	7.7
Land	286.6	37.2
Total	798.1	386.2

a. Including seed, fertilizer, chemicals, and machine operation and repair.

similar in the United States and Brazil, the cost of land in the *cerrado* encourages farmers who move from the United States to Brazil to buy larger plots than the ones they leave behind. In 2001, the average size of a soy-producing farm in the central-*cerrado* state of Mato Grosso was more than 1,000 hectares as compared to 120–150 hectares in the US Corn Belt (Rezende 2001, p. 7). For those who have the capacity and education to engage in large-scale commodity production for export, Brazil is a country with seemingly unlimited land. At the same time, wages in the region are very low. According to one report (Luchiezi n.d.), wages for tractor drivers averaged 78 cents an hour, while common laborers received 50 cents an hour. Managers were relatively well paid at $1.40 an hour. Wages are low in part because of high competition. Although poor Brazilians have flocked to the *cerrado* in recent years, setting up shantytowns and hoping for employment in agricultural areas, few opportunities are to be found. Large-scale, mechanized farms require little labor: one study found that from 1970 to 1985, the number of workers per 100 hectares of land decreased from seven to four (WWF, cited in CEBRAC 2000).[9] Even though the *cerrado* is considered an agricultural frontier and the primary economic activities of the region are related to cattle ranching and soybean production, a higher percentage of the population (approximately 90 percent) lives in cities than any other region of the country, including the highly industrialized and urbanized South and Southeast (Hogan, Cunha, and Carmo 2001).

If the popular demand for land distribution had been realized in the 1960s or if the military government had provided incentives and infrastructure for rural resettlement and supported small-scale cultivation of products for the domestic market, however, large farms would have had little "natural" advantage over small farms in the *cerrado*. Many studies have shown existence of an inverse relationship between farm size and productivity in agriculture (Carter 1984). A recent paper by Stephen Helfand (2003) argues that access to credit, electricity and technical assistance had a greater impact on efficiency than farm size for grain producers in the *cerrado*. Helfand argues that if these public goods were provided to small farmers "an inverse relationship (between farm size and efficiency) could prevail in the Center-West of Brazil even up to about 1,000 [hectares]" (2003, p. 12).

The Political Economy of Agro-Food Development in Brazil

The rapid development of Brazil's soybean industry has to be understood in the context of the world agro-food system after the mid 1940s (Friedmann and McMichael 1989). Brazil has, of course, always been integrated into the global economy through its agricultural production. The first lucrative commodity to be produced was sugarcane in the early 1500s and since then, a majority of Brazil's gross national product has derived from the export of relatively few agricultural or natural resource commodities, including sugarcane, coffee, rubber, cacao, and cotton. In the early 1900s, revenue from coffee production facilitated and encouraged localized industrialization within Brazil, primarily in the state of São Paulo (Dean 1969).

After World War II, however, Brazil became much more tightly integrated into a modern agro-industrial system dominated by the United States (Müller 1985). It was then that modern agricultural production methods and technologies developed in the United States and Europe (the Green Revolution) were disseminated throughout the rest of the world. Without such methods and technologies, intensive grain production in the *cerrado* would not have been possible. Brazilian producers were exposed to Green Revolution technologies through cross-country collaborative efforts. Brazilian farmers traveled to the United States, going to the World Fair in Chicago and then on agricultural tours around the Midwest to learn about mechanization, chemical inputs, direct planting, and computerized organization. Agricultural extension agents with the US Agency for International Development (USAID) worked to promote agricultural development in Brazil. USAID contributed approximately $40 million to support the work of Pedro Sanchez who won the World Food Prize in 2002. A research scientist at North Carolina State University, Sanchez led the campaign to "turn the acidic, tropical soils of the *cerrado* region of Brazil into 75 million acres of productive farmland" (press release, University of California at Berkeley, August 12, 2002). Although Pedro Sanchez is praised for "restoring soil fertility using naturally available resources [that] have dramatically increased crop yields for hundreds of thousands of small farmers from Brazil to Africa" (ibid.), in the *cerrado* natural resources have been manipulated to favor large, highly capitalized farmers.

Channeled through an aid agency, US interest in Brazilian agriculture reflected agro-industry's concern for the development of input consumption markets. Agriculture Research Science National Program Leader for International Programs Rick Bennett put it this way: "If Brazil is going to be buying millions of dollars of our agricultural products and technology, wouldn't it be a good idea to involve their scientists in defining joint problems and finding solutions that can help us both?" (ARS/USDA May 2000). In 1973, the Brazilian Agricultural Research Enterprise (EMBRAPA) was created as a liaison between government, scientists, and agricultural producers, and throughout the 1970s, a majority of the organization's personnel were trained in the United States (Warnken 1999, p. 45). For large farmers who have access to financial resources, the frontier region of the *cerrado* is intimately connected to global export and input markets. The main suppliers of chemical inputs, seeds, irrigation equipment, tractors, and extension advice are multinational corporations primarily based in the United States. As one US farmer said, "if they've got it in the US, we've got it here" (cited in Romero 2002). Two companies that have played significant roles in the spread of agricultural technology and products to Brazil, Ceval (owned and operated by the Dutch company, Bunge) and US-based Cargill, dominate input, processing and distribution markets in western Bahia. The main soybean crushing plant located in the area, operated by Ceval, is the largest in all of South America and controls approximately 75 percent of the soybean market in the *cerrado*.

The development of a competitive grain sector was also due in part to Brazil's desire to foster national wheat production and reduce its dependence on food aid from the United States. In 1954, the US passed the Agricultural Trade Development and Assistance Act (known as "Food For Peace" or Public Law 480), which subsidized grain exports to developing countries as a way of supporting domestic agricultural production and providing foreign assistance. By producing wheat at home with American-led methods, the Brazilian state took advantage of modern technologies being developed in the industrial core countries and built its own highly advanced agro-industrial infrastructure. The production of wheat, a winter crop, stimulated the rise of soybeans, which could be grown on the same field in the summer.[10]

The international economy provided a further impetus to soybean production in the 1970s when Soviet grain purchases depleted US soy stocks, raising world prices and leading to a temporary embargo of soybean exports from the United States (Friedmann and McMichael 1989; Yokota 1997). The embargo affected consumers in Asia and Western Europe who depended on US supplies, and they actively sought out new sources in Brazil. Japan was particularly aggressive in securing new suppliers: in 1974, Japan agreed to provide financing through the Japanese International Cooperation Agency (JICA) to develop soybean production in the *cerrado*. The first phase of the joint Japan-Brazil project (1979–1982) was called PRODECER I (Programa Nipo-Brasileiro de Desenvolvimento do Cerrado). JICA provided roughly US$50 million to clear 70,000 hectares in Minas Gerais and settle 92 "experienced" farming families in three colonization areas to plant primarily corn, soy, and wheat (Osada, n.d. 1; Klink and Moreira 2002, p. 77). In 1985, PRODECER II covered 200,000 hectares with a Japanese investment of approximately US$350 million. These bi-lateral projects were crucial in establishing the high levels of productivity in the *cerrado* today.

The World System in Brazil: US Farmers Move to the *Cerrado*

In recent years, farmers from the United States have moved into the *cerrado* frontier along the western edge of the state of Bahia (figure 9.1). Attracted to Brazil by high profit margins, US farmers see themselves as pioneers opening a new, wild frontier, much as their ancestors did in the American Midwest.

US farmers moving to the region highlight the productive work that uneven development does for the expansion of markets and expropriation of profit (Smith 1990). Uneven development between Brazil and the United States means that US farmers are able to take advantage of low land, labor, and environmental prices even as they utilize the most sophisticated technologies and vertically integrated enterprise networks (maintained by corporations such as Cargill and Bunge). They are able to buy large plots of land with little concern for government intervention over use of the property. Eager to encourage export production, the Brazilian government has placed few effective restrictions on the use of land or water resources. As US farmers feel increasingly burdened by environmental legislation in the United States, they have made new homes and farms in the Brazilian *cerrado*.

A farmer from Iowa who bought more than 7,000 acres as a way of allowing his son to continue the family tradition of farming said: "Expanding in Iowa would have cost much more. . . . My ancestors left Scotland when things looked better in Iowa, maybe the same thing is true for Brazil now." (cited in Perkins 2002) A farmer from Mississippi said: "My family came here to the Delta in the 1830s. . . . Now maybe it's my turn to be a pioneer and open up some new land." (cited in Phillips n.d.) David Kruse, an entrepreneur who established a land-access company in Brazil, said: "Brazil is where we're going to expand Iowa." (cited in Perkins 2002) Although the Brazilian frontier evokes images of wildness, these farmers are willing to brave the difficulties in return for agricultural opportunity. "Before I went down there," one farmer said, "I thought they were a bunch of hicks farming the rain forest and fighting off monkeys, but there have been enough people go down there who've seen it and recognize the potential like I do." (cited in Perkins 2002) Such farmers are seen as bringing the values of the US frontier to Brazil. As Philip Warnken said, "It's like getting a chance to open the Midwest to farming again." And the Brazilian financial magazine, ISTOÉ Dinheiro commented on January 20, 2003:

In the raw countryside of the Brazilian *cerrado*, different faces, blond and sunburnt, are beginning to call attention. They hardly speak Portuguese, but they know exactly what that land has to offer. A legion of American farmers is setting foot in the so-called agricultural frontier, the little-exploited area that sits in the region between Goiás and Bahia. There, they have one objective: to plant soy, that yellow grain that is synonymous with gold for the farmers. Just like their ancestors, who colonized the American Midwest in the nineteenth century, these men are looking for land and opportunity.[11]

In recent years, the unregulated nature of the frontier has had increasing appeal for farmers facing rising land costs and growing environmental regulation in the United States. A farmer from Mississippi said of his recent inquiries into land ownership in Brazil: "Here we're just hanging on. . . . It would be a bit of an adventure, but I think we're up to it. We're looking for an opportunity to make money and maintain a farming life, even if it's in Brazil." (cited in Thompson 2000) Land in the United States is subject to high opportunity costs as a result of competing development interests. Farmland prices are dictated less by the quality of land than by the alternative uses possible. As strip malls, suburbs, and six-lane highways cut into the countryside, it has become difficult for family farmers to remain on the land. Between 1990 and 1998, the average value of farm real estate in the US Corn Belt increased from US$1,111 per acre to US$1,869 per acre.[12] During that same period, the value of farm real estate in the 48 contiguous states increased from US$737 per acre to US$1,000 per acre.

On the Brazilian frontier, however, land prices are low—in 2002, land prices in the *cerrado* were on average as much as nine times lower than in the US Corn Belt. This is one of the main reasons why soy production in the *cerrado* is competitive with other, more established grain-producing regions. (See table 9.1.)

But US farmers are not simply attracted by the low cost of land. Soybean producers moving to Brazil are also attracted by the "complete absence of public regulation on [things like] well drilling" (from the AgBrazil website). Since the beginning of the international environmental movement in the 1970s and the creation of the US Environmental Protection Agency in 1970, there has been increasing awareness of the environmental degradation associated with large-scale intensive farming, and regulations on land and water use have been created to try and protect both private and public property in the country.[13] Much of the concern surrounding high-input intensive farming has been for water sustainability. Farming methods in western Bahia are sophisticated and highly mechanized, as can be seen by the high rate of adoption of pivot irrigation methods, which can be clearly identified in the Landsat images (figure 9.2). Each of the circles is a pivot irrigation field. From 1990 to 2002, pivot irrigation expanded rapidly on large farms in the study area.

Preventive measures like the 1985 Conservation Reserve Program, which provides government funds for farmers who protect fragile farmland by diverting production and planting soil-saving grasses, indirectly increase the cost of land and ultimately raise the cost of agricultural production. Many farmers feel unjustly persecuted by the focus on environmental preservation. As one farmer from Mississippi commented:

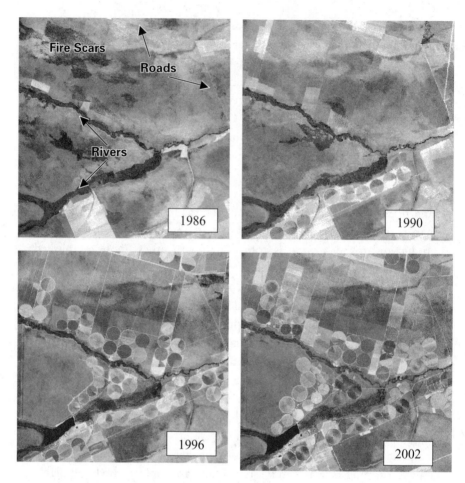

Figure 9.2
Agricultural expansion and pivot irrigation in the raw remotely sensed images
in the area within the bottom blue box (about 20 × 20 km) in figure 9.1. Landsat
images are displayed with RGB = 453. Each of the circles is a pivot irrigation
field. Pivot irrigation agriculture has been expanding rapidly in the study area,
particularly between 1990 and 2002.

"Everything down there is growing; here rural areas are dying" (cited in Thompson 2002). Steven Blank, an economist at the University of California at Davis and the author of *The End of Agriculture in the American Portfolio* (1998), even argues that American "commodity farming is slowly disappearing" because of high production costs he directly attributes to environmental and food regulations.

The perception of relatively strict environmental restrictions in the United States has pushed agriculture and industry alike to find new, less restrictive, areas for production. Legislations regulating livestock production in the United States, for example, are considered a primary driver of forest burning and cutting in the Brazilian *cerrado* (Knight 2002). In a telling comment, the CEO of AgBrazil said: "As the farm bill was being debated and there were attempts to limit program payments for cotton and rice operations, I was getting several dozen calls a day from that part of the country." (cited in Thompson 2002)

Conclusion

For those who have the capacity and education to engage in large-scale commodity production for export, Brazil is a country with seemingly unlimited land. In 2002, EMBRAPA estimated that 61 million of the 204 million hectares that make up the *cerrado* were currently under use, leaving an estimated 66 million hectares available for productive incorporation.[14] For those without the financial or vocational means, Brazil is a country with little available land. In 2002, an estimated 4 million rural families were considered "landless" because they could not afford to buy land or were being squeezed onto insufficient properties. Since 1985, Brazil has been home to the largest grassroots agrarian reform movement in Latin America: the Movimento dos Trabalhadores Rurais Sem Terra (meaning Movement of Landless Rural Workers, and abbreviated MST), whose members organize collective acts of disruption to fight for land distribution. The co-existence of modern export farmers and impoverished landless workers is indicative of Brazil's uneven development trajectory, now playing itself out—and being reinforced—on the *cerrado* frontier. This distributional inequity is intimately tied to an agro-industrial model of production and to serious environmental degradation in Brazil's most sensitive ecosystems. The social movements that have arisen to combat environmental injustices are importantly peasant movements articulating an agrarian populism similar to the populism of the early-twentieth-century United States. At its most general level, the alternative articulated by the MST includes a critique of unequal land tenure relations; a campaign to get back to the land; a desire to re-embed the economy in local (and usually traditional) communities or connections; and the practice of sustainable (also conceived of as traditional) agriculture. Movement leaders argue for land distribution as an economic, social and environmental project. Land reform is economic because it will distribute assets and create growth with equity. It is a social project because it will include the population that has been consistently excluded from development in Brazil: the rural poor. Finally, land reform is an environmental project because movement activists and members argue that small farmers are the natural caretakers of the land and capable of tending to it in a way that will promote environmental health, food security, and national sovereignty. The MST has only recently begun to actively organize in the western region of Bahia, but from its inception, it has critiqued the model of agro-industrial production that led to the *cerrado*'s development.

The environmental justice problem in the *cerrado* is one in which wealthy large-scale farmers have access to land and—whether intentionally or not—their presence furthers environmental degradation in the region. Extractive activities in the *cerrado* raise serious environmental concerns about soil degradation, water contamination, increased CO_2 emissions, and loss of biodiversity. Soil degradation and water contamination are commonly associated with large-scale modern agriculture, but there is added danger in the *cerrado* due to the level of intervention required to transform the soil into productive land. Water resources are also likely to be affected by the dependence on irrigation during the *cerrado*'s dry winter season. Sophisticated irrigation technologies, such as the central pivot systems, draw water from the underground aquifer and drain into the "spinal cord of Brazil's hydrographic system," consisting of the country's three main river basins: the Amazon, the São Francisco, and the Tocantins.

Various non-governmental organizations have responded to these questions about environmental and economic sustainability in the *cerrado* with suggestions for alternative products and production practices that might draw from—rather than suppressing—the ecosystem's natural qualities. Native plants could be cultivated for sale locally and internationally (Abramovay 2000), and small farmers could be brought in to produce a diversified set of crops using more ecologically sustainable methods. These might be ways to preserve the "genetic banks" still to be discovered in the *cerrado* ecosystem while promoting economic development (CEBRAP 2000). But these policy changes will be difficult because production in the *cerrado* reflects (and reproduces) the dualisms that have characterized Brazilian national development since early colonization. The most recent frontier to be colonized, development in the *cerrado* both reflects and reproduces the elite privilege constructed through agrarian capitalism in Brazil.

Notes

1. The idea of a racial democracy was first conceptualized by Gilberto Freyre in the 1930s. It was complicated by subsequent scholarship on slave-owner relations and then rejected after considerable work on Brazilian social relations, but the myth is a pervasive one, and many Brazilians argue that national inequalities are economic and not racially motivated. This is a subject on which there is a considerable literature and much remains to be explored. In this chapter, however, I work with a class-based notion of rightful access to natural resources.

2. There are too many sources on the subject of social mobilization and "actually existing democracy" to cite all of them, but for excellent edited collections on "new" social movements, poor people's politics, and environmentalism in Latin America, see Alvarez and Escobar 1992; Fox and Starn 1997; Eckstein and Wickham-Crowley 2002.

3. Susan Cutter has also referred to this distinction of outcome versus process (Cutter and Holm 1996).

4. One hectare is equal to 2.47 acres.

5. According to the WWF, plant diversity is the biological basis for hotspot designation. See http://www.biodiversityhotspots.org.

6. The inverse was also true: Agricultural establishments with less than 10 hectares constituted 44.0% of all establishments in the state in 1970, but collected only 1.50% of all the public credit disbursed.

7. Cited in Minnesota IssueWatch, January 2003 (http://www.mnplan.state.mn.us).

8. In 1993, the Dutch government was considering transferring 100–150 Dutch hog farming families to the state of Mato Grosso because environmental concerns made hog production increasingly politically and economically impossible in Holland (Stedman-Edwards 2000).

9. The report is available at http://www.worldwideconsulting.org.

10. The production of wheat and soy, in turn, facilitated the development of poultry and companies located in southern Brazil that came to dominate the new field of vertically integrated agro-industrial complexes (Mueller 1985), capturing activities from fertilizer production to feed planting and mixing to livestock processing, packaging, and marketing.

11. See the clipping from ISTOÉ at http://www.mre.gov.br.

12. Figures released March 17,1998, by the National Agricultural Statistics Service (NASS), Agricultural Statistics Board, US Department of Agriculture.

13. Rachel Caron's *Silent Spring* (1962), an indictment of chemically intensive agricultural production in the United States is considered one of the seminal statements of the rising environmental sentiment in the 1970s.

14. 77 million hectares are considered inappropriate for agricultural production.

References

Abramovay, Ricardo. 2000. Preservar para Lucrar com os Cerrados. Gazeta Mercantil, May 22.

Alvarez, Sonia, and Arturo Escobar, eds. 1992.*The Making of Latin American Social Movements in Latin America*. Westview.1

Blank, Stephen. 1998. *The End of Agriculture in the American Portfolio*. Quorum.

Bowen, William M. Mark J. Salling, Kingsley E. Haynes, and Ellen J. Cyran. 1995. Toward Environmental Justice: Spatial Equity in Ohio and Cleveland. *Annals of the Association of American Geographers* 85, no. 4: 641–663.

Bullard, Robert, ed. 1990. *Dumping in Dixie: Race, Class and Environmental Quality*. Westview.

Carter, Michael. 1984. Identification of the inverse relationship between farm size and productivity: An empirical analysis of peasant agriculture production. *Oxford Economic Papers* 36: 131–145.

Cunha, Aércio. 1994. *Uma Avaliação da Sustentabilidade da Agricultura nos Cerrados*. IPEA.

Cutter, Susan, Lloyd Clark, and Danika Holm. 1996. The role of geographic scale in monitoring environmental justice. *Risk Analysis* 16, no. 4: 517–526.

CEBRAC (Fundação Centro Brasileiro de Referência e Apoio Cultural). 2000. Analysis of the Environmental Impact Study (EIA/RIMA) for the Araguaia-Tocantins Hidrovia Project.

Dean, Warren. 1969. *The Industrialization of São Paulo, 1880–1945*. University of Texas Press.

Delgado, Guilherme. 1985. Capital Financeiro e Agricultura no Brasil: 1965–1985. Editora UNICAMP.

Eckstein, Susana Eva, and Timothy Wickham-Crowley, eds. 2002.*What Justice, Whose Justice?* University of California Press.

Fox, Richard, and Orin Starn, eds. 1997 *Between Resistance and Revolution*. Rutgers University Press.

Friedmann, Harriett, and Phillip McMichael. 1989. Agriculture and the state system: The rise and decline of national agricultures, 1870 to the present. *Sociologia Ruralis* 29, no. 2: 93–117.

Goodman, David, Bernardo Sorj, and John Wilkinson. 1984. Agro-industry, state policy and rural social structures: Recent analyses of proletarianizastion in Brazilian agriculture. In *Proletarianisation in the Third World*, ed. B. Munslow and M. Finch. Croom Helm.

Graziano da Silva, José. 1982. A Modernização Dolorosa: Estrutura Agrária, Fronteira Agrícola e Trabalhadores Rurais no Brasil. Zahar Editores.

Grote, Ulrike, Claus Deblitz, and Susanne Stegmann. 2001. International trade in agricultural products: The impact of environmental standards on costs and competitiveness. Prepared for 77th EAAE Seminar/NJF Seminar No. 325, Helsinki.

Helfand, Stephen. 1999. The political economy of agricultural policy in Brazil: Decision making and influence from 1964 to 1992. *Latin American Research Review* 34, no. 2: 3–41.

Helfand, Stephen. 2003. Farm size and the determinants of technical efficiency in the Brazilian center-west. Presented at IX NEMESIS Conference, IPEA, Rio de Janeiro.

Hogan, Daniel J., José Marcos Pinto da Cunha, and Roberto Luiz do Carmo. 2001. Population distribution and environmental change in Brazil's center-west region. Population Studies Center, State University of Campinas, São Paulo.

Holifield, Ryan. 2001. Defining environmental justice and environmental racism. *Urban Geography* 22, no. 1: 78–90.

Klink, Carlos. n.d. The *Cerrado* Loses Ground. brazilnetwork.org.

Klink, Carlos, and Adriana G. Moreira. 2002. Past and current human occupation and land use. In *The Cerrados of Brazil*, ed. P. Oliveira and R. Marquis. Columbia University Press.

Klink, Carlos, Adriana G. Moreira, and Otto Solbrig. 1993. Ecological impact of agricultural development in the Brazilian *Cerrado*. In *The World's Savannas*, ed. M. Young and O. Solbrig. UNESCO and Parthenon.

Knight, Bruce, I. 2002. Address to the USDA Symposium on Natural Resource Management to Offset Greenhouse Gasses, Raleigh.

Kurtz, Hilda. 2003. Scale frames and counter-scale frames: constructing the problem of environmental injustice. *Political Geography* 22, no. 8: 887–916.

Landers, John. 2001. Zero Tillage Development in Tropical Brazil: The Story of a Successful NGO Activity. Bulletin 147, FAO Agricultural Services.

Luchiezi, Álvaro, Jr. n.d. Repercussões Ambientais da Expansão da Soja no *Cerrado* e seus Vínculos com a Liberalização do Comércio e a Política Macro-econômica Brasileira. Paper prepared for Fundo Mundial para a Natureza, World Wildlife Fund.

Martins, José de Souza. 1981. Os Camponeses e a Política No Brasil: As Lutas Sociais no Campo e Seu Lugar no Processo Político. Vozes.

Medeiros, Leonilde.1989. Historia dos Movimentos Sociais no Campo. FASE.

Müller, Guilhermo. 1989. Complexos Agroindustrial e Modernização Agrária. Hucitec.

Osada, Neido Mayumi. n.d. PRODECER: Projetos no *Cerrado* e Dívidas Agrícolas. Núcleo de Pesquisa em Relações Internacionais de la Universidad de San Pablo.

Page, Joseph. 1972. *The Revolution That Never Was: Northeast Brazil, 1955–1964*. Grossman.

Perkins, Jerry. 2002. Iowans bid to broaden farming prospects in Brazil: bountiful Brazil lures Iowans with vast farming prospects. DesMoines Register, November 10.

Philips, Jim. n.d. Heading overseas. ProgressiveFarmer.com.

Pulido, Laura, Steve Sidawi, and Robert Vos. 1996. An archaeology of environmental racism in Los Angeles. *Urban Geography* 17, no. 5: 419–439.

Recuperação do *Cerrado*. Estudos Brasileiros, 21. Rio de Janeiro: Serviço de Informaão Agrícola.

Rezende, Gervásio Castro de. 2001. Inconsistência Espacial da Política de Preços Mínimas e a Questão do Desenvolvimento Agrícola da Região.

Rezende, Gervásio Castro de. 2002. Ocupação Agrícola e Estrutura Agrária no *Cerrado*: O Papel do Preço da Terra, Dos Recursos Naturais e da Tecnologia. Working Paper Number 913. Rio de Janeiro: Instituto de Pesquisa Econômica Aplicada.

Romero, Simon. 2002. US farmers put down roots in Brazilian soil. *New York Times*, December 1.

Smith, Neil. 1990. *Uneven Development*, second edition. Blackwell.

Stedman-Edwards, Pamela. 2000. The Brazilian *Cerrado*. In *The Root Causes of Biodiversity Loss*, ed. A. Wood et al. Earthscan.

Thompson, James. 2000. Investing in Brazil. *Soybean Digest*, January 1.

Towers, George. 2000. Applying the political geography of scale: grassroots strategies and environmental justice. *Professional Geographer* 52, no. 1: 23–36.

Warnken, Philip. 1999. The Development and Growth of the Soybean Industry in Brazil. Iowa State University Press.

World Wildlife Fund (WWF). 2001. Expansão Agrícola e Perda da Biodiversidade no *Cerrado* (Agricultural Expansion and Loss of Biodiversity in the *Cerrado*).

10

Popular Protest and Unpopular Policies: State Restructuring, Resource Conflict, and Social Justice in Bolivia

Tom Perreault

Bolivia now has, for the first time, a Ministry of Water. In January 2006, newly elected President Evo Morales created the ministry in response to calls by social movements and activists to coordinate water management—a job that had previously been carried out in fragmented fashion through a diversity of state agencies and users' groups, and under a proliferation of often contradictory resource laws. Morales' choice for Minister of Water, Abel Mamani, had only months before led street protests against Aguas del Illimani, a subsidiary of the giant French transnational Suez. The "Second Water War," as this protest came to be known, took advantage of governmental weakness and growing national sentiment against neoliberalism, in order to pressure then President Carlos Mesa into rescinding Aguas del Illimani's concession, initially granted in 1998. That Mamani so quickly made the transition from street protestor to government minister indicates the central importance to the new government not only of social movements, but of anti-neoliberal resource politics more generally. Indeed, Morales's popularity stems largely from his move to nationalize natural gas—calls for which had been increasing ever since protests in 2003 over the government's plan to export gas to the United States via a Chilean port. Resource conflicts are often at the center of Bolivian politics. Morales' resounding victory—the most dramatic transformation of Bolivian politics in half a century—attests not only to the widespread rejection of the neoliberal model, but also to the centrality of natural resources and their governance to the Bolivian polity.

The first president of indigenous descent to be elected in Bolivian history, Morales was also the first since the return of democracy in the

1980s to win outright in the first round of voting.[1] That Morales won nearly 54 percent of the popular vote indicates that his popularity extended beyond his traditional base of coca growers, Andean indigenous groups, and *campesinos* to include the urban poor and middle classes, as well as some professionals and intellectuals. Moreover, the victory of Morales and his Movimiento al Socialismo signals the downfall of Bolivia's traditional political parties, and in particular the Movimiento Nacional Revolucionario, which swept to power in the 1952 social revolution and was an ubiquitous presence in Bolivian politics during the subsequent 50 years. Now, however, Bolivians are ready for a change.

The fall of the mainstream political parties[2] can, in large measure, be read as a rejection of the neoliberal policies which together they have promoted during the past generation. Since the late 1990s, resistance to the neoliberal model had been growing in Bolivia, particularly among indigenous and *campesino* groups in the Andes, labor unions, and the urban poor. In this chapter I consider resource politics and protest in Bolivia through the lens of environmental justice, broadly conceived. I do so through a close examination of two major protest movements: the 2000 Guerra del Agua (Water War) in the city of Cochabamba, and the 2003 Guerra del Gas (Gas War), which was centered in the cities of El Alto and La Paz, but spread to many other highland cities as well. These struggles, which in other instances may have remained localized contests over resource management, quickly gained national and international importance. In making this scalar jump, protests over water and gas became venues for the expression of manifold frustrations on the part of a people with a long history of colonial and neocolonial exploitation, marginalization, and poverty. Fundamentally, these were struggles over resource governance, in which protestors articulated a vision of social justice at odds with the state's neoliberal policies. Here I address the question of why and how protests over water and natural gas crystallized a broader set of claims involving livelihood rights, political participation, regional autonomy, and the meanings of citizenship and the nation.

Resource Governance and Neoliberalism

At the heart of Bolivia's recent struggles over water and natural gas are questions of resource governance, conceptualized here as the legal frameworks and institutional arrangements through which decisions about natural resources are taken, and the management practices by which those decisions are enacted. The term "resource governance" has been widely adopted in recent years to signal the institutional diversification of environmental and resource management as a component of political-economic restructuring under neoliberalism. Critical discussions of environmental governance often draw on regulation theory to highlight new institutional configurations of government, law, capital, and civil society. In this perspective, particular institutional configurations—for example, resource rights, policies regarding resource extraction and conservation, or codified social norms and management practices—mediate the metabolic relationship between nature and society, and in so doing serve to stabilize environmental and social regulation within a given regime of accumulation. Such institutional arrangements are seen as responses to, and codifications of, the social and ecological contradictions of capitalism (Bakker 2002; Bridge and Jonas 2002). One central focus of such studies is the movement away from state-centric forms of management toward decentered institutional arrangements involving state, quasi-state, and non-state actors (MacLeod and Goodwin 1999).

It is important to recognize, however, that in the context of a chronically weak and historically corrupt Bolivian state, the governance of many natural resources has never been strongly centralized. In the water sector, for instance, grassroots users' groups (either irrigators' organizations or community-based drinking water associations) have long managed much of Bolivia's rural and urban water supplies. Moreover, transnational development agencies—non-governmental organizations, bilateral aid agencies, and multi-lateral lending institutions—have long been involved with the development and management of Bolivia's drinking water and irrigation systems (Gerbrandy and Hoogendam 1998). Thus, processes of Bolivian neoliberalization, and associated shifts in resource governance, cannot simply be assumed to follow patterns common in North Atlantic states, by which strong central state apparatuses are "hollowed out" and their functions are outsourced to non-state actors (Jessop 2002; Tickell and Peck 1995). As I hope to demonstrate in this chapter, Bolivia's neoliberal reforms led to a pronounced re-scaling and re-institutionalization of natural resource management, albeit in ways distinct from those found in advanced industrial economies. As I argue below, this shift in governance is at the heart of recent resource struggles, and has led to the emergence of resistance movements that have effectively blocked the privatization and export of natural resources.

The application of market principles to resource governance involves a fundamental shift toward private sector norms and institutions such as competition, markets, and efficiency indicators. The privatization of (formerly) publicly controlled natural resources represents one such institutional reconfiguration, what Harvey (2003) calls "accumulation by dispossession." Harvey maintains that the mechanisms Marx (1967 [1867]) described in his discussion of primitive accumulation have in recent years been refined through labor and social policy reform, trade agreements, resource privatization, and economic and political restructuring, all of which have facilitated renewed rounds of accumulation. As Bakker (2002) points out, the institutional realignment toward market principles also necessitates not just transformations in institutions and material practices, but also in the ways that resources are conceptualized and discursively represented. Under neoliberalism, resources such as water are no longer conceived of as public goods that individuals have rights to as citizens, but rather as scarce commodities whose access for consumers is mediated by the market.

In Bolivia, a country with endemic political and economic instability and one strongly influenced by foreign aid agencies, lending institutions, and private firms, the legal and institutional frameworks for governing the management of natural resources are often outdated, incomplete, or easily restructured to favor the interests of foreign and domestic capital. Indeed, this is precisely what has occurred in recent years, as neoliberal policies have ushered in a series of legal and institutional reforms designed to facilitate private investment and roll back state involvement in economic planning (Conaghan et al. 1990; Kohl 2002). Inherent to these new structures of governance are power imbalances and inequalities in the allocation of resource rights, as well as inequitable distribution of benefits derived from resource use. This recognition, then, calls attention to the ways that structural asymmetries in access to and control over natural resources become institutionalized through neoliberalism. Who has the power to allocate resource rights? Through which institutional arrangements, at what geographical scales, and with whose participation are decisions regarding nature and natural resources made? These questions in turn draw attention to the normative basis of environmental conflict, and what may be thought of as environmental justice broadly writ.

In contrast to the Hobbesian struggle over scarce resources depicted in the literature of environmental security (e.g. Homer-Dixon 1999), Bolivia's water and gas wars encompassed more subtle and far-reaching contests over questions of governance: access to and control over resources, and the implications these have for conceptions of livelihood, democracy, and development. These concepts are in turn bound up with understandings of social justice, insofar as they are concerned with the authority to make decisions regarding competing claims to resources, based on differing regimes of value (Zerner 2000). A governance approach to environmental justice focuses on processes of political participation, decision making, and the democratization of resource management and distribution. This signals a move away from the more traditional environmental justice focus on social inequity in industrial location decisions and exposure to pollution (Bullard 1993), socially uneven access to environmental amenities (Heynen 2004), and differential spatial mobility and race-based privilege (Pulido 2000). In this chapter, while acknowledging the immense contribution and continued importance of these approaches, I argue for paying attention to how struggles over nature and natural resources are simultaneously struggles for social justice (Moore 2005). Recent protests in Bolivia may be seen as a variant of what Martinez-Alier (2003) has called "environmentalism of the poor"—a movement that fuses concerns for resource access and environmental conditions with calls for social justice. (See the introduction to this volume.)

Of particular importance to recent Bolivian struggles over water and gas were two sets of claims to social justice. First, protestors demanded procedural justice, calling for greater participation and transparency in decisions over the management of natural resources. Second, protestors demanded distributive justice, calling for more equitable distribution of the benefits deriving from the exploitation of natural resources. As discussed below, the socio-spatial forms these claims took varied considerably, not least because the use values and physical properties of gas and water are fundamentally distinct. Irrespective of these differences,

however, the unifying factor remains: protestors rejected the commodification, privatization, and control by foreign entities of what were
widely perceived (and often, in the case of water, managed) as collective
resources.

"El Agua es Vida": The Guerra del Agua, April 2000

Jallalla usos y costumbres, Kawsachun yaku, Wañachun privatizadores [Power
to customary uses, long live water, die privatizers]
—Quechua slogan from the water war

As the twentieth century drew to a close, the government of former
dictator Hugo Banzer sought new ways to sell off Bolivia's resources.
In late 1999, under pressure from the World Bank, which vigorously
promoted the adoption of market-based practices in water management
(Nickson and Vargas 2002), Banzer granted a concession to Aguas del
Tunari, a transnational consortium controlled by US-based Bechtel
(García et al. 2003). Upon taking charge of the city's water services in
January 2000, Aguas del Tunari increased water rates as much as 200
percent, which the company claimed was necessary to cover the costs of
planned extensions and upgrades to existing infrastructure. Rates were
increased before any improvements were made, however, a move that
angered many and raised suspicions of price gouging. Aguas del Tunari
claimed control over all water systems in the city—including the many
neighborhood-based water cooperatives for which members had provided their labor and ingenuity, and which were collectively managed
without assistance from the city (Finnegan 2002). Residents were even
to be charged for the rainwater collected in their rooftop cisterns.

Cochabamba's social movements began to mobilize in early January to
analyze Aguas del Tunari's contract, as well as the legal reforms put in
place to enable it.[3] The Coordinadora de Defensa del Agua y de la Vida
(Coordinator of Defense of Water and Life, hereafter the Coordinadora),
called for marches and road blockades to protest the concession
(Bustamante 2002). In a referendum held in late March and organized by
the Coordinadora, the population of Cochabamba overwhelmingly
rejected the privatization of the city's water services.[4] In early April,

campesino organizations began blocking roads throughout the Cochabamba valley, and a general strike paralyzed the city. During the following several days, tens of thousands of people gathered in streets and plazas to demand the cancellation of Aguas del Tunari's contract, and a reform of the laws that allowed it. Several members of the Coordinadora were jailed in late night raids, and dictator-turned-democrat Banzer declared a 90-day state of emergency and sent the military into the streets of Cochabamba. Ensuing confrontations resulted in one death and dozens of injuries, but also forced Banzer's government to concede to the protestors' demands. On April 9, the government cancelled its contract with Aguas del Tunari, and announced that the consortium would leave the country and that management of Cochabamba's water services would once again be controlled by SEMAPA (the municipal water service), with a greater role for social movement participation in oversight and administration. The government hurriedly issued a revised drinking water law.

Many structural problems remain, however, as some 40 percent of the city's population is not served by the municipal water system, and must rely on expensive and often unsafe water sold by private vendors (García et al. 2003). Issues of water scarcity in semi-arid and drought-prone Cochabamba have not yet been resolved. Meanwhile, water rights for peasant irrigators remain insecure (Perreault 2005). Importantly, many of the protestors who took to the streets were relatively recent migrants without domestic connections to the city's supply of drinking water. Thus, their involvement in the Guerra del Agua was not a defense of secure resource access, or of a just and efficient municipal service. Rather, it was a rejection of the privatization of Bolivia's natural resources, and their control by foreign interests. This point was emphasized by Óscar Olivera, the leader of the Coordinadora:

I would say [the water war] was clearly a regional struggle, but . . . naturally it began with the irrigators' sector, that is, with the Quechuas, the indigenous people who also have a very different conception of water . . . from that of businessmen and politicians. But in the cities the first to join the struggle were the migrants . . . that is, people who do not have water since they live in neighborhoods that were populated by the massive migration that has taken place since 1985, that is people I believe that fight so that the water is not privatized, they fight so that the [water] company does not fall into the hands of the transnationals, they fight so that the [communal] water networks do not become property of the transnationals, they fight for the usos y costumbres of the *campesinos*, but these are people who do not manage nor enjoy [access to] water.[5]

As this statement shows, *usos y costumbres* (customary uses) were conceptually central to this struggle, and constituted a moral economy of water rights for irrigator associations and neighborhood water cooperatives involved in the struggle. Customary uses, recognized throughout Andean Bolivia in the management of common-property resources, are established and enforced through traditional, commonly agreed upon practices, and are inherently local, collective, idiosyncratic, and mutable. As such, they subscribe to a fundamentally different logic from that of privatized, individualized resource rights regimes, a recognition with bearing on questions of governance—the ways in which rights to water are allocated and enforced, how decisions regarding water are taken, and how water itself is managed—as well as forms and scales of social organization for water management (Laurie et al. 2002).

Though the water war was largely a regional struggle (with the exception of a few scattered road blockades in the Altiplano, all major actions occurred in and around the city of Cochabamba), it quickly grew to national importance. Protestors forced the government to cancel its contract with Aguas del Tunari, return water services in Cochabamba to public control and amend the legislation that permitted concessions of this type—the world's first instance of public protest reversing water privatization (Barlow and Clarke 2002). Emboldened by their success in Cochabamba, activists and intellectuals in Bolivia subsequently turned their attention to the concession granting Aguas del Illimani (owned by French giant Suez) control over water services in La Paz and El Alto. Thus, protestors have been able to place their concerns squarely on the national political agenda, thereby engaging a politics of scale that continues today in the form of social organizing, legal proposals, and public education campaigns (Perreault 2005).

"El Gas es Nuestro": The Guerra del Gas, October 2003

Despierta Bolivia, despierta. Los Gringos nos quieren robar el gas. [Wake up Bolivia, wake up. The Gringos want to steal our gas.]
—slogan used during the gas war

Three and a half years after the Guerra del Agua, Bolivia once again erupted as widespread protests swept the country. At issue this time was the government's plan to allow the export of natural gas through a Chilean port. Under the rules for oil and gas exploitation established by the revised hydrocarbons law of 1996 (Law 1689), financial benefits of gas export were to accrue overwhelmingly to the consortium of transnational firms involved, while the state received relatively little by way of royalties, taxes or fees. The law dramatically lowered the rate of royalties exporting firms would pay the state, and established conditions of shared risk, in which royalties were to be paid to the state only in cases of profitability, in contrast to the previous requirement of payment for any oil or gas extracted, regardless of market conditions. In this way, the new law created regulatory conditions that strongly favored transnational capital, while significantly decreasing the benefits accruing to the state (Orgaz García 2002). Indeed, the government reported in December 2003 that the Bolivian operations of BP Amoco and Repsol YPF benefited from the world's lowest operating costs for oil and gas exploration and production (Hylton and Thomson 2004).

The Guerra del Gas must be viewed against the historical backdrop of Bolivia's colonial past and neocolonial present, with their systemic processes of rapacious resource exploitation, social exclusion, and impoverishment. The return of democracy in the early 1980s brought little change in this condition, and the almost immediate turn to neoliberalism deepened poverty and led to an exodus from the countryside, swelling the ranks of the urban underclass in cities that could not provide adequate services or employment. It was from these populations in El Alto, La Paz, Cochabamba, and Oruro that protestors rose up against a state they viewed as profoundly undemocratic, and a government they perceived as irreparably corrupt. These processes also contributed to the rise of radicalized social movements in response to what Cortés Hurtado (2003, p. 4) calls the "crisis of representivity" in Bolivian politics. Following the decline of the traditional miner-led labor union system, a suite of social movements emerged, organized around class, ethnicity, neighborhoods, sectoral interests, or various combinations of these, and assumed a leading role in representing a re-energized civil society in making demands against a weakened state.

The Guerra del Gas can be traced in part to the formation of Pacific LNG, a transnational consortium established in Paris in 2002. Pacific LNG was formed with the expectation of transporting natural gas from the Margarita oil and gas field in southernmost Bolivia via a pipeline to a Pacific port. It was to be transformed cryogenically into liquefied natural gas (LNG) at a plant on the Chilean coast (to be constructed by Pacific LNG), allowing it to be shipped to markets in California (Miranda Pacheco 2002). At a meeting in Washington in 2002, Pacific LNG signed an agreement with Sempra energy for the distribution of Bolivian gas in North America, a signing overseen by then Bolivian president Jorge "Tuto" Quiroga. Shortly after leaving office in August 2002, Quiroga—a young Texas-educated technocrat known for his conservative pro-business positions—quietly declared his support for exporting the gas through a Chilean port (Guzmán 2002). It was to Chile that Bolivia lost its coast in the War of the Pacific in the 1870s, leaving its people land-locked and embittered (Klein 1992). The Chilean option, though rejected by the armed forces, nationalist politicians, and the majority of the country's population, was favored by Pacific LNG as closer to Bolivia's gas fields, and therefore more cost effective, than any Peruvian alternative.

When Gonzalo Sánchez de Lozada assumed the presidency for the second time, in August 2002, he followed his predecessor's advice.[6] "Goni," as he is universally known, is a mining magnate who had spent much of his life living in the United States (and who speaks Spanish with a pronounced Gringo accent), and is precisely the kind of cosmopolitan elitist that Glassman (1999) identifies as essential to the internationalization of the state. Unburdened by nationalist sentiments, he strongly favored the economic expediency of the Chilean option. It is worth noting, however, that in 2001 José Guillermo Justiniano—a member of Goni's National Revolutionary Movement (MNR) party, and later his Minister of the Presidency—foresaw the revolutionary potential of conflicts over natural gas: "One shouldn't think that everything with gas is resolved; one cannot forget that if gas facilitates things in the political system, it can also become the motive for revolutionary change for those outside the system" (quoted in Guzmán 2003b; translation mine). Indeed.

In mid September 2003, the newly formed Coordinadora Nacional por la Defensa del Gas (headed by Óscar Olivera) began working with other social movements to intensify the pressure already placed on the government by ongoing protests in El Alto and on the Altiplano. These latter protests, which were diffuse, disparate, and lacking in widespread support, were fused into a more generalized opposition movement by the government's heavy-handed mission to "rescue" hundreds of Bolivian and foreign travelers who, owing to the road blockades on the Altiplano, could not leave the tourist town of Sorata. The large police and military presence sparked *campesino* resistance near the Aymara town of Warisata, and the ensuing confrontation left one police officer and five *campesinos* dead, including an 8-year-old girl killed in her home by a stray bullet (Espinoza and Guzmán 2003; Guzmán 2003a). The killings in Warisata unified and radicalized Aymara *campesinos* throughout the Altiplano, who reinforced the road blockades and declared strikes, both in rural areas and in the cities of El Alto and La Paz (Espinoza 2003b). Strikes paralyzed El Alto, a city of more than 800,000—some 80 percent of whom are Aymara—situated at the edge of the Altiplano, overlooking La Paz. The radicalization of the protests, and the sympathy of urban workers for the *campesino* struggle, was articulated by Roberto de la Cruz, a labor leader in El Alto:

The objective was to initiate the struggle for gas and in a meeting of the *Campesino* Federation of La Paz, where they only wanted to block roads, we discussed how was it possible that in the countryside people continue cooking with animal dung, while Goni wants to sell the gas? This discussion was key for the *campesinos* to react and start to join [the struggle]. (quoted in Espinoza 2003a, p. 17; translation mine)

Here de la Cruz articulates the conceptual linkage between natural gas and political-economic and development models. The gas protests were not only a struggle over natural resources but also a struggle over *national* resources. At the heart of these struggles was an overriding sense of the ways in which the structural inequalities that have marked Bolivian society throughout its history were being reproduced by plans to allow foreign firms to export what was widely viewed as national patrimony. This was expressed by an El Alto protestor, in reference to the southern (and lower elevation) portion of La Paz, home to the country's rich and powerful:

These capitalist people do not know what this country is. There [in the southern zone of La Paz] they don't know bad weather, they don't know the noise of the airplanes and airport when they sleep, nor have they swallowed the police's teargas because they don't ever have to struggle for their rights. There, they have everything. (quoted in Espinoza 2003a, p. 17; translation mine)

By October 12, when the military killed more than 20 people in El Alto (Espinoza 2003c), the demands of the protesters had already shifted from their original position. What began as calls for "Gas por Perú"—demands that the government alter its plans so as to export natural gas through a Peruvian rather than Chilean port—had transformed into a widespread rejection of export plans altogether. Protestors now called for the recovery and industrialization of the nation's gas reserves—that is, the strengthening of state control and the simultaneous weakening of private, foreign influence over natural gas, together with coordinated, state-led efforts to use the gas for the country's social development (del Granado and Zaratti 2003). These demands were discursively bundled with calls for the re-founding of the country ("refundar el país")—a concept linked to calls for greater democratization based on new forms of social organization. Importantly, these demands came both from the Aymara groups of the Altiplano, and from the Cambas of the Amazonian city of Santa Cruz—white and *mestizo* urban middle- and upper-class people who wanted nothing to do with the highlanders they perceived as poor, indigenous/*campesino*, and radicalized.[7] Thus, through calls for the re-founding of the country, regional autonomy emerged as an important leitmotif that ran through the remainder of the gas war and its aftermath (Lora 2003b).

The massacre in El Alto, like the one in La Paz the following day, provoked outrage throughout the country. On October 14, the former head of the government's human rights office (Defensor del Pueblo) initiated a hunger strike in La Paz. Over the next three days, she was joined by more than 1,000 others, mostly white middle-class urban intellectuals, artists, and activists. On October 16, more than 8,000 miners converged on the village of Patacamaya, in the northern Altiplano, and began a march to La Paz. On the morning of the following day, the high command of the armed forces withdrew its support for Goni, sending the clearest signal yet that his time was short, and his options few (Lazarte 2003).

Even the US embassy, which until that point had shown its support for Goni through absurd condemnations of the protestors' apparent "disregard for democracy," recognized that he had outlived his usefulness. By the time the miners reached La Paz on the afternoon of October 17, Goni had already resigned, and, having fled the presidential palace in the back of an ambulance, was in the Santa Cruz airport awaiting his flight to Miami (Cortés Hurtado 2003).

That evening, Carlos Mesa, Goni's vice president, assumed the presidency. He took his oath of office at precisely the same moment that Goni's aircraft was taxiing down the runway in Santa Cruz, an almost surreal convergence of events that was shown on split television screens across the country. Personally shaken by the violence that had convulsed Bolivia and in a politically vulnerable position, Mesa, a political independent, set out to form a broadly inclusive government that eschewed traditional party alliances. He immediately promised to fulfill three political demands articulated by the social movements involved in the uprising: a referendum on the governance and export of natural gas, passage of a revised hydrocarbon law more favorable to the Bolivian state and people, and, most contentious, the formation of a popularly elected Asamblea Constituyente (Constitutional Assembly) to re-write the Constitution (Lazarte 2003).[8] In his first year in office, Mesa presented a (deeply flawed and much criticized) revised hydrocarbon law, and organized a referendum on gas (also widely criticized). The Asamblea Constituyente would have to await the election of Evo Morales.

In direct contrast to the post-facto interpretations proffered by the exiled Goni and his North American apologists, protestors were neither "narco-terrorists" nor anti-democratic.[9] During the 21 years of neoliberal "democracy" between 1985 and 2003, the Bolivian people suffered some 280 deaths,[10] nearly 700 injuries, and more than 10,000 illegal detentions during protests (*Opinión* 2003). The spasms of violence that marked Goni's last days in office may thus be read as the latest expression of what has been dubbed by Bolivians as "democradura"—that is, democracy in form but *dictadura* (dictatorship) in style. Democratic in only the barest sense, Bolivia's political system has, since the return to civilian government, fostered impunity for military violence and official corruption. This system, lacking as it is in meaningful participation and representation, amounts to a politics of domination and systemic violence thinly veiled in democratic formalities.

Uneven Geographies of Protest and Justice

Despite many underlying similarities the water and gas wars had distinctly different spatial dynamics. Here I offer two brief observations regarding the uneven geographies of resource protest in Bolivia.

First, the water war was primarily a regional struggle. With the exception of isolated road blockades in the Altiplano and a few protests in La Paz, the vast majority of actions took place in and around the city of Cochabamba. Although Aguas del Tunari's concession held clear implications for other cities in the Bolivia, it was, to a large degree, a local struggle over a locally produced and consumed resource. Protestors emphasized the place of water in everyday practice, a daily necessity of universal importance, and the central slogan of the protest, "el agua es vida" ("water is life") directly connected the resource to livelihood and survival. Similarly, the irrigators' emphasis on usos y costumbres linked water rights not only to the biological functions of life, but also to the social aspects of living. Water is, in this sense, a daily necessity as essential for communities and cultures as it is for bodies, and was discursively represented and physically defended as such.

The gas war was a more national and a more nationalist uprising. The center of the protests was the Altiplano, and in particular El Alto, with several protests and more than two-dozen deaths occurring in La Paz. Road blockades, hunger strikes, marches and rallies quickly spread to other cities, most notably Cochabamba, Oruro, Potosí, and Sucre, though these were markedly less violent. Tellingly, the area of natural gas production—the Chaco region of eastern Tarija department—was relatively calm during the protests. The elites of Tarija, like those of Santa Cruz, favored gas export and with Goni denounced the protests as the work of narco-terrorists and radical leftist indigenous organizations. Tarija's *campesino* organizations and the indigenous Guaraní of the Chaco—those most directly affected by gas production—remained largely silent during the protests, though they supported the basic positions of the organizations that led the protests in the Altiplano (Lora 2003a; Orduna 2004).

Why, then, did the gas war so quickly become a national struggle, with the center of gravity in the Altiplano, far from the areas of gas production? By the same token, in view of the universal importance of water, why did the water war remain largely a regional struggle? In short, what accounts for this uneven geography of protest? In part, the answer to these questions is rooted in regional and national histories of mobilization and conflict, and have much to do with the very different political economies of water and oil. For all its importance to biological and social reproduction, water is of comparatively little importance to international financial markets and geopolitics. As Selby (2005) points out, hydrocarbons, being central to economic well-being, dwell close to the center of state policy. In contrast, water management is a more spatially and administratively dispersed affair—locally important, but of little consequence to international trade or geo-strategic interests.

But the differing geographies of Bolivia's protests over water and gas also have much to do with the very materiality of the resources themselves, and the means by which they enter into circuits of capital and social reproduction. Though the insertion of water into society is in general mediated by complex networks of canals, pipes, reservoirs, legal frameworks, and social institutions—making it what Bakker (2002) calls a "hydrosocial resource"—it can be, and in Bolivia often is, brought into cycles of social reproduction through relatively simple technological mediation: hand dug wells, roof-top cisterns, earthen and stone canals. Water has long been considered by many Bolivians to be a collective good and a social right, both instrument and product of their labor; its use value is not in doubt. Water, then, is viscerally material (as well as potently symbolic) in its importance.

In contrast with water, natural gas enters into society only through more technologically sophisticated means. Its use value is profoundly different from that of water, and is always socially mediated. The expansive, volatile nature of natural gas means that its entry into daily life must be brought about through complex engineering systems oriented toward its extraction, transport, storage and combustion. As Bridge (2004, p. 396) points out, natural gas "may have use-value and be in plentiful supply, but producing its exchange value requires the labours of science, capital and law." The importance of natural gas as a unifying factor in social struggle is, then, as much symbolic as material. Gas came to symbolize the kind of exploitative practices Bolivians know so well—the theft of national wealth—that enrich a few foreign and national elites while further impoverishing those who labor for them. Those who have been most excluded by these processes and, crucially, most organized politically, were those who first protested the government's plans to export yet another of Bolivia's resources. Gas may be, as Bridge (2004, pp. 395) avers, a "commodity with geographical ambition," but this is an exclusionary geography littered with poverty, underdevelopment and violence.

My second observation concerns the socially uneven character of protest politics. Ramonet notes that the uprisings "are based in centuries of historical experience. The export of natural riches (silver, tin, petroleum) never improved the condition of the poor nor allowed the modernization of the country. . . . The Bolivian population, in overthrowing Sánchez de Lozada, reject an economic model that throughout Latin America has aggravated corruption, destroyed populations and increased social exclusion. (2003, pp. 32; translation mine) Ramonet is right to point to the exclusionary nature of neoliberalism as experienced in Bolivia. However, the exclusionary nature of the protests is worth noting. The water war permitted irrigators, led by Cochabamba's departmental irrigators' federation, FEDECOR, to consolidate their influence. But, as Laurie et al. (2002) observe, they did so in a way that largely obscured the needs of Cochabamba's urban migrant population, which has only precarious access to water and shares in few of the collective political and social benefits enjoyed by more organized sectors, such as irrigators, miners, and factory workers. Moreover, only a particular "elite" class fraction of the peasantry has benefited from these processes. It must be recognized that irrigators as a group are privileged relative to the majority of Bolivian *campesinos* who have no access to irrigation. FEDECOR thus represents the interests of a relatively privileged class fraction of the peasantry. Moreover, FEDECOR is composed primarily of irrigators in the lower and central valleys of Cochabamba, that is, those with access to wells, high-quality valley-bottom land, and good access to large urban markets. Through the water war, FEDECOR was able to consolidate its organizational capacity and gain political and social influence, important and hard-won achievements to be sure. But the benefits of these achievements are distributed in a socially and spatially uneven fashion among Cochabamba's *campesino* population.

Similarly, both in terms of the discursive framing of the struggle and the protestors in the street, the gas war was dominated by Aymara communities in the Altiplano and by urban social movements in La Paz and Cochabamba. Thus, struggles over natural gas were defined and enacted by people and places distant from the actual centers of production, while the Guaraní communities directly affected by gas extraction were (and remain) largely excluded from discussions and demands circulating in the Andes. Neither the government nor the social movements took seriously the possibility that the Guaraní themselves might have something to say about the extractive practices occurring on their lands. These relations are embedded in broader, historically constituted regional antagonisms between Andean and Amazonian groups, both indigenous and *mestizo*, which transcend class and ethnic divisions (Gustafson 2006). Thus, a complex politics of scale is at work in these struggles, which cannot be explained by recourse to a romanticized local, neither can it be attributed solely to the work of trans-local activist networks.

Conclusion

As the water and gas wars demonstrate, questions of environmental governance and resource rights are found at the heart of protest politics in Bolivia. However, in many ways, these conflicts were less about the best way to manage water and natural gas than they were about what Bolivia is and should be as a nation. The two are inseparable, in that water and gas (like silver, tin, nitrates, and oil) are seen not only as natural resources, but as national resources as well, that is, resources that properly belong to the nation and its people, and that should not (indeed cannot) be exploited for the benefit of a few private interests—particularly if those interests are foreign (and all the more so if they are Chilean or North American).

Despite the uneven nature and occasional incoherence of protest during these uprisings, it is possible to identify three over-arching and integrative themes among the demands made by protestors in the water and gas wars.

First, protestors demanded broader forms of participation, and the democratization of decision-making processes regarding natural resources. Long histories of exclusionary rule by an elite caste of white landowners, foreign domination of the country's resource wealth, and seemingly intractable poverty have made many Bolivians understandably wary of recent waves of neoliberal reform. That privatization and associated reforms have increased foreign control over the country's natural resources and key industries is viewed by many Bolivians as merely a continuation of historical patterns of colonialism and foreign domination (Cortés Hurtado 2003; Orgáz García 2002). Protests over water and gas, then, are not only struggles over how best to manage those resources. They are, more broadly, contests over the right to participate both in the management of resources, and in the benefits deriving from them. To this extent, they may be seen as struggles over environmental justice, broadly conceived.

Second, protestors demanded more secure livelihoods and resource rights. This was perhaps most apparent during the water war, during which slogans such as "el agua es vida" were ubiquitous. The universal, bodily and daily need for water gave this struggle an immediacy and intimacy that the gas war did not have, as irrigators and urban residents alike invoked a moral economy of water rights. In particular, the concept of usos y costumbres was central to demands by both irrigators and some urban water-user groups for local, collective control over water systems. The use value of natural gas is distinctly different from that of water, however, and claims to it sit uneasily in an individualized, moral framework. But claims to livelihood and resource rights were to be found at the heart of the gas war, if perhaps in unexpected ways. Whereas protestors in the water war could credibly argue that "water is life," the cry of the gas war was "Gas para los bolivianos" ("Gas for Bolivians"). In making this call, protestors argued that national development and social welfare—livelihood security writ on a national, collective scale—and not the profits of transnational firms, should be the first priority of the government's plans to develop its huge gas reserves. This is, at heart, a call for distributive justice.

Third, these protests clearly called for an alternative model of economic development. Neoliberalism has, for most Bolivians, led to growing insecurity and poverty, and the disruption of well established forms of production, resource rights, and social organization (Arze and Kruse 2004). As collective forms of resource management and social organization came under intense pressure from the atomizing forces of neoliberalism, social movements called for distributive justice and a more social model of national development. The Guerra del Agua sowed the seeds of the Guerra del Gas, which in turn created the political conditions for the so-called "second water war," against Aguas del Illimani's concession for water services in El Alto and La Paz. Protestors toppled two neoliberal governments, forcing the resignation of Gonzalo Sánchez de Lozada in October 2003, and his successor, Carlos Mesa, in June 2005. These events set the stage for the election in December 2005 of Evo Morales, who has promised to reverse Bolivia's neoliberal policies by disallowing private concessions for water services, and nationalizing the country's natural gas reserves.[11]

Though these demands were woven through the water and gas wars, bringing together diverse coalitions of social actors to oppose the neoliberalization of Bolivia's natural—and national—resources, the protests were in many respects divisive and exclusionary. As I have argued here, honest analysis of the water and gas wars must recognize the uneven geographies of resource protests, and the ways in which these events exposed and accentuated enduring social asymmetries in Bolivia. To acknowledge these disparities is not to diminish the accomplishments of these struggles and the social movements and individuals that took part in them. Rather, it is to argue for attention to the limitations, as well as the liberatory potentials, of oppositional movements, and, with Watts and McCarthy (1997), to caution against ascribing to them more than they are capable of achieving. Struggles for justice in Bolivia are far from over, and efforts to construct more equitable political and social systems must involve more inclusive forms of social organization, not just in the realm of formal politics but, crucially, within civil society as well. It remains to be seen whether the seeds of such structures have yet been sown.

Acknowledgments

Portions of this chapter appeared under the title "From the *Guerra del Agua* to the *Guerra del Gas*: Resource governance, neoliberalism and popular protest in Bolivia" in *Antipode* (38, no. 1: 150–172) and are published here in revised form with the kind permission of Blackwell Publishing. This chapter is based on personal observation, open-ended interviews with activist leaders, and document analysis during, and subsequent to, a 10-month period in Bolivia, from August 2003–June 2004, funded by a Fulbright-Hays Fellowship, and supported by the Department of Geography and the Maxwell School of Syracuse University. I would like to thank David Carruthers for his assistance and support in including this work in the present volume.

Notes

1. In the Bolivian electoral system, if no presidential candidates wins more than 50 percent of the popular vote, the newly elected Congress selects the new president from among the two candidates with the highest vote totals.

2. In addition to the Movimiento Nacional Revolucionario, these include the Movimiento Izquierdista Revolucionario, Acción Democrática Nacional, and the Nueva Fuerza Republicana.

3. It is not my intention to provide an in-depth analysis of this struggle, which has received considerable attention already. Rather, I wish merely to provide a rough sketch of the protest, as a basis of comparison for the less well documented Gas War, which is considered in more detail below.

4. The referendum drew 48,276 people, who voted on the following questions: "Do you accept the water fee increase?" (to which 99 percent responded "no"), "Should the contract with Aguas del Tunari be canceled?" (to which 96 percent responded "yes"), and "Do you agree that water is private property, as stated in Law no. 2029?" (to which 97 percent responded "no") (Bustamante 2002).

5. Interview with Óscar Olivera, Cochabamba Bolivia, February 12, 2004. Translation by author.

6. Sánchez de Lozada had served as president from 1993 to 1997, during which time he had implemented sweeping neoliberal reforms under the heading of Plan de Todos (Plan for Everyone).

7. This sentiment was expressed clearly, if naively, by 21-year-old Gabriela Oviedo Sarrete of Santa Cruz, who competed as Miss Bolivia in the Miss Universe contest in May 2004. Before the pageant, in response to a question regarding the most common misperception about the contestants' home countries, Oviedo responded: "Unfortunately, people who don't know Bolivia very much think that we are all just . . . poor people and very short people and Indian people. . . . I'm from the other side of the country, the east side and we are tall and we are white, and we know English, so all that misconception that Bolivia

is only an 'Andean' country, it's wrong, Bolivia has a lot to offer. . . ." (quoted in *Pulso*, May 28, 2004, p. 3) Predictably, Oviedo's comment merely inflamed regional tensions, leading the Vice-Minister of Culture to issue a denunciation, and garnering harsh—at times vicious—responses from journalists and political cartoonists in La Paz.

8. In an eleventh-hour attempt at conciliation, Goni promised these same reforms on October 15. By then, however, he had lost all credibility, and protestors remained firm in their demands for his resignation.

9. Accusations that the protestors were "narco-terrorists" was a rhetorical tactic adopted by Goni (and subsequently by his US supporters) to vilify Evo Morales, leader of the coca growers' union and head of the Movimiento al Socialismo party. The well-documented importance of coca to Bolivia's economy and indigenous cultures has been a source of ongoing tension—and at times open conflict—with Washington (Farthing and Ledebur 2004). "Narco-terrorist" was also a reference to Felipe Quispe's past as an armed insurgent, for which he spent several years in prison.

10. Nearly all of these have been civilians killed by the police or military. During protests in February 2003, against a package of taxes and budget reforms imposed by Goni and the IMF, nearly 60 people were killed, including eleven policemen and four soldiers who died in a gun battle between police and military that took place in La Paz's Plaza Murrillo, in front of the parliament building.

11. Morales fulfilled this promise on May 1, 2006, when he announced Presidential Decree 28701 "nationalizing" Bolivia's natural gas. In fact, however, this is less a true nationalization than it is a forced re-negotiation of the terms of rents and taxes.

References

Arze, Carol, and Tom Kruse. 2004. The consequences of neoliberal reform. *NACLA Report on the Americas* 38, no. 3: 23–28.

Bakker, Karen. 2002. From state to market? Water mercantilización in Spain. *Environment and Planning* A 34: 767–790.

Barlow, Maude, and Tony Clarke. 2002. *Blue Gold: The Fight to Stop the Corporate Theft of the World's Water*. New Press.

Bridge, Gavin. 2004. Editorial: Gas and how to get it. *Geoforum* 35: 395–397.

Bridge, Gavin, and Andrew E. G. Jonas. 2002. Governing nature: The reregulation of resource access, production and consumption. *Environment and Planning* A 34: 759–766.

Bullard, Robert D., ed. 1993. *Confronting Environmental Racism: Voices from the Grassroots*. South End.

Bustamante, Rocio. 2002. The "Water War" in Cocahabamba: A war against privatisation. In *Water Law and Indigenous Rights—WALIR* studies, volume 2. Wageningen University/IWE and United Nations/CEPAL.

Conaghan, Catherine, James Malloy, and Luis Abugattas. 1990. Business and the "boys": The politics of neoliberalism in the Central Andes. *Latin American Research Review* 25, no. 2: 3–30.

Cortés Hurtado, Roger. 2003. Reflexiones sobre la rebelión boliviana: El fracaso definitivo del Gonismo. *Le Monde Diplomatique "el Dipló"* (Bolivian edition) 14: 4–5.

del Granado, Hugo, and Francesco Zaratti. 2003. La industrialización del gas: ¿Mito o realidad? *Pulso* (La Paz) 217: 9.

Espinoza, Claudia. 2003a. El Alto: La ciudad rebelde y sin límites. *Pulso* (La Paz) 218: 16–17.

Espinoza, Claudia. 2003b. "Plan Añutaya": La respuesta comunal. *Pulso* (La Paz) no. 216: 16.

Espinoza, Claudia. 2003c. Villa Ingenio, una historia de massacre y terror. *Pulso* (La Paz) 220: 22–23.

Espinoza, Claudia, and Gustavo Guzmán. 2003. Reconstrucción no official de los hechos sucedidos en Warisata: "Operación Rescate." *Pulso* (La Paz) 216: 12–13.

Farthing, Linda, and Kathryn Ledebur. 2004. The beat goes on: The US war on coca. *NACLA Report on the Americas* 38, no. 3: 34–39.

Finnegan, William. 2002. Leasing the rain. *New Yorker*, April 8.

García, Alberto, Fernando García, and Luz Quitón. 2003. *La "Guerra del Agua" Abril de 2000: La Crisis de la Política en Bolivia.* PIEB.

Gerbrandy, Gerben, and Paul Hoogendam. 1998. *Aguas y Acequias: Los Derechos al Agua y la Gestión Campesina de Riego en los Andes Bolivianos.* Plural Editores.

Glassman, Jim. 1999. State power beyond the "territorial trap": The internationalization of the state. *Political Geography* 18: 669–696.

Gustafson, Bret. 2006. Spectacles of autonomy and crisis: Or, what bulls and beauty queens have to do with regionalism in Eastern Bolivia. *Journal of Latin American Anthropology* 11, no. 2: 351–379.

Guzmán, Gustavo. 2002. El gas, una partida de tres jugadores. *Pulso* (La Paz) 163.

Guzmán, Gustavo. 2003a. Han asesinado a una niña boliviana. *Pulso* (La Paz) 216: 11.

Guzmán, Gustavo. 2003b. Un presidente sitiado y un desafío nacional: El gas. *Pulso* (La Paz) 215: 12–13.

Harvey, David. 2003. *The New Imperialism.* Oxford University Press.

Heynen, Nikolas. 2004. The scalar production of injustice within the urban forest. *Antipode* 35, no. 5: 980–998.

Homer-Dixon, Thomas. 1999. *Environment, Scarcity, and Violence.* Princeton University Press.

Hylton, Forrest, and Sinclair Thomson. 2004. Insurgent Bolivia. *NACLA Report on the Americas* 38, no. 3: 15–19.

Jessop, Bob. 2002. Liberalism, neoliberalism, and urban governance: A state-theoretical perspective *Antipode* 34: 452–72.

Klein, Herbert S. 1992. *Bolivia: The Evolution of a Multi-Ethnic Society.* Oxford University Press.

Kohl, Benjamin. 2002. Stabilizing neoliberalism in Bolivia: Popular participation and privatization. *Political Geography* 21: 449–472.

Laurie, Nina, Robert Andonlina, and Sarah Radcliffe. 2002. The excluded "Indigenous"? The implications of multi-ethnic policies for water reform in Bolivia. In *Multiculturalism in Latin America*, ed. R. Sieder. Palgrave.

Lazarte, Jorge. 2003. Insurgencia civil y ceguera "culpable" del poder. *Pulso* (La Paz) 220: 8–9.

Lora, Miguel. 2003a. Habla el Chaco: El gas no se rifa, aunque patalee Tarija. *Pulso* (La Paz) 224:13.

Lora, Miguel. 2003b. Ya no es solo gas, ahora la gente exige refundar el país. *Pulso* (La Paz) 218:14–15.

Marx, Karl. 1967 [1867]. *Capital*, volume 1. International Publishers

MacLeod, Gordon, and Mark Goodwin. 1999. Space, scale and state strategy: Rethinking urban and regional governance. *Progress in Human Geography* 23, no. 4: 503–527.

Martinez-Alier, Joan. 2003. Mining conflicts, environmental justice, and valuation. In *Just Sustainabilities*, ed. J. Agyeman et al. MIT Press.

Miranda Pacheco, Carlos. 2002. El Puerto boliviano en el Pacífico. *Pulso* (La Paz) 157: 8–9.

Moore, Donald S. 2005. *Suffering for Territory: Race, Place, and Power in Zimbabwe.* Duke University Press.

Nickson, Andrew, and Claudia Vargas. 2002. The limitations of water regulation: The failure of the Cochabamba concession in Bolivia. *Bulletin of Latin American Research* 21, no. 1: 99–120.

Opinión. 2003. 280 muertos, 700 heridos y 10.000 detenidos son cifras de la democracia. *La Opinión*, Cochabamba, October 21.

Orduna, Victor. 2004. Margarita y los Guaranís. *Pulso* (special report) (La Paz) 246: 1–8.

Orgáz García, Mirko. 2002. *La Guerra del Gas: Nación versus Transnacionales en Bolivia.* OFAVIN.

Perreault, Tom. 2005. State restructuring and the scale politics of rural water governance in Bolivia. *Environment and Planning* A 37, no. 2: 263–284.

Pulido, Laura. 2000. Rethinking environmental racism: white privilege and urban development in southern California. *Annals of the Association of American Geographers* 90, no. 1: 12–40.

Ramonet, Ignacio. 2003. Bolivia. *Le Monde Diplomatique "el Dipló"* (Bolivian edition) 14: 32.

Selby, Jan. 2005. Oil and water: The contrasting anatomies of resource conflicts. *Government and Opposition* 40, no. 2: 200–224.

Tickell, Adam, and Jamie Peck. 1995. Social regulation after Fordism: Regulation theory, neo-liberalism, and the global-local nexus. *Economy and Society* 24, no. 3: 357–386.

Watts, Michael, and James McCarthy. 1997. Nature as artifice, nature as artifact: Development, environment and modernity in the late twentieth century. In *Geographies of Economies*, ed. R. Lee and J. Wills. Arnold.

Zerner, Charles. 2000. Toward a broader visions of justice and nature conservation. In *People, Plants, and Justice*, ed. C. Zerner. Columbia University Press.

11

The Struggle for Environmental Justice in Vieques, Puerto Rico

Katherine T. McCaffrey

In 2003, the US Department of Fish and Wildlife announced the opening of a new National Wildlife Refuge on the site of a former US Navy bombing range. The department announced that the Vieques Wildlife Refuge, with 14,573 acres, was the largest and most ecologically diverse refuge in the Caribbean.

According to promotional materials, the Vieques Wildlife Refuge is a "unique area" that includes "beaches used by threatened and endangered sea turtles for nesting, subtropical dry forest, mangrove lagoons, salt flats and bioluminescent bays."[1] The Department of Fish and Wildlife promotes Vieques as a great place for a family vacation:

From mountain biking on the dirt roads to swimming in the turquoise waters, Vieques National Wildlife Refuge offers all types of recreational opportunities. Playa Caracas and Playa la Chiva are an escape from reality. There's no high rise, no hustle or bustle just a quiet destination where you become one with nature. Sometimes you can find a few others. The swimming and snorkeling are fantastic. The waters are crystal clear and the variety of color found in the undersea life is astounding. Vieques National Wildlife Refuge offers more than just swimming, snorkeling, hiking, biking bird watching. It's a place where family and friends can eat "arroz con gandules," play Puerto Rico's national pastime—dominoes or a place to lounge under a palm tree and see no one. Summer is coming! So, make Vieques National Wildlife Refuge your destination. An escape from the everyday life; a place to revive your soul and bond with loved ones![2]

Yet this same tropical fantasy island is also a newly declared Superfund site, a designation reserved for the nation's most hazardous waste sites. Its coral reefs are shattered by explosions and its clear turquoise waters littered with bombs. Stormy waters wash bullets up on its white sand beaches. Its mangroves are contaminated by oil, battery acid, and live munitions. According to the US Environmental Protection Agency (EPA), 60 years of live fire exercises have left a toxic legacy on its land and surrounding waters that may include "mercury, lead, copper, magnesium, lithium, perchlorate, TNT, napalm, depleted uranium, PCBs, solvents, and pesticides."[3] Most of the refuge is closed to public access indefinitely due to the presence of thousands of unexploded bombs. Cleanup is underway, so quiet nature walks may be punctuated by the open detonation of 500-pound bombs.

Vieques is a 51-square-mile island (roughly twice the size of Manhattan) where for more than 50 years a civilian population of 10,000 was wedged between a US Navy ammunition depot and a US Navy maneuver area. The Navy controlled three-fourths of the island and used Vieques for live fire practices, air-to-ground bombing, shelling, artillery fire, ship-to-shore bombing, and maneuvers. After years of conflict, a social movement erupted after the accidental bombing of a civilian security guard. Four years of mass mobilization, thousands of arrests for civil disobedience, and international media attention halted live bombing exercises on the island.

True victory, however, has proved elusive. Residents long aspired not only for the eviction of the Navy, but also for the recovery of land for public use. When the Navy left, however, jurisdiction over the land shifted to the US Department of Interior, with the former base land to be operated and managed as a National Wildlife Refuge. The conversion of former base land into a nature reserve represents an incomplete realization of residents' dreams and institutionalizes their exclusion from island land. Consequently, land ownership, land use, and environmental contamination remain highly contested.

Several articles have explored environmental justice as a framework for interpreting Vieques's struggle to halt live bombing exercises (Berman Santana 2005; McCaffrey and Baver 2006) and to understand the cleanup process now faced by islanders (Baver 2006). This chapter considers Vieques's struggle in classic environmental justice terms as unequal exposure to environmental risk. Risk is interpreted as residents' subjection to live fire practices, the contamination of military training activity, and continued exposure to toxins left behind by the Navy. The chapter considers not only resistance to exposure to environmental harm but also the struggle for equal access to environmental good as important dimensions of the struggle for environmental justice. By considering two interconnected processes—the imposition of a wildlife refuge on Vieques and the gentrification of the former civilian sector—the chapter considers how environmental justice is not only about the struggle against unequal exposure to environmental harm, but also a struggle against exclusion and marginalization. Environmental justice, in a Latin American context, is inseparable from broader issues of foreign domination and external control of the landscape. By examining the case of Vieques, environmental justice is broadly interpreted to include people's desire to have some control over the development of their environments (Collinson 1997).

Environmental Justice

In the United States, environmental justice emerged from the civil rights movement as a powerful movement that challenged the class and racial dimensions of environmental problems. Proponents of environmental justice are concerned with socially unequal exposure to environmental risk. They argue that poor people and people of color suffer the unequal burden of exposure to environmental hazards, and a lack of voice in shaping environmental policy (Gibbs 1982; Bullard 1990; Camacho 1998; Faber 1998; Harvey 1999; Cole and Foster 2000). While scholarship has tended to focus on the unequal siting of industrial pollution, hazardous waste, and the negative environmental consequences of commercial development on minority and low income communities (Pellow 2004; Checker 2005), a growing number of works examine the unequal distribution of military toxics and exposure to military hazards, particularly on Native American land (Grinde and Johansen 1995; Kuletz 1998; LaDuke 1999; Hooks and Smith 2004).

Latin American environmentalism, in comparison with US mainstream environmentalism, analyzes environmental problems in relation to larger social and political inequalities. Lynch (1993, p. 115) argues that "the deepest roots of Latin American environmentalism come from resistance to conquest." In Vieques, conflict with the Navy is inseparable from broader issues of the United States' colonization and domination of

Puerto Rico. Vieques, an inhabited bombing range, a residential island simultaneously serving as a theater of war, is a fundamental expression of Puerto Rico's colonial status, the usurpation of its national territory, the pillaging and destruction of its natural resources, the unequal treatment of its citizens, and the state's disregard for their lives and aspirations. At its core, Vieques's struggle is about sovereignty. Who controls the land and for what purpose? What power does the state possess to determine what unfolds within its borders? What voice do citizens have in the state that governs them? The US Navy's control of Puerto Rican territory, the destruction of the environment, the subjection of civilians to bombs and toxic residues, and the lack of public voice in influencing military policy are inseparable from Puerto Rico's colonial status.

Vieques fits into a pattern of unequal distribution of military hazards and toxins. Residents have historically faced dramatic risk in terms of their exposure to military live fire practices and toxins, and now to its legacies of unexploded ordnance and contamination. Pro-statehood Puerto Rican Governor Pedro Rosselló, referring to the live bombing of an island inhabited by 10,000 American citizens, commented: "I think if this were happening in Manhattan, or if it were happening in Martha's Vineyard, certainly the delegations from those states would make certain that this would not continue."[4] Although the US Navy argued that Vieques was like many other communities near live fire ranges, there is no other parallel to its experience.

Unequal Risk, Unequal Exposure

The US Navy conducted maneuvers and target practice in Vieques from 1941 to 2003. The military expropriated three-quarters of island land and squeezed a resident civilian population of about 10,000 between an ammunition depot and a maneuver area. The Navy conducted artillery and small-arms firing, naval gunfire support, and missile shoots. It rehearsed amphibious landing exercises, parachute drops, and submarine maneuvers. The Navy bombed Vieques from air, land, and sea. In the 1980s and the 1990s, the Navy trained an average of 180 days and dropped or fired an average of 1,464 tons of bombs and explosives per year on the island (Shanahan and Lindsay-Poland 2002, p. 2). In 1998, the last year before protest interrupted maneuvers, the Navy dropped 23,000 bombs on the island, the majority of which contained live explosives (US Navy 1999).

The Navy argued that Vieques was only one of 56 live fire ranges operated by the US military. Thus, according to the Navy, the island's share of the burden of national defense was not unusual: in fact there were a number of other communities in the United States with residents living closer to weapons ranges (US Navy 1999). Vieques, however, was only one of two naval sites in the United States where both air-to-ground and ship-to-shore bombardment were practiced, and "the only inhabited island under the US flag ever to have a bombing range" (Giusti 2000). Most US bombing ranges, "especially those with air-to-ground fire, lie deep within huge military bases between five and ten times the size of Vieques. The large military bases with bombing ranges often adjoin vast national forests or wilderness reserves that further isolate the bases' bombing ranges." (Giusti 2000) The Vieques civilian zone was 8.7 miles from the "live impact area." According to Giusti (2000), "while in the United States there may be communities just outside the gates of bases with bombing ranges, those communities are a considerable distance from the actual ranges, which lie deep inside the bases." The intensity of military exercises, the proximity of live fire practices to the civilian population, and the environmental destruction caused by the Navy were unparalleled (ibid.).

The US military originally planned to use Vieques as a part of a major operating base in the Caribbean that would have extended from eastern Puerto Rico to the islands of Culebra and Vieques. Instead, Vieques became a training site, used for live fire practices and the amphibious landings of tens of thousands of sailors and Marines. Residents struggled to subsist on an island strangled by the military. The Navy controlled the majority of the land, water, and air surrounding Vieques. Its takeover shut down the island's sugar cane industry, and stifled the local economy. The Navy controlled nautical routes, flight paths, aquifers, and zoning laws in civilian territory. It blocked developers from establishing a resort on the island. It held title to the resettlement tracts in the civilian sector, where the majority of the island's population lived under constant threat of eviction (McCaffrey 2002).

The Navy planned eventually to eradicate not only the residents' presence on the island but also their history. Recognizing the incompatibility of military training exercises on an inhabited island, the Navy drafted secret plans in 1961 to remove the entire civilian population of 8,000 from the island; even the dead were to be dug up and removed from their graves (Fernández 1996). The plan would have allowed the Navy to expand the base without interference. Governor Luis Muñoz Marín intervened and a presidential order from President John F. Kennedy eventually blocked the Navy from carrying out its plans but the tension between the military and civilian population persisted.

In the late 1970s, protest erupted in Vieques in response to the intensification of maneuvers and live-fire exercises on the island. Between 1978 and 1983, fishermen led a dramatic grassroots struggle against the military presence in Vieques. Despite winning several important concessions from the Navy and broadcasting Vieques's plight to the world, the movement was ultimately unsuccessful in its goal of evicting the Navy and recovering land (McCaffrey 2002).

Discontent with the military presence continued and in the early nineties, activists began grassroots organizing around themes of health and the environment. The intensification of weapons firing and live bombing exercises over time increasingly put the civilian population at risk. Military jets, traveling between 500 and 1,300 miles per hour, bombed the easternmost part of the island. A miscalculation of several seconds thus exposed residents to significant risks of accidental bombings, such as when a mishap in October 1993 exploded bombs near the center of town.[5]

While the Navy emphasized the importance of Vieques for rehearsing high-altitude bomb drops, it was precisely these high altitudes runs that increased the possibility of error and thus risk to the civilian population dwelling beneath bomb-toting jets. "An error in four seconds of fire from a ship can land up to 14 or 20 miles from the target, while a four second error from an aircraft pilot could drop a bomb up to 50 miles from a target." (Shanahan and Lindsay-Poland 2002, p. 3) An increasing number of mishaps suggested that the relatively small target area (the Vieques target range was 982 acres, roughly the size of New York's Central Park, and was only 8.7 miles upwind from the residential sector) was too small to handle the powerful long-distance missiles in the Navy's arsenal (Shanahan and Lindsay-Poland 2002, p. 3).[6]

Not only were residents exposed to risk posed by jets practicing bomb drops from increasingly high altitudes; they were also subject to the toxic residue of bombs. One of the first studies to raise warning flags was published in 1988 in a Puerto Rican engineering journal (Cruz Pérez 1988). This article documented high concentrations of explosives in the local drinking water. Because Vieques's water is piped in from Puerto Rico, the study hypothesized, airborne contaminants were traveling from the bombing area into the civilian sector.

Residents were increasingly concerned about rising cancer rates and their possible connection to contamination from military explosives. Studies by the Puerto Rican Health Department eventually verified Vieques's cancer rate as significantly higher than that of the main island. Vieques's incidence of cancer for 1995–99 was 31 percent above that of the main island.[7]

The secretive nature of military activity and the community's lack of access to information intensified fear and suspicion. When the Navy imposed a radar installation on the island in the mid 1990s, local activists rallied renewed opposition to the Navy and built consciousness of the health and safety risks of the military presence.

In 1999 conflict erupted anew when a Navy jet on a training mission mistakenly dropped its load of 500-pound bombs not on the intended target range, but on the military observation post a mile away. The explosions injured one guard and killed a civilian employee of the base, David Sanes Rodríguez. Outrage over Sanes's death reignited the decades-long conflict.

Sanes's death came after 6 years of mobilizing and organizing against the threat military practices represented to civilian community. Within days of his death protestors occupied a military target range littered with live ordnance and shut down all Navy training exercises for more than a year. Tens of thousands of Puerto Rican marched in the streets of San Juan, demanding a halt to military training exercises in Vieques. Over the course of the next 4 years, mass mobilizations, constant pickets, thousands of acts of or civil disobedience, international solidarity and media attention eventually succeeded in halting live bombing exercises on the island.

The Navy's Pullout

Base land was decommissioned and converted to civilian use in two installments in May 2001 and May 2003. In response to mass protest, President Bill Clinton issued an executive directive in January 2000 that instructed the Navy to return all 8,000 acres on the former Naval Ammunition facility on the western side of Vieques to the government of Puerto Rico. In western Vieques, the Navy maintained a small operational base and dozens of magazines used for ammunition storage.

In military terms, western land was less significant than eastern land where maneuvers and bombing exercises were carried out. From a civilian perspective, however, the western part of the island was particularly valuable because it represented the closest transportation point between Vieques and Puerto Rico. Land turnover in the west seemed designed to quell protest and maintain the status quo in the strategically more important east.

Political developments, however, eroded the islanders' apparent victory. Congress altered the Clinton directive when it translated the order into law. Rather than returning land to the municipality, Congress ordered 4,000 acres returned to the municipality, 3,100 acres to the federal Department of the Interior, and 700 acres to the Puerto Rican Department of Natural Resources, with the remaining 200 acres (the site of a military radar installation) to remain under the control of the Navy. By the terms of the law passed by Congress, the Navy was responsible for cleaning up contaminated land according to future plans for its use.

The turnover of land failed to put an end to protest, which had built momentum around rising public concern about the risks to public safety, health and the environment created by live bombing exercises. Congress ultimately ordered the Navy to leave eastern Vieques and transfer its training activities elsewhere. Yet according to the terms of the Floyd D. Spence National Defense Authorization Act, 14,573 acres (40 percent of all island land) of eastern Vieques land was not returned to Puerto Rico. Instead, it was transferred to the US Department of Interior to be operated and administered as a National Wildlife Refuge. The 982-acre live impact range on the easternmost tip of Vieques was designated a Wilderness Area, the most protected status, and blocked from public access.

Fish, Wildlife, and Bombs

The idea of a bombing range turned overnight into a wildlife preserve on its face seems incongruous. Historically, however, many National Wildlife Refuges in United States and its territories were once military ranges, sites for military production, or bases (Lindsay-Poland 2006). In Vieques, the creation of the wildlife refuge is inseparable from a history of struggle against the US Navy's presence, and represents an incomplete realization of residents' desires to remove the Navy and recover island land. The establishment of the wildlife refuge represents a continuity of patterns of colonial usurpation and external control of the landscape.

Most fundamentally, the Vieques National Wildlife refuge enshrines unequal power relations that exclude the resident Viequense population from access to the land. The majority of island territory is placed under the jurisdiction of an external authority and the residents' access to land is curtailed. This approach to the land draws on a fortress model of conservation, which regards humans as a threat to the environment. According to this model, access to nature must be restricted by a paternalistic state, and the environment should be preserved and protected from human influence which is inherently negative (Adams and McShane 1997; Brockington 2002; Neumann 2004).

The fortress model of conservation assumes that the environment is static and ignores historic relations between people and the environment. Yet for thousands of years people have lived on Vieques Island and interacted with the ecology. Archaeological evidence suggests that several different cultural groups inhabited Vieques for at least 4,000 years before the Spanish conquest. Spanish and English colonists were attracted to the island because of its tropical forests and water supply. The land that is now under federal authority was dramatically transformed by human culture. Spain used Vieques as a hunting preserve until danger from Carib raids caused authorities to ban access to the island (Rouse 1952, p. 555). Sugar cane monoculture deforested land and cattle grazing programs initiated by the Navy contributed to soil erosion and the unchecked growth of mesquite. Navy construction of roads along the coast and interior of the island closed channels between lagoons and the sea, altering salinity levels and leading to the slow destruction of lagoons

(García Martínez 1979). Live bombing exercises blew away topsoil, contributing to the sedimentation of coral reefs. Human activity thus has fundamentally altered the pre-Columbian landscape.

Not only does the Wildlife refuge envision the environment as static, but also as pristine. In fact, the Wilderness Act of 1964, 16 USC. § 1131, et seq., under which the Vieques refuge was established, explicitly defines a wildlife refuge as a landscape "untrammeled by man" and "retaining its primeval character and influence." The designation of "wildlife refuge" therefore informs a land-use ethic that is focused on conservation, on maintaining the status quo, rather than remediation. Yet even the military acknowledges that "a natural progression of vegetative types from coastal areas to higher elevations has been lost and present day vegetation on the island is characteristic of the dry coastal zone vegetation of mainland Puerto Rico" (US Army Corps of Engineers 1998, quoted in Arbona 2004, p. 75). Centuries of human exploitation of the environment has reduced natural diversity to such an extent that one study suggested that "approximately eighty percent of the original vegetative cover ... has been greatly modified by man" (Woodbury 1972, quoted in Arbona 2004, p. 74). The Department of Fish and Wildlife is constructing as pristine a landscape that has already been fundamentally altered by centuries of human activity.

Rather than focusing on restoration, then, the Wildlife refuge premises that land needs to be protected from human intrusion, and implies that local use practices are responsible for ecological degradation. Instead, the state has been responsible for overwhelming destruction of the environment. The "wildlife refuge" is the same land that was bombed 180 days a year, that is littered with both spent shells and live bombs, that is pockmarked with bomb craters. The most devastated terrain, the 980-acre live impact area, is officially designated as a "wilderness preserve," the most protected environmental status, and blocked from public access.

The military is using environmental designation as a cloak to evade its legal and ethical responsibility to clean up waste. Legally, cleanup of unexploded ordnance and other military waste is determined by projected land use. Land designated for "conservation use" requires only a superficial cleanup, since presumably no humans would inhabit it. The wilderness designation to the live impact range, bombed by air, land,

and sea for 60 years, has less to do with the quality of the ecosystem than with the nature of responsibility for environmental remediation. Land inhabited by pelicans and sea turtles, simply put, is not a national priority for cleanup. Reality is turned on its head as residents are fined for collecting a sack of crabs, while the military, which has annihilated whole ecosystems, walks away from responsibility for environmental catastrophe.

Fish and Wildlife officials have protested that the Department of Interior never wanted Vieques land, and that it was imposed on them by Congress. (Lindsay-Poland 2006, p. 3). By the terms of the Wilderness Act, a wilderness area should appear "to have been affected primarily by the forces of nature, with the imprint of man's work substantially unnoticeable" and have "outstanding opportunities for solitude or a primitive and unconfined type of recreation." The former bombing range on Vieques clearly does not meet these statutory criteria.

The Department of Fish and Wildlife has become the lightning rod for local resentment because residents see the department as acting as handmaiden to the Navy, blocking access to land for which residents have struggled for decades. Although Fish and Wildlife argues that it restricts access to land out of necessity due to the threat of contamination and the danger of unexploded ordnance, it is imposing restrictions above and beyond what is required by law. Technically, only the 982-acre former bombing range has been designated with the most restrictive category of Wilderness area, but these access standards are being applied wholesale to the entire refuge. For example, the eastern beaches, which lie outside the former bombing range, are blocked from public access (Lindsay-Poland 2006). Moreover, the Department says that access depends upon a Navy certificate that land is cleared. In fact no such legal requirement exists. A number of wildlife refuges in the United States that have a history of military use and remaining problems of cleanup yet allow public access to land (Lindsay-Poland 2006).

Cleanup

The military used the two sides of Vieques very differently, and contamination and cleanup issues on western and eastern Vieques reflect different patterns of military use. In the west, where the Navy maintained an ammunition depot and a small operational base, cleanup is connected to the storage and disposal of munitions. Nearly two million pounds of military and industrial waste—oil, solvents, lubricants, lead paint, acid, and other refuse—were disposed of in different sites in mangrove swamps and sensitive wetland areas. A portion of this waste contained extremely hazardous chemicals. One 200-acre site was used for open detonation and burning of excess and defective munitions (Márquez and Fernández Porto 2000; UMET et al. 2000).

The Navy initially identified 17 sites for investigation and engaged in surface removal of munitions. By March of 2005, however, the military committed itself to continued investigation and surface ordnance explosion at only three of the 17 sites. The Navy argued that "no further action" was required at nine of the 17 sites. Of the remaining eight sites, the Navy argued that five had only minimal contamination and posed no significant risk (Bearden 2005, p. 14). In a controversial move, the Navy argued that toxic contamination did not, in fact, originate from military activity, but rather from naturally occurring processes related to the island's geology.[8]

The military's resistance to cleaning up the relatively limited amount of contamination on the western "clean" side of Vieques indicates how contentious the cleanup process in the east may become. The cleanup on the eastern side of the island is much more dramatic in scope. The 14,573-acre eastern area was used for naval bombing exercises and maneuvers since the 1940s. In the military base conversion process, the cleanup of firing ranges has proved one of the most dangerous, expensive and challenging tasks (Sorenson 1998). The point of the most intense destruction is the live impact range, which constitutes 982 acres, about the size of New York City's Central Park, on the island's eastern tip. According to the EPA, extensive unexploded ordnance and remnants of exploded ordnance remain in this range and its surrounding waters. "Hazardous substances associated with ordnance use may include mercury, lead, copper, magnesium, lithium, perchlorate, TNT, napalm, and depleted uranium among others. At Camp Garcia, and in the NASD, the hazardous substances present may also include a range of chemicals such as PCBs, solvents, and pesticides."[9] A 1998 EPA survey cited by the Military Toxics Project noted that most former firing ranges have significant contamination. The survey discussed widespread health dangers at 206 closed, transferred, and transferring (CTT) and inactive military ranges. The report concluded that: "contamination resulting from used or fired munitions including UXO [unexploded ordnance] is found on almost all ranges. . . . UXO has been found on 85 percent of the ranges and chemical or biological weapons are known to exist or are suspected at over 50 percent of the ranges. The risks from contamination resulting from ordnance use are widespread. Ranges in this report potentially pose significant risks to human health and safety because of their proximity to growing surrounding populations."[10]

Most unexploded ordnance in Vieques is concentrated in this easternmost former target area, yet some ordnance is likely to have strayed off target and into adjacent land, beaches, and water. In addition, land based maneuvers involving live fire exercises took place in different locations in the east, making it unclear how extensive the spread of munitions is outside the live impact area (Bearden 2005, p. 15).

The cleanup of eastern land will be expensive and time consuming. Over time live ordnance sinks beneath the surface of the land, requiring cleanup crews to remove both surface and subsurface soil. Depleted uranium, which was fired on the range in violation of federal law, poses its own unique problems for cleanup. Because of its mass and the size of the guns that fire it, depleted uranium can penetrate the earth to depths of hundreds of feet, requiring the removal of enormous amounts of soil to recover lost rounds (Sorenson 1998, p. 83, n. 174).

In addition, the groundwater has been contaminated by nitrates and explosives (Márquez and Fernández Porto 2000). Cleaning groundwater is also difficult and expensive. Subterranean water must first be located under thousands of acres of land, which is in itself a difficult process, then pumped to the surface, cleaned with scrubbing devices, and returned to the ground (Sorenson 1998, p. 81). Coral reefs and sea grass beds have sustained significant damage from bombing, sedimentation, and chemical contamination (Márquez and Fernández Porto 2000; Rogers, Cintrón, and Goenaga 1978). Despite the existence of numerous bombs off the shores of Vieques, cleaning the water is outside the purview of military cleanup requirements.

On February 11, 2005, the EPA responded to Puerto Rican Governor Sila Calderón's request to identify Vieques as a "Superfund site," a designation given to some of the nation's most hazardous waste sites. Placing Vieques on the National Priority List of hazardous sites did not, however, determine the stringency of the cleanup process, nor guarantee the availability of funds (Bearden 2005, p. 2). The cleanup process is ultimately contingent upon the designation of funds by Congress. Priority is established by the threat toxic waste poses to human health and the environment. This caveat is crucial because the extent to which people are barred access to the land reduces contact with hazardous sites and thus military responsibility for cleanup.

Establishing a pathway of human exposure to contamination, however, is another way to compel the military to clean up its waste. "If contamination has leached from munitions and migrated to present a pathway of exposure, removal of more munitions may be required to protect human health. Possible pathways include consumption of contaminated groundwater and contaminated fish or shellfish" (Beardon 2005, p. 2). Two studies (Massol and Díaz 2000a,b) suggest that toxic heavy metals have entered the Vieques food chain. The first study documented high levels of lead, cobalt, nickel and manganese in violin crabs and in plants near the Vieques impact area. The second study found vegetables and plants growing in some civilian areas of Vieques are highly contaminated with lead, cadmium, copper, and other metals.

In a major setback to community groups, however, the Agency for Toxic Substances and Disease Registry (ATSDR), the federal public-health agency responsible for determining human health effects associated with toxic exposure, announced that it found no toxic contamination in Vieques.[11] The agency's findings of no significant contamination after more than 60 years of bombing outraged community members who found this conclusion completely at odds with common sense and the fact of drastically increased cancer rates.[12] Indeed research data suggests a correlation between the onset of live bombing exercises in the 1970s, and the escalation of cancer rates in Vieques (Nazario et al. 1998). In this context, ATSDR's findings of no significant contamination and no danger to the health of the Vieques community, not withstanding 60-plus years of bombing, stood out as remarkably convenient for the Navy.

Seductive Fantasies and the Politics of Exclusion

Another pernicious consequence of the US government designating roughly half of Vieques Island as a wildlife refuge is that it has triggered a land grab in the existing civilian sector. This land grab is occurring in a context of impoverishment and marginalization of the overall population.

According to the 2000 US Census, the municipality of Vieques is one of the poorest in all of Puerto Rico, with 65 percent of the population living below the poverty level. Vieques has the highest child poverty rate in Puerto Rico, with 81 percent of its children living below poverty level (Mather 2003, p. 7). It has among the highest rates, 20 percent, of teenage high school drop outs (ibid., p. 7). Health indicators are poor, with high rates of cancer, and infant mortality compared to the rest of Puerto Rico. In 2001, the Puerto Rican Department of Health reported that death rates from cardiac illness, diabetes, HIV/AIDS, strokes, hypertension, liver disease, and cancer were substantially higher than on the main island of Puerto Rico.[13] The island suffers from a serious lack of infrastructure. Transportation to the mainland of Puerto Rico is poor, and there is no system of public transportation on a 52-square-mile island. Trash pickup and disposal have suffered from a lack of revenue due to a poor tax base. A 1999 Special Commission to the Governor of Puerto Rico concluded that the Navy's control of land, water and island resources caused high unemployment and economic stagnation on the island.

Although little has changed in the material conditions of the municipality since the departure of the Navy in 2003, the military's exit has removed the principal obstacle to development and has triggered wild speculation. Investors seek out homes and land that can be renovated and developed and resold for substantial profit. Housing prices and sales in beachfront neighborhoods have soared.

A recent article analyzed housing sales in the Esperanza neighborhood of Vieques. The article detailed frenzied buying in an 18 month period between 2003 and the first 6 months of 2004. During this period, 36 properties were sold—22 to buyers from the United States, eight to buyers from the Puerto Rican mainland, and only two to buyers from

Vieques. (The other buyers could not be classified.) During this same 18-month period, housing prices in the neighborhood rose by 50 percent.[14]

One unusual aspect of Vieques's real estate market is that a large amount of property is untitled, the legacy of decades of insecurity created by the military presence. In the 1940s, the Navy evicted residents and relocated them to resettlement plots without title. Later, residents' frustration with cramped and uncertain living quarters and resentment of the Navy's hold on three-fourths of the island spurred land takeovers in the idle lands of the military buffer zone. Today whole neighborhoods in Vieques, with water, roads, and electrical service, are effectively squatter communities where thousands of families live without title. Yet land sales in these areas are dizzying. Non-coastal lots sell for $70,000 an acre and beachfront property sells for $1 million an acre.[15] Vieques's mayor, Dámaso Serrano, proclaims himself powerless in the face of this frenzy: "The fact is that properties without land titles are being sold two and three times in a two-month period, reaching higher prices each time, and there is nothing we can do about it."[16]

Vieques is a classic scenario of gentrification: "Housing speculation thrives in rapidly changing markets, where properties turn over quickly, where low-income, often elderly original residents are anxious to pull out new found equity, or where original residents may not have sufficient information to understand the increasing value of their homes." (Kennedy and Leonard 2001, p. 11)

Perhaps the most striking indicator of the rapid gentrification of the island was a listing in the Escape section of the *New York Times* featuring a three-bedroom house with a guesthouse for sale in Vieques for $2.5 million. The owner was quoted as saying: "We love the beach, we love the Caribbean. Vieques, though, is very different from many of the other islands. Two-thirds of the island is a wild preserve, and there are a lot of beautiful beaches with no development—that's what is special to us."[17]

North American investors are surprisingly satisfied to overlook Vieques's troubled environmental history and to embrace the fantasy of a tropical, undiscovered Eden advanced by developers. Connections Real

Estate owned and operated by North Americans, paints an idyllic picture of Vieques in its promotional literature. With a pitch designed to appeal to soul and pocketbook, the island is marketed as a tropical Eden and an irresistible investment:

Owning a piece of paradise is a seductive fantasy that many of us dream about and some of us turn into reality. The Vieques real estate market is an opportunity to make that dream come true. Come and see Vieques Island, Puerto Rico, known as one of "the Spanish Virgin Islands," and find the opportunity to make your dream come true.

Vieques offers an attractive investment on a beautiful Caribbean island reminiscent of the "discovered" islands of at least thirty years ago. Development has not yet started and there are several properties with an amazing variety of views available.

Come and enjoy our beaches that are preserved in their natural form, where one can enjoy white sand beaches, gentle breezes, incredible vistas, and an inviting turquoise sea, as well as many species of birds, turtles, dolphin, manatee, and whales as they travel through the Caribbean.

Describing Vieques as one of the "Spanish Virgin Islands" is highly charged. Local Viequenses bristle at a North American invention that they see as a thinly veiled racist attempt to distance Vieques from its association with Puerto Rico. "Spanish Virgin Islands" connects Vieques to the US-controlled English-speaking islands to the east, and away from "problematic" associations with Spanish-speaking, culturally unassimilated Puerto Ricans. Marketing Vieques as a "Virgin Island" draws a metaphorical connection between Vieques and a neighboring underdeveloped island, St. John. In the 1950s, Laurence Rockefeller bought up half of St. John and imposed a national park upon the island, excluding the Afro-Caribbean residents from access to land and wealth (Olwig 1986). Vieques's real estate propaganda mirrors the celebratory St. John tourist literature, marveling at the beauties and tranquility of the undeveloped terrain. Yet Vieques, with its toxic legacy of bombs and pockmarked terrain, is probably better compared to Love Canal than to its Caribbean neighbor St. John.

Reality has very little to do with real estate marketing campaigns, which are firmly planted in the realm of fantasy. Rainbow Realty, advertised to progressive circles as a gay-owned and gay-friendly business, markets Vieques as a laid-back alternative to life on the fast track:

Located in the turquoise Caribbean waters off the southeast coast of Puerto Rico is the small tropical island paradise called VIEQUES!! The place for a simple, casual, relaxing, and "laid back" get-a-way. No casinos, clubs, or glitz here . . . spend a night in San Juan for that. We have no traffic lights and no fast food. We do have wild horses and plenty of chickens. The coqui frog will serenade you and our Bioluminescent Bay will enchant you! Bring those books you have wanted to read and find a hammock. Sit on deserted beaches, watch dazzling sunsets, snorkel, dive the reefs, fish, or just float, all in perfect weather. All of this . . . and affordability!

Of course, "affordability" is relative. For North Americans who have access to capital and can draw second mortgages on homes up north to come up with the cash necessary to buy real estate on untitled land in Vieques, such real estate is attractive. For Vieques residents who earn $5.15 an hour cleaning hotels rooms in Martineau Bay Resort, island real estate prices are soaring out of reach.

Crow's Nest, another real estate competitor, sells its vision this way:

Vieques is a miracle. An unspoiled Caribbean island off the coast of Puerto Rico, easily reached from the United States and Canada. There are no traffic lights, no movie theatres and no bowling alley. We do have many fabulous restaurants, beautiful white sand beaches and a sky full of stars at night. There are no hawkers on the beach, no fast food joints, no neon signs. Under the US flag, Vieques is safe for property owners and for tourists.

Vieques, conveniently located under the US flag, is apparently ideal for "Americans," but will Puerto Rican Americans be able to own the land on which they were born? The immediate effect of military pull-out on the resident Viequense population has been an intensification of the island's housing crisis. For years, the military's control of island land and failure to issue title to residents relocated to military resettlement tracts created a housing crunch on the island. Now, rising real estate values threaten to further exclude the local population from access to affordable homes. Existing housing programs are underfunded and inadequate in addressing housing needs in this impoverished island. In 2004, 260 families were on the waiting list for Section 8 housing subsidies. Even families who have subsidies may be priced out of the rental market by escalating prices.[18]

Designating Vieques as a National Wildlife Refuge has added a premium to property values in the civilian sector. Value is based fundamentally on exclusion. By cordoning off parkland from the working class, Puerto Rican population, the new wildlife refuge has effectively attracted off-shore capital that is displacing the working-class residents from the island. Thus residents are doubly excluded, by the refuge and the housing frenzy that it stimulated.

Although state intervention can constrain gentrification through control of zoning and code enforcement, both the municipal and commonwealth governments have been slow to enforce existing laws in Vieques. Plans to develop a land trust that might slow the pace of gentrification have not yet materialized. While the municipality approved an ordinance that imposed a fine of up to $10,000 and jail time on any person buying or selling property without title, it is not clear how effective a deterrent this has been. Additionally, while Puerto Rican law provides for equal access to the coasts and beaches of the islands, a Starwood resort opened on the northern coast of Vieques with financing from the Puerto Rican government, even though the resort blocked public access to the shore in violation of the law. And across the north coast of island wooden shacks and Moorish-style estates perched on cliffs behind high white walls block public access to the coast. Three story homes are built in defiance of zoning regulations. A public beach on the island's north coast is completely consumed by a newly constructed vacation rental property that pipes its sewage directly into the sea. Community groups, overwhelmed by the increasing complexity of struggle against the Navy, various federal agencies and market forces, have been slow to respond to these developments.

The Struggle for Inclusion

I was always afraid during maneuvers. I was always worried that they'd make a mistake, miss, and drop a bomb on us and that would be the end of us. I was always worried about this. . . . [Now] there aren't anymore bombs! The planes aren't flying overhead dropping bombs, cracking the foundations of houses. It's a big change. It's great!
—Felicita Solís Solís, Vieques resident, 2004

Vieques residents committed to the sustainable development of the island and the integration of the predominantly working-class residents with socioeconomic development of their island are rightfully concerned with twin forces of privatization and state usurpation that are challenging the victory that the military eviction represented. Despite the victory that the end of bombing represents, the cessation of live fire exercises in and of itself was never the goal of the movement. Activists had long sought the recovery of land. This aspiration has yet to be realized and is challenged by the transformation of former base land into a National Wildlife Refuge and the concurrent rapid gentrification and privatization of the civilian sector.

I have argued for a broader interpretation of environmental justice, to include access to the positive aspects of the environment. Environmental justice should ensure that people who have suffered the greatest harm should be compensated at the very least by full access to the richness of the land and its resources.

Acknowledgments

Many thanks to Neeraj Vedwan, who gave me thoughtful feedback on an earlier draft of this article, and to Howard Fischer for his editorial comments and support.

Notes

1. US Fish and Wildlife Service, South East Region 4, "Vieques National Wildlife Refuge Welcomes the Public to the Eastern End of the Island," April 30, 2003, http://www.fws.gov.

2. US Department of Fish and Wildlife, 2006, "Come and Enjoy Vieques National Wildlife Refuge This Summer," http://www.fws.gov.

3. US Environmental Protection Agency, Superfund, "EPA Proposes the Atlantic Fleet weapons Training Area on Vieques and Culebra for Inclusion on the Superfund National Priorities List," August 2004, http://www.epa.gov.

4. CBS News, "60 Minutes," August 15, 2000.

5. Vieques Times, November 1993.

6. A Special Commission appointed by the Governor of Puerto Rico concluded that the training accident that killed security guard David Sanes was "the last in a series of errors that prove that it is possible for an explosive or dangerous artifact to be discharged near or in the civilian population area, thus jeopardizing the life and safety of the citizens of Vieques." The Attorney General of Puerto Rico testified that "in 1998 alone, by the Navy's own admission, five separate live fire events . . . occurred during training exercises." He added that "this

pattern of live fire events has been repeated virtually every year," and concluded that "all of these incidents show that the Navy cannot ensure the safety of the population of Vieques. Source: report to the Secretary of Defense of the Special Panel of Military Operations in Vieques. June 1999, http://www.defenselink.mil/news.

7. *Miami Herald*, May 7, 2004.

8. Source: http://www.forusa.org.

9. Source: http://www.epa.gov.

10. Source: www.miltoxproj.org.

11. *Puerto Rican Herald*, November 6, 2001.

12. "The ATSDR inspires little confidence among environmental health activists," writes John Lindsay-Poland of the Fellowship for Reconciliation, "because its methodology has made it nearly impossible to find causality between contamination and illness. According to Linda King of the Environmental Health Network, who has monitored the agency for more than ten years, only one ATSDR study among hundreds showed a link between contaminants in the community and health problems." (http://www.forusa.org)

13. *Caribbean Business*, April 15, 2004.

14. *Claridad*, July 8–14, 2004.

15. *Puerto Rico Herald*, April 15, 2004.

16. Ibid.

17. *New York Times*, May 20, 2005.

18. *Claridad*, July 8–14, 2004.

References

Adams, Jonathan, and Thomas McShane. 1997. *The Myth of Wild Africa: Conservation without Illusion*. University of California Press.

Arbona, Javier. 2004. Vieques, Puerto Rico: From Devastation to Conservation, and Back Again. Master's thesis, Massachusetts Institute of Technology.

Baver, Sherrie L. 2006. Environmental justice and the cleanup of Vieques. *CENTRO Journal* 18, no. 1: 3–19.

Bearden, David. 2005. Vieques and Culebra Islands: An analysis of cleanup status and costs. Report for Congress, Congressional Research Service Report, Library of Congress. http://www.fas.org.

Berman Santana, Déborah. 2005. Vieques: The land, the people, the struggle, the future. In *The Quest For Environmental Justice*, ed. R. Bullard. University of California Press.

Brockington, Dan. 2002. *Fortress Conservation: The Preservation of the Mkomazi Game Reserve*. Indiana University Press.

Bullard, Robert. 1990. *Dumping in Dixie: Race, Class, and Environmental Quality*. Westview.

Camacho, David. 1998. *Environmental Injustices, Political Struggles: Race, Class, and the Environment*. Duke University Press.

Checker, Melissa. 2005. *Polluted Promises: Environmental Racism and the Search for Justice in a Southern Town*. New York University Press.

Cole, Luke W., and Sheila R. Foster. 2000. *From the Ground Up: Environmental Racism and the Rise of the Environmental Justice Movement*. New York University Press.

Collinson, Helen, ed. 1997. *Green Guerrillas: Environmental Conflicts and Initiatives in Latin America and the Caribbean*. Black Rose Books.

Cruz Pérez, Rafael. 1988. Contaminación producida por explosivos y residuous de explosivos en Vieques, Puerto Rico. *Dimensión* 8, no. 2: 37–42.

Faber, Daniel, ed. 1998. *The Struggle for Ecological Democracy: Environmental Justice Movements in the United States*. Guilford.

Fernández, Ronald. 1996. *The Disenchanted Island: Puerto Rico and the United States in the Twentieth Century*. Praeger.

García Martínez, Neftalí. 1979. Consecuencias Histórico-Naturales de la Presencia de la Marina en Vieques. Comité Nacional pro Defensa de Vieques.

Gibbs, Lois. 1982. *Love Canal: My Story*. SUNY Press.

Giusti Cordero, Juan. 2000. One-stop shopping for Navyfacts: A response to the Navy's Vieques website. Puerto Rico Update, Fellowship for Reconciliation Puerto Rico Campaign, www.forusa.org.

Grinde, Donald A., and Bruce E. Johansen. 1995. *Ecocide of Native America: Environmental Destruction of Indian Lands and Peoples*. Clear Light.

Harvey, David. 1999. The environment of justice. In *Living with Nature*, ed. F. Fischer and M. Hajer. Oxford University Press.

Hooks, Gregory, and Chad L. Smith. 2004. Treadmill of destruction: National sacrifice areas and Native Americans. *American Sociological Review* 69, no. 4: 558–575.

Kennedy, Maureen, and Paul Leonard 2001. Dealing with Neighborhood Change: A Primer on Gentrification and Policy Choices. Brookings Institution Center on Urban and Metropolitan Policy. http://www.brookings.edu.

Kuletz, Valerie. 1998. *The Tainted Desert: Environmental and Social Ruin of the American West*. Routledge.

LaDuke, Winona. 1999. *All Our Relations: Native Struggles for Land and Life*. South End.

Lindsay-Poland, John. 2006. Refuge for whom? Vieques and the uses of a bombing area. Paper presented at Latin American Studies Association Congress, San Juan, Puerto Rico.

Lynch, Barbara. 1993. The garden and the sea: US Latino environmental discourses and mainstream environmentalism. *Social Problems* 40, no. 1: 108–124.

Márquez, Lirio, and Jorge Fernández Porto. 2000. Environmental and Ecological Damage to the Island of Vieques due to the Presence and Activities of the United States Navy. Special International Tribunal on the Situation of Puerto Rico and the Island Municipality of Vieques.

Massol Deya, Arturo, and Elba Díaz. 2000a. Biomagnificación de Metales Carcinógenos en el Tejido de Cangrejos de Vieques, Puerto Rico. Casa Pueblo de Adjuntas y Departamento de Biología del Recinto de Mayagüez, Universidad de Puerto Rico.

Massol Deya, Arturo, and Elba Díaz. 2000b. Metales Pesados en la Vegetación Dominante del Area del Impacto de Vieques, Puerto Rico. Casa Pueblo de Adjuntas y Departamento de Biología del Recinto de Mayagüez, Universidad de Puerto Rico.

Mather, Mark. 2003. Children in Puerto Rico: Results from the 2000 Census. Annie E. Casey Foundation and Population Reference Bureau. http://www.aecf.org.

McCaffrey, Katherine. 2002. *Military Power and Popular Protest: The US Navy in Vieques, Puerto Rico*. Rutgers University Press.

McCaffrey, Katherine, and Sherrie Baver. 2006. Ni una bomba mas: Reframing the Vieques struggle. In *Beyond Sun and Sand*, ed. S. Baver and B. Lynch. Rutgers University Press.

Nazario, Cruz María, Erick L. Suárez, and Cynthia Pérez. 1998. Análisis Crítico dle Informe Incidencia de Cáncer en Vieques del Departamento de Salud de Puerto Rico. Recinto de Ciencias Médicas, Universidad de Puerto Rico.

Neumann, Roderick. 2002. *Imposing Wilderness: Struggles over Livelihood and Nature Preservation in Africa*. University of California Press.

Olwig, Karen Fog. 1986. *Cultural Adaptation and Resistance on St. John: Three Centuries of Afro-Caribbean Life*. University Press of Florida.

Pellow, David Naguib. 2004. *Garbage Wars: The Struggle for Environmental Justice in Chicago*. MIT Press.

Rogers, Caroline S., Gilberto Cintrón, and Carlos Goenaga. 1978. The Impact of Military Operations on the Coral Reefs of Vieques and Culebra. Report submitted to Department of Natural Resources, San Juan, Puerto Rico.

Rouse, Irving. 1952. *Porto Rico Prehistory*. New York Academy of Sciences.

Shanahan, John, and John Lindsay-Poland. 2000. Vieques: Is It Needed by the Navy? Vieques Issue Brief. http://www.prorescatevieques.org.

Sorenson, David. 1998. *Shutting Down the Cold War: The Politics of Military Base Closure*. St. Martin's Press.

UMET (Universidad Metropolitana), New Jersey Institute of Technology y el Centro de Acción Ambiental. 2000. Resumen de Estudios y Datos Ambientales en Vieques.

US Navy. 1999. Commander, US Second Fleet, National Security Need for Vieques.

12

Cultural Politics and the Essence of Life: Who Controls the Water?

Stefanie Wickstrom

Is a river alive, endowed with spirit, integral to the well-being of the interconnected biotic and supernatural communities created in the land-scapes where it flows? Or is it a resource that, properly managed, creates wealth for nations and individuals? Is water a commodity that can be managed most efficiently by markets? Cultural politics has been defined as conflicts between meanings and practices of different cultural groups (Alvarez, Dagnino, and Escobar 1998). Indigenous communities, govern-ments, and transnational business represent conflicting cultural groups fighting "water wars" over meanings related to water. This chapter examines the cases of Chile, Bolivia, and Mexico to ascertain which of the three contending groups or combinations of groups is winning and the ends toward which the winners exercise their control over water. Once the context is set, the influences of the different regimes on indig-enous communities and the kinds and effectiveness of indigenous move-ments responding to the outcomes will be examined.

Who Controls the Water?

Water, conceived as a resource, is used for an expanding array of eco-nomic activities in Latin America today, from electric power generation to high-tech irrigation for specialty export crops. It is important to remember that before it became a "resource," water was "managed" for hundreds of years by indigenous communities through what expert observers today characterize as either "single-community" or "multi-community" "self-managed, autonomous systems." For example, sophis-ticated infrastructure and management regimes for irrigation were developed by communities in the Andes well before the Incas flexed their imperial muscle (Gelles 2000; Mitchell and Guillet 1994). In some places in Mexico, communities managed water autonomously and cooperatively. In arid regions, water management was "heavily dependent on terraces, diversion dams, aqueducts, and canal networks within valley-limited drainages which were knit together by expanding empires" (Scarborough 1993, p. 18). Mexico City was a marvel of water engineering when Hernán Cortés and his forces arrived to conquer the Aztec Empire.

These indigenous Latin American communities and empires encouraged respect for power and sacredness inherent in other beings and interconnected natural and supernatural systems upon which they depended for life. They maintained spiritual bonds with water that helped shape individual and collective productive activities and related behaviors, responsibilities, and rights. Water use was governed by beliefs about appropriate behavior toward a revered spirit of a spring or river. Scarce rains were coaxed or courted by sacrifice or ceremony. Many peoples also recognized concepts we now associate with the emerging science of ecology.

Today political and economic elites wield a shifting combination of state and market power to manage water for utilitarian and profit-making purposes: power generation, large-scale agriculture, industrial applications, drinking, and sanitation. In the global marketplace, water is a valuable commodity; demand is increasing as the supply of clean, fresh water is decreasing. Different settler state regimes throughout the Americas are influenced by different values and understandings of rights,[1] which has resulted in a variety of experiences when it comes to managing water resources. All settler states, however, have imposed their respective values and systems of governance on the indigenous communities of the Americas with little regard for indigenous people's water use or for indigenous cultures' ecologically sustainable systems of productive activity. They exhibit even less regard for indigenous values and rights, and they totally disregard anything as laughably irrational as the spirit of a spring or river that might be offended by disregard. But indigenous movements are fighting back.

Trends in Controlling Water Resources in Latin America

Indigenous values and political cultures and the complex systems of rights and responsibilities where they have any status at all have been reduced to what social scientists call "common-law normative frameworks" that are superseded by property rights and resource-management regimes imposed by settler states. Indigenous normative frameworks ground water use in spiritual beliefs, prohibit transfer of water rights apart from land, recognize community entitlement to (as opposed to individual ownership of) water, and rely to some extent on consensus but also empower traditional authorities to organize maintenance of infrastructure in cooperation with authorities from other communities when joint management of infrastructure is necessary. After independence in Latin America, states had no interest in promoting emulation of indigenous systems of productive activity. State and market systems of water-resource management "ignore or deny the existence or importance of common-law normative frameworks regarding local indigenous rights and uses and water resource management" (Gentes 2002b, p. 36). States continue to annihilate or forcibly integrate indigenous communities as cheap labor, especially wherever their valuable water can be made available to settlers.

Latin American settler states became concerned with water-resource management in the twentieth century as populations, urbanization, and industrialization increased dramatically, as public administration matured and communications and information technologies took root, and as water supplies were threatened by decades of unsustainable development. Until at least the mid 1970s, water-resource management was carried out by governments, which engaged primarily in construction of infrastructure to supply the increasing demands of expanding economies. Governments identified, directed, and helped to finance the construction of major water works projects. With help from international financial and development institutions, governments also funded research into innovative uses of national water resources (especially potential for generating hydroelectric power) and traditions governing water use in different places (Dourojeanni and Jouravlev 2002).

Sustainable development became a buzzword on the international scene in the 1980s. As water regimes evolved, Latin American bureaucracies began to engage in integrated water-resource management. Integrated water-resource management defined water as a commodity, but valuing and allocating rights to a commodity in order to facilitate both maximum efficiency and social justice would still require that a variety of responsibilities be exercised by regulating authorities (Bauer 2004). By the late 1980s, however, just when it was arguably most necessary and most viable in Latin America, the regulatory authority of the state in resource-management activities was undermined by global market mania. In the neoliberal global economy, the role of the Latin American state has become protection of private investment and promotion of international trade so that market forces might provide for basic needs. Control of public networks for monitoring and managing water resources was sold to multinational corporations that would transform old and insufficient infrastructure. Profitable forms of water-resource management, especially hydroelectric power generation and provision of drinking water and sanitation, became private-sector endeavors. Funding for research in integrated water-resource and watershed management is now largely a thing of the past. International financial and development institutions like the World Bank and the Inter-American Development Bank implemented programs to make water-resource management more "efficient" and to upgrade infrastructure through investment by multinational corporations that would have long-term contracts to provide water and sanitation services on behalf of state agencies.

Some administrative systems are in worse shape than others, but in general little is being done in Latin America to facilitate effective governance for sustainable water-resource management (Dourojeanni and Jouravlev 2002). Negative externalities associated with water-resource management have become "gray areas" in systems of public administration and diverse administrative sectors have to deal with them case by case. Social equity and conflict resolution are not typically addressed by water-resource-management systems (Bauer 2004). When private companies invest in providing water and sanitation services in poor countries, "full cost recovery" for investment in infrastructure and provision of water and sanitation services is usually part of the package. Accompanying fee increases are rarely affordable for consumers. In Latin America today, "free" trade and the interests of multinational corporations are protected by governments, and conflict is intensifying between MNCs and governments and communities struggling to protect their rights as they lose control over water.

Chile: Transnational Dominance Supported by the State

Chile's 1981 Water Code,[2] implemented by the military dictatorship (1973–1990), privatized water rights and restricted governmental regulatory authority. It also separated water resources from land ownership. The objectives of the Code were to create markets that enabled the free and unprioritized transfer of water rights, to secure water use rights as property that could be used to further economic development, and to reduce the regulatory role of the state in water-resource management.

The current legal and institutional framework of water-resource management is controlled by the central government's[3] General Water Directorate.[4] It has been successful in strengthening private economic rights and restricting government regulatory authority. This system is regarded for its efficiency at allocating relatively scarce water resources and Chile has been lauded by neoliberal economists as a case of successful allocation of water rights and of coping with water scarcity. Proponents claim Chilean water-resource-management regimes and development policies are based on balanced and realistic macroeconomic policies (Solanes 2006).

Restructuring has resulted in major transfers of wealth and a significant redefinition of property rights. As a result of privatization, water and infrastructure are being used in ways and places that are profitable, but not in the public interest. For example, the Water Code established a new class of "nonconsumptive" water rights that promote hydroelectric development,[5] but failed to establish norms or institutions to promote river basin management. This has resulted in environmental degradation, "a major transfer of wealth from irrigators to electric companies, and a significant redefinition of property rights, on the basis of legal reasoning of dubious quality" (Bauer 2004, p. 111).

Market incentives have failed to promote efficiency in water use, obviate the need for government subsidies for irrigation works, make water rights more secure or tradable (in practice), or benefit small agricultural producers (Bauer 2004). The majority of the water rights in Chile are now held by power-generating, mining, and fruit exporting corporations (Bauer 2004; Boelens 2003). With the government's role reduced to protection of private property, a transnational corporate elite was empowered to pursue profit-making in rural Chile while ignoring the concerns of the vast majority of people who depend for their well-being on water (Boelens 2003). Because "individual property owners are not sanctioned for polluting their property" (ibid.), the country's water resources are being degraded. *Campesino* communities and indigenous communities throughout Chile have been adversely affected, and analysts concerned with preservation of traditional indigenous cultures point to Chile's neoliberal water law as a threat to customary and indigenous water use regimes (Boelens 2003).

Given these impacts on many segments of the Chilean economy and society, well-qualified analysts[6] and some state agencies have recommended that the country's water law be modified to promote more effective governance and sustainable use of water and allocation of water rights (Natural Resources and Infrastructure Division 2003). With re-democratization concerns for the environment and indigenous rights began to take more precedence in the public arena. Following the United Nations Conference on Environment and Development in 1992, the Chilean legislature approved changes to the Water Code[7] to protect aquifers, ensure continued hydration of fragile highland ecosystems, and protect water sources that had been used traditionally by some indigenous communities (Gentes 2002a; Yañez and Gentes 2005). Nonetheless, the Code's economic concerns could not effectively balanced with social and environmental concerns by Chile's new Environmental Law[8] passed in 1994. Its implementation has done little to protect water.

In May 2005, President Ricardo Lagos signed into law some reforms of the Code. These provisions came into force beginning in 2006 in most regions of the country. The main objective of the reforms was a better balance between the public interest and property rights. The revised Code obliges the General Water Directorate to consider environmental issues in the future establishment of water rights, in order to promote more sustainable water flows and aquifer management. The new legislation also permits the Chilean president to "protect the public interest by excluding water resources from economic competition when they need to be reserved for public supply in the absence of other means of obtaining water or, in the case of non-consumptive rights, in the event of exceptional circumstances of national interest" (Natural Resources and Infrastructure Division 2005). Revisions to the Code were intended to return control to the state and encourage a stronger role in public decision making by user organizations (Natural Resources and Infrastructure Division 2005).

From the beginning, however, policymakers agreed that market incentives should remain the basis of water-resource management: "On many different occasions, the Government stated that free commercialization of water use rights tends to be an appropriate way of achieving more economically efficient water use and allocation" (Natural Resources and Infrastructure Division 2005). Water rights allocation criteria remain structured to grant control over water to actors that guarantee they will use it to promote activities with the highest productivity per cubic meter. Reforms have primarily been designed to put an end to hoarding and speculation. One measure is the incorporation of licensing fees charged for unused water rights. New requests for water rights allocation must now be accompanied by an explanation of how water will be used and the General Water Directorate will have the authority to limit the amount of water users can control, though allocation criteria will remain "strictly economic" (Natural Resources and Infrastructure Division 2005).

In Chile, the elite interests the government now represents exercise effective control over water resources. From 1951, when the first water code was implemented, until the coup of 1973, a variety of interests and actors struggled to control the government and so implement policies that would promote development and social justice. After 1973, aspirations for social justice were forcibly thwarted, and the military dictatorship that seized control of the state radically reshaped public administration to foster neoliberal development. Since re-democratization, the governing Concertación coalition has expressed interest in promoting sustainable development, but water remains under the control of an increasingly powerful transnational elite, which is aware of the importance of environmental protection, but mostly unwilling to compromise economic advantage even to enact substantive protections for natural capital.

Protecting indigenous rights yields little economic or political gain, but placing the burden of development on indigenous peoples and the ecosystems they have managed since before the Conquest yields profits for big business and fosters national economic "growth." Despite the odds against their success, indigenous communities that have borne the costs associated with the economic and political gains of Chile's middle and upper classes since re-democratization are contesting control of water. Today many enjoy the support of an active and well-organized advocacy community that makes clear connections between indigenous rights, environmental protection, and sustainable development in Chile.

Bolivia: The Indigenous Majority Wins Control of the State

The Republic of Bolivia is a unitary state, with some authority in decision making devolved by the central government to the departmental level since the Administrative Decentralization law passed in 1995. Bolivia currently has no national water law or policy (Natural Resources and Infrastructure Division 2003). Water resources are managed by sector (irrigation, provision of drinking water, and provision of sanitation services) with regional oversight. In 1997, the World Bank made privatization a condition of a loan to the Bolivian government (Bloom 2005) resulting in a new law that privatized the provision of drinking water and sanitation services.[9] (For more on the causes of the water wars, see Perreault's chapter.)

The ultimate response to privatization was a popular uprising in Cochabamba, Bolivia's third largest city, from February to March 2000. Thousands of people took to the city's streets to protest the privatization of their water that included the communities' cooperatively built and cooperatively managed domestic water systems and family wells. Violent repression by the state left more than 100 people wounded and five dead. When the tear gas cleared, however, President Hugo Banzer announced on April 11 that the privatization law had been revised.[10] In the short-term, activism paid off. Control of Cochabamba their water was returned to the communities. Activists succeeded in redefining water as a public trust resource. The former Municipal Autonomous Drinking Water and Sewer Service (SEMAPA)[11] resumed providing water and sanitation services and the contract with the Bechtel subsidiary was canceled.[12] In early 2006 Abengoa of Spain, a Bechtel co-investor, sued the Bolivian government for $50,000,000 in the World Bank's International Centre for Settlement of Investment Disputes (ICSID), but when the case was settled in January 2006 Bolivia paid only 30¢ for damages suffered by the corporation—another victory.[13]

Part of the explanation for the success of the popular uprising in Cochabamba is earlier opposition organized by *campesino* and indigenous farmers to the 1999 law that privatized their water and prohibited traditional water practices in rural areas. Their Coalition in Defense of Water and Life[14] played a leading role in organizing the opposition to privatization of the Cochabamba municipal water system (Olivera and Lewis 2004).

After the popular uprising, the Bolivian government began to revise water law to make possible more democratic, holistic management, with coordinated participation by a broad spectrum of private and public entities. The Bolivian Commission for Integrated Water Resource Management[15] is the lead agency in the ongoing restructuring of water-resource-management regimes.

Indigenous rights are now being explicitly delineated. The Bolivian legislature has recognized indigenous peoples' customary rights to use and develop water resources for drinking and sanitation. Indigenous rights and traditional authorities and customs now have legal standing in water-resource management. Furthermore, when ambiguity exists as to substantive recognized rights and practices that might actually guarantee their implementation, the tendency is now to protect the interests indigenous communities have in local natural resources within recognized traditional territories (Yañez and Gentes 2005).

Bolivian organizations and communities working to promote more just and sustainable water-resource management have allied with transnational NGOs and experts from around the world. After the "water wars" of 2000, transnational NGOs began to replace the World Bank and transnational business as advisors to Bolivian government agencies on how to restructure water-resource-management regimes. The

International Development Research Centre (IDRC), for example, supported a research project organized by the Commission for Integrated
Water Resource Management. The project created a database of existing
water rights and used computerized replicas of water systems to simulate
various approaches to allocating water. Input was collected from irrigation councils and farmers to help determine the most efficient approaches
to water-resource management. Ultimately, the project results were
employed by the Bolivian government in drafting a new irrigation law.[16]
Because it was designed using input from the public, it gained widespread
acceptance—the importance of which should not be underestimated,
given the levels of activism concerning resource management in Bolivia
today.[17] Another transnational NGO involved in promoting inquiry into
water-resource management in Bolivia is The Democracy Center, which
is organizing a major study that includes a comparison of water-resource
management by private companies in El Alto and La Paz and public
agencies now managing Cochabamba's water (Shultz 2005).

In early 2005, new protests and civic strikes broke out in La Paz and
Cochabamba. Facilities owned by Aguas del Illimani, S.A., a subsidiary
of the French corporation Suez-Ondeo/United Water were seized. The
unrest led to the temporary takeover of provision of water and sewer
services in La Paz and El Alto by SEMAPA until reorganization could
take place to permit more citizen participation in company business
(Bloom 2005).

Having succeeded in defending their water, the indigenous majority
elected Evo Morales as Bolivia's first indigenous head of state. In keeping
with campaign promises, he is leading the Latin American revolt against
neoliberalism. For example, on May 1, 2006 he announced a nationalization of Bolivia's petroleum reserves. (See Perreault's chapter.) But whether
Morales' government will be capable of implementing policies that
promote just and sustainable water use remains to be seen. Ongoing
water shortages and increasing demands for water by both farmers and
urban dwellers have the potential to fuel conflict, and a coherent policy
on water has yet to be formulated and implemented. Different sectors of
the population and the organizations that represent them, government
agencies, international financial and development institutions, and transnational business are still competing for control over Bolivia's water.

These conflicts must be resolved before sustainable use of water based on indigenous values can be implemented by a reformed state.

Mexico: The Corporate State in Control under Siege

In Mexico, the national government, the states, and municipalities are all involved in water-resource management. The country has also been a textbook case of corporatism.[18] Mexico claimed water resources as state property for the first time in 1902.[19] Beginning in 1915, as the Mexican Revolution was coming to an end, agrarian reform resulted in restructuring of water-resource management to take into account social justice concerns, including those brought to the negotiating table by historically disenfranchised indigenous communities. The Mexican constitution of 1917 defined surface waters as federal property and directed the national government to act as trustee in overseeing their management.[20] Rights to groundwater resources were originally connected to land ownership, but the constitution specified that landowners could use groundwater only in ways that did not adversely impact other users. It was amended in 1946 to permit the federal government to intervene in management of groundwater and then in 1983 a Supreme Court decision made groundwater national property (Wester, Merrey, and De Lange 2003).

The Federal Water Law of 1971[21] represents the federal government's first comprehensive effort to manage water resources. It gave the Hydrological Resources Secretariat[22] sole authority to issue rights to national water resources and established the first forward-looking regulatory procedures designed to take into account scarcity, especially in the irrigation sector (Aguilar n.d.). At about the same time, water-resource managers in Mexico began to consider river basin management (Wester, Merrey, and De Lange 2003). Water resources were managed sectorally by functional ministries with vested interests in particular types of water use (Natural Resources and Infrastructure Division 2003). The Mexican government's federal water-resource-management agency, the National Water Commission (CONAGUA),[23] was established in 1989 to formulate and implement a neoliberal integrated water-resource-management regime, incorporate a broader range of societal actors in decision making, and limit intensifying conflicts that arose as water became more scarce.[24] Since that time, water policy has been driven increasingly by over-exploitation and interests of Mexican elites and transnational capital (Wester, Merrey, and De Lange 2003).

By the late 1980s, policymakers in Mexico were anticipating the liberalization of trade that would accompany passage of the North American Free Trade Agreement (NAFTA). A new Federal Water Law was passed in 1992 (Aguilar n.d.; Wester, Merrey, and De Lange 2003). Although its purposes were to develop infrastructure needed to improve water and sanitation services where they existed and to extend them, as well as to restore and improve the quality of water in watersheds and aquifers affected by pollution, to ensure ongoing availability of clean, fresh water (Aguilar n.d.), its primary intent was to "introduce the use of economic incentives for improved management" (Natural Resources and Infrastructure Division 2003). The law serves the interests of transnational business in that it commodifies rights to water to promote more "efficient" use through private investment in development of water resources (Aguilar n.d.).

The Federal Water Law also encourages decentralization of water-resource management and stakeholder participation. State water commissions have existed since 1991 and aquifer management councils were established in 1995. The main responsibilities of such regional authorities, however, are assisting CONAGUA in carrying out its duties and bringing stakeholder concerns to the table. CONAGUA retains control over water licensing, taxation, and water investment programs and has resisted further decentralization. Modification of the Federal Water Law in December 2003 that requires basin-level administration and encourages more active participation by aquifer management councils[25] in water-resource management (Wester, Merrey, and De Lange 2003), does not seem to have changed this pattern. Essentially, corporatism still prevails in Mexico, even if the PRI (Institutional Revolutionary Party) no longer dominates the system.

Vicente Fox, the PAN (National Action Party) candidate who won the presidency in 2000, adopted a neoliberal approach to dealing with water shortages that daily affect the lives of millions of Mexicans. Privatization was an essential component of Fox's national development plan for 2001–2006. During Fox's tenure, CONAGUA received two World Bank loans that push "public private partnerships" and cost recovery for private investors. The World Bank loans make it possible for CONAGUA to provide loans to municipalities and states to upgrade their water systems via partnerships with investors.[26] Critics contend that transnationals Suez, Vivendi, and Bechtel (United Utilities) are using PROMAGUA to seize control of Mexico's water resources (Public Citizen n.d.; Grusky 2003).

Indigenous communities in Mexico have been organized by the state as *campesino* communities, institutionalized after the Mexican Revolution as *ejidos*. Rural lands were distributed to thousands of peasant communities—many of them indigenous—to be held and administered in common. Article 27 of the 1917 constitution prohibited the sale or rental of *ejido* lands. The federal government owned the lands and communities held use use-right titles. In other words, *ejidos* have rights to manage lands and resources communally, but the state retains ownership and control. "In effect, the government institutionalized the indigenous land system that the liberals and positivists had attempted to destroy" before the Revolution (Camp 2003, p. 45).

The Lázaro Cárdenas administration (1934–1940) issued collective land titles to thousands of communities throughout the country. Cárdenas saw the *ejido* system as a way to prepare communal regimes for participation in the capitalist economy as actors that could maximize efficiency in resource use and, perhaps most importantly, incorporate formerly excluded rural communities into the corporatist political structure.

Water rights are tied to "productive" use of *ejido* lands—primarily in forestry and agriculture. *Ejidos* with recognized use-right titles to lands have been granted concessions to exploit or use associated water resources (Yañez and Gentes 2005), but when development plans involve *ejido* water resources, the standard practice has been to bribe *ejido* leaders to agree to them (Rodríguez Santos 2006). Agrarian reform provisions of 1992 altered Article 27 of the constitution to make possible the privatization of *ejidos*. Even foreign nationals can now hire Mexican lawyers with expertise in guiding *ejido* communities through the bureaucratic processes established to privatize their lands and resources so as to "regularize" them—in other words, to make them available for sale and private development.[27]

The state has recognized that water resources are being used unsustainably, but has accomplished little in the way of establishing effective policies for resource management that promote solutions to environmental or social problems. Meanwhile, communities all over the country having recognized that neoliberal development threatens their well-being and are demanding more control over water.

Impacts of Water-Resource Management on Indigenous Peoples

Chile: Rear-Guard Action

The productive activities of indigenous agricultural communities pursuing semi-autonomous development in Chile have been negatively impacted by the 1981 Water Code, which separated land ownership and water rights. Now the state can expropriate "unregistered" rights to water associated with lands owned by or titled to indigenous people and communities. Scattered and isolated indigenous communities attempting to remain engaged in small-scale farming, animal husbandry and fishing endeavors must often sell their water rights to powerful elites and corporations pursuing water-intensive regional development plans supported by the Water Code. Since 1981, conflicts over water have intensified as powerful economic actors gain control of the water the people and their crops and pasture animals have relied upon for centuries (Boelens 2003). More than 75 percent of the available water rights in Mapuche territory have been appropriated by the state, and only about 2 percent of those with water rights are Mapuches (Toledo in Aylwin 1998).

Since re-democratization, indigenous organizations and indigenous rights advocates have attempted to use laws and policies to protect their interests. Many hoped Articles 20 and 21 of the 1993 Indian Law[8] would protect indigenous communities' water rights—those of Aymara and Atacameña communities in the arid north in particular (Gentes 2002a), but victories in their struggles to gain more control over water by legal means have been mostly symbolic. For example, in 2003, a Mapuche-Lafkenche community in the Coi Coi Valley in south-central Chile had a retaining wall removed that had flooded 12 hectares (about 29 acres) of their agricultural land off and on for 43 years. The wall was constructed illegally by a wealthy estate owner seeking protection from future tsunamis after a 1960 tsunami flooded some of his land. It blocked drainage of the Mapuche-Lafkenche community's land. The community had attempted for years to get regional authorities to condemn the wall. It was not until March 2003 that the Newen pu Lafkenche Association could convince the General Water Directorate that the estate owner had no right, according to the 1981 Water Code and earlier legislation, to create infrastructure that flooded an adjoining property. The Association had finally employed a strategy that, with a modicum of good luck thrown in, drew attention to their rights (Boccara 2004). It is also important to note that the new estate owner had little to lose in complying with the law.

Whenever real interests of powerful political and economic actors are at stake, the Water Code supports them and trumps the 1993 Indian Law. Although the Indian Law guarantees indigenous communities both property and use rights over water resources within their traditional territories, non-indigenous people and corporations are granted those same rights by the Water Code. The Chilean government remains most responsive to the demands of the corporations and non-indigenous landowners that exercise firm control over the country's development agenda. It has backed hydroelectric development and parceled out mining, aquaculture and forestry concessions in Mapuche territory in south-central Chile. Forestry companies have turned most of central Chile into radiata pine and eucalyptus plantations that deplete aquifers for miles around. This development near legally recognized Mapuche lands has substantively diminished water supplies. Wells have run dry and irrigation systems have been adversely impacted.

The ENDESA consortium, using the 1981 Water Code[9] purchased and came to control 80 percent of the country's available rights associated with hydroelectric development through 2020 (Jouravlev 2003). In the 1990s, Mapuche-Pehuenche people who live along the Bío Bío River in the foothills of the Andes mountains organized to demand recognition of their rights. They demanded the re-democratized Chilean state not follow through with hydroelectric development instigated during the military dictatorship. ENDESA's Pangue and Ralco hydroelectric projects on the Bío Bío River were being constructed with virtually no regard to environmental and human rights impacts. The projects were even allowed without emergency response plans in a region prone to frequent seismic and volcanic activity (Office of the Compliance Advisor/Ombudsman 2003). When the Indian Law was invoked to protect Mapuche-Pehuenche interests, it was superseded by the Electrical Law of 1982.[30] Despite well-organized resistance, a strong legal case, and international support, the Mapuche-Pehuenches were relocated by the Chilean government in 2004 and ENDESA completed construction of the dams.

In perceived life and death situations Mapuche activists have resorted to violence. Sabotaging roads, attacking logging equipment, and occupying lands they have claimed for centuries are tactics activists have used against forestry companies. Those who employ such tactics emphasize their connections to their militant ancestors that held the Incan and the Spanish empires at bay and believe they have the right to keep developers from destroying Mapuche communities and stealing their resources. The Chilean government protects property rights acquired by economic elites by cracking down on Mapuche leaders and organizations. It uses an anti-terrorism law implemented during the military dictatorship[31] to prosecute even peaceful protesters and community leaders who attempt to draw the attention of policymakers and the Chilean public to their concerns. Mapuche activists assert that during the last eight years, the Frei and Lagos governments have jailed 500 Mapuche political prisoners using the law (UPI 2006).

Where environmental impacts of expanding non-indigenous settlement are least severe, indigenous communities have enjoyed slightly greater success at maintaining traditional political culture and systems of productive activity as they adapt to externally driven economic and political change (Castro-Lucic 2002). Highland Andean communities in what is today northern Chile have adapted with some success to intensified non-indigenous development in or near their traditional territories. In May 2004, the Atacameña community of Toconce was able to reclaim some ancestral waters from ESSAN/Aguas de Antofagasta, a corporate entity that had diverted the community's river to provide drinking water (as a profit-making endeavor) for coastal cities in the region. The people of Toconce, like others in the area, depend on terraced agriculture and herd camelids and sheep. The loss of their water meant that many could no longer remain engaged in traditional productive activities and were forced to emigrate. The Chilean Supreme Court ruled in their favor, invoking the authority of the 1993 Indian Law and required a flow rate of 100 liters per second to the community.[32]

Protecting economic security by remaining engaged in traditional productive activities may help indigenous communities continue to effectively govern themselves, even when pressured to adapt to change. But, as thirsty non-indigenous populations expand in the arid northern regions of Chile and to the extent that investors empowered by institutionalized or widely accepted policies secure rights to control and use their water,[33] Andean communities and the fragile highland ecosystems they have inhabited for thousands of years are at risk.

Indigenous communities and organizations in Chile continue appealing to courts, policymakers and government agencies, publicizing their struggles, attempting to preserve traditional systems of productive activity and strengthen community control over water, and protesting state actions that enable Chilean elites and transnational capital to usurp rights to water on or under indigenous lands. Sporadic victories since the implementation of Chile's 1993 Indian Law and support from government programs for community development projects encourage some indigenous organizations and activists to continue working within the state system to regain control over their water, despite problematic interpretations of the 1981 Water Code and Chile's Indian Law when it conflicts with other laws, and refusal of Chilean authorities to enforce laws that could protect communities and the environment.

Indigenous organizations and activists are also becoming better informed about changing international norms regarding indigenous peoples and better connected with the international indigenous movement. Some have appealed to prominent inter-governmental organizations (such as the United Nations and the Inter-American Commission on Human Rights) and forged partnerships with both Chilean and transnational NGOs working to promote human rights and environmental protection. Since re-democratization in 1990, the Chilean indigenous rights movement has pressured the Chilean government to ratify the International Labour Organization's Convention No. 169 concerning Indigenous and Tribal Peoples in Independent Countries. Indigenous organizations and activists see Convention No. 169 as a means of loosening state control over indigenous nations' lands and resources.[34] It is likely for this very reason, however, that Chile's government has refused to ratify the Convention. On November 16, 2005, in a televised debate during her campaign for office, Chile's new president, Michelle Bachelet, promised she would lead Chile to ratify the Convention. Indigenous rights advocates are waiting to see if she will keep her promise.

Bolivia: Majority Power

Because Bolivia has a significant indigenous population, many communities still survive by engaging in traditional productive activities. Even though they are the majority, indigenous peoples there have been ruthlessly exploited and almost completely excluded from both citizenship and decision making until after 1952 Bolivian National Revolution. The revolution was designed to incorporate the formerly disenfranchised indigenous communities as part of the nation state—but as *campesinos* without indigenous identity (Yashar 2005). Despite attempts to incorporate them, indigenous *ayllus* (communities that live together and manage their traditional territories communally) continue to exist in the Andean highlands alongside the *campesino comunidades* organized under the 1953 Agrarian Reform program (Claure, Gutiérrez, and Hoogendam 2002).

Indigenous identity, communal management of land, water, and productive activities, and traditional forms of political culture that support inter-communal cooperation have formed the basis for an indigenous movement in Bolivia, which is bolstered by changing international norms influenced by indigenous peoples' movements around the world. Constitutional reforms in the mid 1990s included acknowledgment of the multiethnic and multicultural nature of the country's population and protections for the ethnic, social, and cultural rights of Bolivia's indigenous peoples. While the constitutional reform process did not involve a constituent assembly and indigenous leaders did not engage directly in negotiations, the government's ethnic affairs office consulted with indigenous leaders during the process (Van Cott 2001). The 1994 Public Participation Law also gave indigenous communities, along with farming communities and neighborhood groups, explicit rights to participate in local governance by organizing as territorial base communities.[35] Observers concerned with water-resource management assert that the law has empowered these groups and increased the coverage of water and sanitation services (Alberto Crespo of Water Portal of the Americas, in International Institute for Sustainable Development 2006).

Resource-management policies still do not enable indigenous communities to participate in decision making about water, however, and Bolivia's indigenous communities and *campesino* activists are fighting against ongoing exclusion by organizing an extensive network of mobilization and joint action at the regional, provincial, and state levels (Olivera and Lewis 2004). The world saw that mobilization in action in the "water wars" of Cochabamba. The conflict illustrated the divide between elite civic and business groups allied with transnationals and the growing indigenous movement they characterize as "extremist and obstructionist" (Ballvé 2005), which is working to bridge the divides between different indigenous communities in Bolivia (Olivera and Lewis 2004).

The indigenous movement brought down presidents Gonzalo Sánchez de Lozada in 2003 ("water wars") and Carlos Mesa in 2005 (natural gas) as civic groups like the Federation of Neighborhood Boards (FEJUVE) in El Alto, and provincial labor federations continued to organize strikes and protests. In the midst of ongoing conflicts over control of water and petroleum resources, civic, labor, and indigenous organizations are attempting to work together to re-envision development, but much remains to be accomplished. *Campesino* and Indian leaders like Felipe Quispe and Evo Morales have created organizations that more effectively channel indigenous dissent, resist neoliberalism, and participate in decision making, but rural and urban people and rainforest peoples of the Bolivian Amazon and the Andean peoples to the west are still at odds.

Indigenous political parties established to unify the indigenous majority in order to gain more control over the state helped win the election of Evo Morales to the presidency of Bolivia. He has established a Ministry of Water, headed by Abel Mamani, former leader of FEJUVE. The new ministry is playing a leading role in the global debate about water and privatization, asserting at the fourth World Water Forum in Mexico City in March 2006 that "water is declared a human right and that it must be managed by public entities" (Buxton 2006). With a "radical" and "leftist" Indian as president, Bolivia will likely face significant opposition from transnational capital and international financial and development institutions. In the age of "peak oil," securing control over resources (especially petroleum) too often justifies invasion and occupation. It remains to be seen whether Bolivia's indigenous majority will be able to retain and use the power of the state and/or find other ways to bring about more just and sustainable uses of water.

Mexico: Responding to Neoliberalization of the Mexican Revolution

As the Mexican population grows and as transnational corporate agriculture, mining, tourism and other environmentally destructive forms of development intensify, water resources are becoming more scarce and polluted. Since Mexico liberalized its trade policies and implemented a whole host of free-market reforms in conjunction with NAFTA, control over resources is again becoming extremely concentrated, as it was before the Revolution. As banks foreclose on *ejido* properties and elites buy up the land, agricultural production can become more efficient in contexts created by increasing trade liberalization and economic globalization (Levy and Bruhn 2001), but many indigenous communities lose control over water in their traditional territories through this disenfranchisement of their *ejidos*. These trends undermine indigenous lifeways, increase vulnerability to exploitative development, and destabilize communities. But they are also bringing indigenous communities together to resist injustice and organize for sustainable development.

Mazahuas, Purépechas, Mayas, and other indigenous peoples in Mexico recognize the injustices and inequities inherent in the state's restructuring of water-resource management. They also still remember their traditional values and stories about living springs and water as the source of all life. The state's failure to sustainably manage water resources and its willingness to surrender control over the country's resources to transnational capital have, especially since the mid 1990s, inspired indigenous rebellion and new visions for the future of development based on indigenous values and systems of productive activity.

The 1994 Zapatista uprising was a high-profile response to neoliberal disempowerment of Mexico's indigenous and *campesino* communities. Over the past 12 years, the Zapatistas have sustained a well-organized struggle to secure autonomous control over resources for indigenous communities in Chiapas and elsewhere. The Zapatista Army of National Liberation (Ejército Zapatista de Liberación Nacional, EZLN) and its political arm, the Zapatista Front of National Liberation (Frente Zapatista de Liberación Nacional, FZLN), along with other organizations in the indigenous autonomy movement, including the Plural National Indigenous Assembly for Autonomy (Asociación Nacional Indígena Plural por la Autonomía—ANIPA) and the Chiapas State Council of Indigenous and Peasant Organizations (Consejo Estatal de Organizaciones Indígenas y Campesinas—CEOIC), have inspired and supported movements for autonomous control of resources by indigenous communities across the country.

Using Zapatista-inspired tactics, Mazahua Indian activists brought the Mexican government to the bargaining table to discuss problematic impacts of the Cutzamala water system, which provides drinking water to the residents of Mexico City. The activists and the community they represent contend that the Cutzamala water system administered by CONAGUA has polluted local water supplies, destroyed crops, and forced people living in the western reaches of the state of Mexico to pay the costs of providing water for an ever more thirsty Mexico City. Organized as the Zapatista Women in Defense of Water (also known as the Mazahua Women's Front), they dress in traditional clothing and carry fake rifles to gain publicity for their cause and the attention of policymakers. After meeting with the head of CONAGUA and the Secretary of the Environment, the activists signed an agreement in October 2004 that promised to indemnify landowners for losses, promote investment in infrastructure for the provision of potable water for the community, and reforest the area (Bensinger 2004; Dellios 2005). Additional agreements to provide water for the community and implement a sustainable development plan were signed in June, 2005. But observers and activists are still waiting for the Mexican government to follow through on its promises. Some observers contend that the activism has benefited non-indigenous people in the area even more than it has helped the Mazahua community recover from damages caused by the Cutzamala system (Bensinger 2004), but others point out that the movement for more control by communities over water cannot succeed if it is limited to indigenous communities (Ferrier 2006). Meanwhile, the activists that organized the Mazahua Women's Front remain active, making well-publicized appearances at the March in Defense of Water and other gatherings organized to coincide with the fourth World Water Forum in Mexico City in March 2006.

Purépecha Indians who live along the shores of Lake Zirahuén in the state of Michoacán also look to the Zapatistas for inspiration and assistance. Lake Zirahuén has become increasingly threatened by mining, commercial agriculture, logging, and tourism development (Davies et al. 2005). Dissatisfied with the Mexican government's failure to protect the lake and promote just and sustainable development in the region, the Purépechas organized a Zapatista-inspired *caracol* (autonomous municipality) in October 2003 (Bellinghausen 2006). Their primary objective is to promote sustainable use of water in their traditional territory. They are hoping to block development of a resort planned for the lake and prevent over exploitation by interests that have been granted concessions by CONAGUA to use lake water (Tilly and Kennedy 2004). Zapatista leader Subcomandante Marcos (known during the campaign for the 2006 general elections as "Delegado Zero") has expressed support for the community and encouraged the Purépechas to open their movement for autonomous and sustainable regional development to non-indigenous people in the area (Bellinghausen 2006).

Demands by indigenous communities for autonomous control of water are intensifying in Mexico. The fourth World Water Forum's meeting held in Mexico City served as a catalyst for indigenous peoples' protests against unsustainable exploitation, privatization and usurpation of control of water. The multinational gathering of civic organizations held at the same time as the World Water Forum, provided opportunities for Mexico's indigenous communities and organizations to meet people with similar concerns from around the world. Autonomous control of water has become a prominent theme in the Zapatistas' Other Campaign and indigenous organizations and communities from all over Mexico are demanding the right to employ traditional practices to "show that another form of water management is possible" (Coalición de Organizaciones Mexicanas por el Derecho al Agua 2006). Before they can do that, however, most indigenous communities in Mexico will have to gain more control over scarce water resources from a state determined to sell them to the highest bidder.

The Mexican political system has been in transition since the PRI lost control of the Chamber of Deputies in 1997 and lost the presidency to the PAN in 2000. The corporatist system is eroding, and the state has been increasingly challenged to coopt or eliminate leaders of organizations that demand substantive rights to land and resources for indigenous communities. The Zapatistas' regional Juntas de Buen Gobierno (Councils of Good Government) and autonomous municipalities (*caracoles*) are models of autonomous control of local development. They cooperatively design and implement locally managed programs for education, health, and agriculture, but remain challenged by lack of financing and oppression by the state and the elite interests that have traditionally controlled their homelands. Their effective organization, has, however, provided an increased sense of political security and legitimacy to attempts to control community resources for both indigenous and non-indigenous people in some of Mexico's most marginalized communities. They have also made progress in shaping norms for the involvement of transnational NGOs in local development by implementing a 10 percent development tax on aid, which is designed to ensure that Zapatista communities benefit equitably (Earle and Simonelli 2004). The Fox administration even had to concede that the establishment of juntas and *caracoles* probably does not violate the Mexican constitution (Stahler-Sholk 2005). For the time being, indigenous activists in Mexico are able to both assert community control over resource management and incorporate traditional cultural perspectives that hold water to be a human right and democratic, just, equitable and sustainable resource management to be essential to development.

Conclusions

Today we call the ongoing expansion of the capitalist world system "globalization." Globalization of the Americas began when settlers from Europe arrived at the end of the fifteenth century and began to construct a "New World" with their meanings and practices as the foundation. Since the Conquest, the definition, allocation, and enforcement of values and rights has been shaped by a dominant culture that itself has been both a cause and effect of globalization. Indigenous peoples progressively lost control over lands and resources as they were forcibly removed whenever their traditional territories became of interest to the conquerors. Today the rewards of development continue to accrue primarily to members of the dominant culture even as indigenous movements take advantage of changing values about justice and development itself to assert claims to traditional territories and resources in the political arena.

At the dawn of the twenty-first century, Chile, Bolivia, and Mexico are facing water shortages and increasing demands for water. Paradoxically, at roughly the same time that Latin American state agencies in charge of development began to recognize the importance of sustainable development, but before state-led development could successfully promote sustainable or just management of water resources, powerful outsiders began to take advantage of their indebtedness to impose neoliberal development models that de-emphasized both the public interest and the environment. In the 1960s Chile's liberal governments experimented with reallocation of rights to water to incorporate new technology and planning criteria and to promote transformative social justice aims. This was too much. The country was forcibly neoliberalized in the 1970s and the 1980s by a military dictatorship backed by the United States. Mexico's neoliberalization came about a decade later, and was implemented by Mexican elites working with transnational capital and the United States and Canada to promote a hemispheric program of "free" trade. Mexican elites have attempted to deconstruct the corporatist political culture of the Mexican Revolution, but have yet to replace it with a new political culture. The neoliberalization of Bolivia has failed. Attempts by elites in control of the state to privatize control of water resources there began in earnest in the mid 1980s and came to a screeching halt in 2000.

Because they are the poorest and most politically disenfranchised groups in all three countries, indigenous communities struggling to remain engaged in traditional productive activities have been disproportionately impacted by neoliberalism. They also typically face the most immediate threats associated with unsustainable management of water resources. Indigenous communities dependent upon agriculture are at risk, along with those displaced by hydroelectric development and those who see their waters depleted and polluted by intensified industrial development. The Zapatistas and other disenfranchised Mexicans, Mapuches and other indigenous peoples of Chile, like the Bolivians who staged the Cochabamba "water wars," are working both within and around the political structures of settler states to promote more just and sustainable use of water. To work within the system, they must, as individual stakeholders, assert convincing claims based on dominant cultural values. This tactic has met with limited success because elites control politics by imposing their own values, especially the prioritization of individual rights over community rights. *Ejidos* in Mexico and Mapuche and highland Andean communities in Chile have lost their control over water and even been displaced when individuals and corporations backed by the state assert claims to it. Elites and multinational corporations can purchase their rights to water, but individuals who comprise indigenous communities cannot usually afford to exercise their rights or protect them when they are violated—even when backed by prominent inter-governmental organizations or transnational NGOs. When nature is commodified and privatized, elites create wealth for themselves and poverty for others whose life ways have depended on natural relationships for centuries.

Dominant cultural values and notions of rights conflict with meanings and practices that support community and indigenous peoples' capacities to engage in ecologically sustainable development. In Mexico, the Zapatista movement has worked around the state's authority by constructing autonomous local and regional resource-management regimes that prioritize community stewardship of water over individual rights and draw at least symbolic strength from indigenous values about water. Indigenous movements and organizations in Bolivia are exerting control over the state and they—along with the new indigenous president of the country—are busy imagining a new approach to politics and resource management and restructuring from the community to national levels to promote decision making based on indigenous meanings and practices. The challenge seems to be the implementation of viable policies that can be agreed upon by all stakeholders. Indigenous communities and organizations in Chile continue to resist exploitative development projects backed by the state and to seek redress for environmental injustice both nationally and internationally. Implementing autonomous and sustainable uses of water will be especially challenging there because the state's water-resource-management regime has so effectively empowered transnational business.

The cases examined here suggest that when indigenous communities and organizations can effectively impede exploitative development schemes that usurp community control of water and undermine indigenous cultures, they may open the door to new possibilities for preserving meanings and practices and creation of more just and sustainable resource management—so long as states and elite interests can be dissuaded from using violence to crush their movements. Changing dominant culture values about indigenous peoples, global communications, and the weakening of the state by neoliberalism have recently offered indigenous movements in Latin America opportunities to promote sustainable development. In all three countries, assistance from the international indigenous movement, environmental and human rights organizations, and transnational NGOs that work across international borders to support indigenous rights and promote sustainable development and environmental justice have helped indigenous communities in attempts to gain more control over water and pursue autonomous and sustainable development. Some attribute this support to successful "framing" by indigenous movements that involves foregrounding indigenous values that appeal to environmentalists. Some research suggests that non-indigenous groups facing similar problems have not received the same level of support from transnational actors (Transnational Communities Programme n.d.). Zapatista communities and institutions of autonomous government have been especially adept at gaining support from global civil society and making sure it doesn't undermine movement solidarity.

For Bolivians who organized the "water wars," for Zapatista communities and others that emulate their tactics in Mexico, and for exploited indigenous communities of Chile, environmental justice has not been achieved by ensuring their inclusion as stakeholders in resource-management regimes loosely managed by states. Environmental justice in Latin American is more than a movement by disenfranchised people to enjoy fuller benefits of environmental protection. The communities of indigenous peoples that still remain in the Americas have long-term experience organizing themselves politically, economically, and socially and interacting with nature to establish ecologically sustainable productive activities that enable survival and well-being in the landscapes that comprise their traditional territories. For them, environmental justice means control over what the dominant culture calls "resources." Preservation and cultivation of that along with authority to manage development rooted in indigenous meanings and practices (as well as freely chosen non-indigenous values and practices) are key. The emergence of just and sustainable water use in the contemporary context is contingent upon the successful incorporation of indigenous cultures' meanings and practices as resource-management regimes adapt to changing political, economic, and environmental realities. Environmental justice will be achieved only when answers to fundamental questions about how we ought to interpret and interact with nature are constructed by all peoples.

Acknowledgment

Special thanks to Rex Wirth for carefully reviewing the manuscript and suggesting revisions.

Notes

1. For more perspective on these differences, see Boelens and Hoogendam 2002 and Groenfeldt n.d..
2. Código de Aguas, D.F.L. No. 1.222.
3. Chile is a democratic unitary state, which means that governmental affairs are carried out by the central government and that provincial, municipal and other governmental bodies are branches of the national government selectively vested with autonomous decision-making power.
4. Dirección General de Aguas.
5. ENDESA, now a privatized electricity generating corporation, but formerly the Chilean government's hydroelectric development corporation, has been granted approximately 80 percent of the available nonconsumptive rights to water in the country (Aylwin 2003).
6. Carl J. Bauer is the most recognized expert on Chilean water law (in English). See Bauer (2004). Ingo Gentes and Nancy Yañez are other noted experts in Chilean water law and its impacts on indigenous peoples.

7. Ley 19.145 modified Articles 58 and 63 of the Code.

8. Ley No. 19.300.

9. Ley No. 2029, "Ley de Servicios de Agua Potable y Alcantarillado Sanitario."

10. It was replaced by Ley No. 2066, also denominated "Ley de Servicios de Agua Potable y Alcantarillado Sanitario."

11. Servicio Municipal de Agua Potable y Alcantarillado. See http://www.semapa.com.bo.

12. For more on these events, see Assies 2003 and Olivera and Lewis 2004.

13. For more on the settlement, see "Bechtel vs. Bolivia" at http://democracyctr.org.

14. Coordinadora de Defensa del Agua y de la Vida.

15. Comisión para la Gestión Integral del Agua en Bolivia (CGIAB). See http://www.aguabolivia.org.

16. Ley No. 2878, de Promoción y Apoyo al Sector Riego.

17. International Development Research Centre 2005.

18. Corporatism is a political system wherein the state controls all segments of society by creating formal relationships that regulate interactions, expectations, and rewards.

19. Ley sobre Régimen y Clasificación de Bienes Federales, antecedente de la Ley General de Bienes Nacionales (Aguilar n.d.).

20. Article 27 of the constitution sets forth the legal and administrative ground rules for water-resource management. Articles 28, 73, 115, 116, and 133 also contain provisions affecting water-resource management.

21. Ley Federal de Aguas de 1971476.

22. Secretaría de Recursos Hidráulicos

23. Comisión Nacional del Agua. See http://www.cna.gob.mx.

24. See http://www.cna.gob.mx/eCNA/Espaniol/Directorio/Default.aspx.

25. Consejos de Cuenca.

26. PROMAGUA (Programa para la Modernización de los Prestadores del Servicio de Agua y Saneamiento) is responsible for implementing the loan programs. The subloans are provided by BANOBRAS, the Mexican development bank (Comisión Nacional del Agua 2002). For more on PROMAGUA (Programa para la Modernización de los Prestadores del Servicio de Agua y Saneamiento), see http://www.cna.gob.mx.

27. PROCEDE (Programa de Certificación de Derechos Ejidales y Titulación de Solares) is the federal government's program that converts communal ejido lands to fee simple lands owned by individual members of the communities. See http://www.pa.gob.mx.

28. Ley No. 19.253.

29. ENDESA, S.A. was formerly Chile's National Energy Enterprise but, privatized during the Pinochet dictatorship, it is now owned by Spanish and Chilean investors. ENDESA España, which claims to be one of the largest private electrical groups in the world, with more than 20.5 million customers in 12 countries (ENDESA España n.d.), took control of ENDESA in Chile in 1998 (Aylwin 2002).

30. ENDESA, under the authority of the 1982 Electrical Law, convinced the Chilean Ministry of Economics, Development and Reconstruction to appoint a commission to determine fair compensation for Mapuche lands. ENDESA then deposited the designated amount in a bank account, and claimed—successfully—that it had complied with necessary requirements for condemning Mapuche lands. According to the Indian Law, exchanges of or restitution for communally titled lands be unanimously approved by all community members before any transactions go forward. Such approval was never forthcoming.

31. Ley No. 18.314.

32. Analysts have suggested that Chile's formal recognition of water as a basic human right via its ratification of the International Covenant on Economic, Social and Cultural Rights may have been one factor that influenced the decision (Vallenas Rojas 2004). The interest of prominent scholars in the impacts on highland Andean cultures of water-resource development may have also played a role in swaying public opinion. Mining activities in the same region had also recently dried up the nearby Inacaliri wetlands, which had served as a main source of pasture for animals traditionally herded by pastoral Aymara and Atacameña communities in the region. Many of them were also forced to emigrate (Castro-Lucic 2002).

33. Perhaps the most recent example of environmentally problematic and exploitative development in the Andes is the Pascua-Lama project of the transnational Barrick Gold company. The corporation plans to mine what is believed to be one of the world's largest unexploited gold deposits. Environmentalists, NGOs, and indigenous and *campesino* communities along the Chilean-Argentine border above the Huasco valley in the country's Third Region (north of Santiago and south of Antofagasta) have carried out a well-coordinated campaign to get the Chilean government to reject this plan. Opponents of the project, including the indigenous Diaguita community, appealed to the Canadian government and the Canadian public to put pressure on Barrick Gold, headquartered in Canada, not to proceed with the project. The gold-mining project was to involve the removal of 20 hectares of glacial ice (three glaciers). In February, 2006, the Chilean government's Regional Environment Commission (Comisión Regional Metropolitana del Medio Ambiente [COREMA], an adjunct of the country's National Environmental Commission [Comisión Nacional del Medio Ambiente—CONAMA]) decided Barrick Gold's project could proceed, as long as the company does not relocate any glaciers and treats all waste. The project threatens downstream wildlife and human communities with arsenic and other types of contamination.

34. Convention No. 169 requires that ratifying countries protect the rights of indigenous peoples to participate in the use, management and conservation of "the natural resources pertaining to their lands" (Article 15 at International Labour Organization 1989). Even when states retain ownership of certain resources or rights thereto, they must consult with indigenous peoples who could be affected by exploitation of resources to determine how their interests might be prejudiced before proceeding. Indigenous peoples must be compensated for their losses and, "wherever possible", awarded a share of any benefits associated with exploitation of state-owned resources.

35. Organizaciones Territoriales de Base.

References

Aguilar, Enrique. n.d. Water Resources Management Legal and Institutional Tool-kit for Latin America and the Caribbean. World Bank Group.

Alvarez, Sonia, Evelina Dagnino, and Arturo Escobar, eds. 1998. *Cultures of Politics, Politics of Cultures: Re-Visioning Latin American Social Movements.* Westview.

Assies, Willem. 2003. David versus Goliath in Cochabamba: Water rights, neo-liberalism, and the revival of social protest in Bolivia. *Latin American Perspectives* 30, no. 130: 14–36.

Aylwin, José. 1998. Indigenous peoples rights in Chile: Progresses and contradictions in a context of economic globalization. Paper read at Canadian Association for Latin American and Caribbean Studies (CALACS) XXVIII Congress, Simon Fraser University, Vancouver.

Aylwin, José. 2002. The Ralco dam and the Pehuenche people in Chile: Lessons from an ethno-environmental conflict. Paper read at Toward Adaptive Conflict Resolution: Lessons from Canada and Chile, Centre for the Study of Global Issues, University of British Columbia, Vancouver.

Aylwin, José. 2003. Interview in offices of Instituto de Estudios Indígenas, Universidad de la Frontera, Temuco, Chile, August 6.

Ballvé, Teo. 2005. Bolivia's separatist movement. *NACLA Report on the Americas* 38, no. 5: 16–17.

Bauer, Carl J. 2004. Siren Song: Chilean Water Law as a Model for International Reform. Resources for the Future.

Bellinghausen, Hermann. 2006. Defienden purépechas pertenencia del lago y las tierras de Zirahuén. *La Jornada* (Mexico City), April 5.

Bensinger, Ken. 2004. Want a successful protest in Mexico? Arm your women. Christian Science Monitor, November 18.

Bloom, David. 2005. Al Alto: Protests oust water company. Weekly News Update on the Americas, January 18.

Boccara, Guillaume. 2004. The struggle of the Mapuche peoples: Deepening democracy in Chile. *ReVista: Harvard Review of Latin America* 3, no. 3: 31–33.

Boelens, Rutgerd. 2003. Local rights and legal recognition: The struggle for indigenous water rights and the cultural politics of participation. Paper read at Third World Water Forum, Kyoto.

Boelens, Rutgerd, and Paul Hoogendam, eds. 2002. *Water Rights and Empowerment.* Koninklijke Van Gorcum.

Buxton, Nick. 2006. Interview with Abel Mamani, Upside Down World (http://upsidedownworld.org), April 3.

Camp, Roderic Ai. 2003. *Politics in Mexico: The Democratic Transformation.* Oxford University Press.

Castro-Lucic, Milka. 2002. Local norms and competition for water in Aymara and Atacama communities (Northern Chile). In *Water Rights and Empowerment,* ed. R. Boelens and P. Hoogendam. Koninklijke Van Gorcum.

Claure, Washington, Zulema Gutiérrez, and Paul Hoogendam. 2002. Design and water rights: Small scale irrigation experiences in Oruro, Bolivia. In *Water Rights and Empowerment,* ed. R. Boelens and P. Hoogendam. Koninklijke Van Gorcum.

Coalición de Organizaciones Mexicanas por el Derecho al Agua. 2006. Joint declaration of the movements in defense of water. Paper read at International Forum in Defense of Water, Mexico City.

Comisión Nacional del Agua. 2002. Programa para la Modernización de Organismos Operadores de Agua. Comisión Nacional del Agua, http://www.cna .gob.mx.

Davies, Sarah J., Sarah E. Metcalf, Fernando Bernal-Brooks, Arturo Chacón-Torres, John G. Farmer, A. B. MacKenzie, and Anthony J. Newton. 2005. Lake sediments record sensitivity of two hydrologically closed upland lakes in Mexico to human impact. *Ambio* 34, no. 6: 470–475.

Dellios, Hugh. 2005. Villagers fight for access to water. http://www.americas .org.

Dourojeanni, Axel, and Andrei Jouravlev. 2002. Evolución de políticas hídricas en América Latina y el Caribe. Economic Council on Latin America and the Caribbean, División de Recursos Naturales e Infraestructura.

Earle, Duncan, and Jeanne Simonelli. 2004. The Zapatistas and global civil society: Renegotiating the relationship. *Revista Europea de Estudios Latinoamericanos y del Caribe,* April: 119–125.

ENDESA España, n.d. Company homepage (http://www.endesa.es).

Ferrier, Van. 2006. Potable politics. The Dominion: News from the Grassroots (http://dominionpaper.ca).

Gelles, Paul H. 2000. *Water and Power in Highland Peru: The Cultural Politics of Irrigation and Development.* Rutgers University Press.

Gentes, Ingo. 2002a. Estudio de la legislación oficial Chilena y del derecho indí-gena a los recursos hídricos. United Nations Commission for Latin America and the Caribbean.

Gentes, Ingo. 2002b. Water law and indigenous rights in the Andean countries: Conceptual elements. Paper read at International Water Law and Indigenous Rights Seminar-Towards Recognition of Indigenous Water Rights and Management Rules in National Legislation, Wageningen, Netherlands.

Groenfeldt, David. n.d. Water development and spiritual values in Western and indigenous societies. http://www.indigenouswater.org.

Grusky, Sara. 2003. Pushing water privatization in Mexico. Public Citizen's International Water Working Group Water for All Campaign (http://www .organicconsumers.org).

International Institute for Sustainable Development. 2006. Implementation of IWRM in National Plans 2005. http://www.iisd.ca.

International Labour Organization. 1989. C169 Indigenous and Tribal Peoples Convention: Convention concerning Indigenous and Tribal Peoples in Independent Countries. http://www.ilo.org.

Jouravlev, Andrei. 2003. Interview in offices of the Division of Natural Resources of the United Nations Economic Commission for Latin America and the Caribbean, Santiago, July 15.

Levy, Daniel C., and Kathleen Bruhn. 2001. *Mexico: The Struggle for Democratic Development*. University of California Press.

Mitchell, William P., and David Guillet, eds. 1994. *Irrigation at High Altitudes: The Social Organization of Water Control Systems in the Andes*. American Anthropological Association.

Natural Resources and Infrastructure Division. 2003. Latin American and the Caribbean preparatory process for the twelfth session of the commission on sustainable development—effective water governance in the Americas: A key issue. Economic Commission for Latin America and the Caribbean.

Office of the Compliance Advisor/Ombudsman. 2003. Assessment by the Office of the Compliance Advisor/Ombudsman in relation to a complaint filed against IFC's investment in ENDESA Pangue S.A.: International Finance Corporation.

Olivera, Oscar, and Tom Lewis. 2004. *¡Cochabamba! Water War in Bolivia*. South End.

Public Citizen. n.d. French multinational wants Mexico's water. http://www .citizen.org.

Rodríguez Santos, Bertha. 2006. The Zapatistas join Querétaro's struggle to defend its water. Narco News Bulletin (http://www.narconews.com).

Scarborough, Vernon L. 1993. Water management in the southern Maya lowlands: An accretive model for the engineered landscape. In *Research in Economic Anthropology*, ed. V. Scarborough and B. Isaac. JAI.

Shultz, Jim. 2005. E-mail correspondence from Executive Director Jim Shultz to Stefanie Wickstrom.

Solanes, Miguel. 2006. Editorial Comments. *Network for Cooperation in Integrated Water Resource Management for Sustainable Development in Latin America and the Caribbean Newsletter*, April: 1–2.

Stahler-Sholk, Richard. 2005. Time of the snails: Autonomy and resistance in Chiapas. *NACLA Report on the Americas* 38, no. 5: 34–38.

Tilly, Chris, and Marie Kennedy. 2004. Indigenous land struggles in Michoacán, Mexico: "We've fought for the land since time immemorial." www.peaceworkmagazine.org.

Transnational Communities Programme. n.d. Research Briefing No. 6: Transnational Communities. Economic Social and Research Council.

United Nations Economic Commission for Latin America and the Caribbean, Natural Resources and Infrastructure Division. 2005. Meaning and Scope of Water Code Reform in Chile. Santiago de Chile.

UPI. 2006. Mapuches marchan por la capital para exigir libertad de "presos políticos" de su pueblo. http://www.latercera.cl.

Vallenas Rojas, Kantuta. 2004. Derechos Humanos: El Derecho al Agua y los Pueblos Indígenas: A Propósito de una Sentencia de la Corte Suprema de Justicia de Chile Comisión Andina de Juristas. http://www.cajpe.org.

Van Cott, Donna Lee. 2001. Explaining ethnic autonomy regimes in Latin America. *Studies in Comparative International Development* 35, no. 4: 30–58.

Wester, Philippus, Douglas J. Merrey, and Marna De Lange. 2003. Boundaries of consent: Stakeholder representation in river basin management in Mexico and South Africa. *World Development* 31, no. 5: 797–812.

Yáñez, Nancy, and Ingo Gentes. 2005. Derechos locales sobre las aguas en Chile: Análisis jurídico y político para una estrategia de gestión pertinente en territorios indígenas. Water Law and Indigenous Rights Initiative, Wageningen University, and Economic Council for Latin America and the Caribbean.

Yashar, Deborah J. 2005. *Contesting Citizenship in Latin America: The Rise of Indigenous Movements and the Postliberal Challenge*. Cambridge University Press.

About the Contributors

Henri Acselrad is a Professor in the Institute of Urban and Regional Research and Planning at the Federal University of Rio de Janeiro.

David V. Carruthers is an Associate Professor in the Department of Political Science at San Diego State University.

Jordi Díez is an Assistant Professor of Political Science at the University of Guelph.

Katherine T. McCaffrey is an Assistant Professor in the Department of Anthropology at Montclair State University.

Sarah A. Moore is an Assistant Professor in the Geography Department and in the Latin American Studies Program at the University of Arizona.

Peter Newell is a Professor of Development Studies at the University of East Anglia and a James Martin Fellow at the University of Oxford Centre for the Environment.

Tom Perreault is an Associate Professor in the Department of Geography at Syracuse University's Maxwell School of Citizenship and Public Affairs.

Carlos Reboratti is a Research Professor in the School of Agronomy at the University of Buenos Aires.

Reyes Rodríguez is a Research Associate at the Centro de Estudios Espinosa Yglesias in Mexico City.

Juanita Sundberg is an Assistant Professor in the Department of Geography at the University of British Columbia.

Stefanie Wickstrom is an independent researcher and multidisciplinary lecturer at Central Washington University.

Wendy Wolford is an Assistant Professor in the Department of Geography at the University of North Carolina.

Michele Zebich-Knos is a Professor of Political Science and International Affairs at Kennesaw State University.

Urban and Industrial Environments

Maureen Smith, *The U.S. Paper Industry and Sustainable Production: An Argument for Restructuring*

Keith Pezzoli, *Human Settlements and Planning for Ecological Sustainability: The Case of Mexico City*

Sarah Hammond Creighton, *Greening the Ivory Tower: Improving the Environmental Track Record of Universities, Colleges, and Other Institutions*

Jan Mazurek, *Making Microchips: Policy, Globalization, and Economic Restructuring in the Semiconductor Industry*

William A. Shutkin, *The Land That Could Be: Environmentalism and Democracy in the Twenty-First Century*

Richard Hofrichter, ed., *Reclaiming the Environmental Debate: The Politics of Health in a Toxic Culture*

Robert Gottlieb, *Environmentalism Unbound: Exploring New Pathways for Change*

Kenneth Geiser, *Materials Matter: Toward a Sustainable Materials Policy*

Thomas D. Beamish, *Silent Spill: The Organization of an Industrial Crisis*

Matthew Gandy, *Concrete and Clay: Reworking Nature in New York City*

David Naguib Pellow, *Garbage Wars: The Struggle for Environmental Justice in Chicago*

Julian Agyeman, Robert D. Bullard, and Bob Evans, eds., *Just Sustainabilities: Development in an Unequal World*

Barbara L. Allen, *Uneasy Alchemy: Citizens and Experts in Louisiana's Chemical Corridor Disputes*

Dara O'Rourke, *Community-Driven Regulation: Balancing Development and the Environment in Vietnam*

Brian K. Obach, *Labor and the Environmental Movement: The Quest for Common Ground*

Peggy F. Barlett and Geoffrey W. Chase, eds., *Sustainability on Campus: Stories and Strategies for Change*

Index